"Dave Taylor explains how Google works for your [_____] in algorithmic science. This book is straightforward, useful, and designed for the entrepreneur—because you are the one who needs to understand this well enough to make it work, make the most of it, and then well enough to know that others are doing it right on your behalf."

—Jim Sterne, author, *Advanced Email Marketing* and *Web Metrics*

"How can a company known best for its search engine possibly help a business? Google AdSense changed my publishing model (of five years) in less than five minutes. Google has created a powerful system for you to use, but without a guide … you'll lose money making opportunities instead of making money."

—Chris Pirillo, technology evangelist, Lockergnome.com

"Are you trying to build a business on the Internet? Then this is the book for you. … Google (and other search engines like Yahoo! and MSN, which now really work very similarly to Google) today is the modern-day equivalent of the Yellow Pages. … This book will ensure that customers find *you* instead of your competition."

—Robert Scoble, Microsoft evangelist

"Given the choice among your smart nephew, that friend from your reading club, the person who designed your website, the slick, unsolicited sales pitch from a "search engine optimization" company, or Dave Taylor, whose advice should you trust when it comes to marketing your business online? Dave's, of course! … Although it focuses on Google and is purported to be for 'idiots,' this book should be required reading for all online entrepreneurs."

—Andrew Goodman, author of *Winning Results With Google AdWords*

"Dave Taylor has written an inspired book on growing your business online. By placing Google center stage he is striking a blow for common sense and pointing the way to a foolproof approach to succeeding online."

—Nick Usborne, author of *Net Words*, www.nickusborne.com

"You better stock up the refrigerator with Diet Coke, Skittles, and sandwich meat before you crack open Dave Taylor's book for the first time … because once you start reading, you're not going to want to stop! You'll be amazed at what you learn, and you'll want to get started applying what you've learned right away. No matter how much you think you know (or think you don't know) about marketing on the Internet … this book is a real eye-opener, and a real page-turner."

—Gregg Stebben, co-author of *Internet Privacy for Dummies*

"Dave Taylor's book takes the confusion and the hype out of Internet marketing. Written for business owners—not computer geeks or direct marketers—the book … explains the steps you must take to put your business on the web, get it found, and make your website a profit center."

—Janet Attard, CEO, BusinessKnowHow.com

"Dave provides tools and strategies that you can use tomorrow to increase the 'findability' of your business. A must-read for everyone looking at leveraging the web to grow their business"

—Rajesh Setty, president, CIGNEX Technologies, and author of "Beyond Code"

"Findability is the key element that establishes the value of your business on the Internet; if you can't be found, you don't exist. Dave recognizes this essential requirement and focuses like a laser beam on this goal to help you achieve the greatest Internet visibility for your company, product, or service."

—Bill French, co-founder, MyST Technology Partners

"The most intelligent book I've seen on how to leverage the power of Google for your own business. Focus on 'findability,' follow Dave's insightful tips on content, and you'll win!"

—Debbie Weil, president, WordBiz.com, Inc., and publisher of BeginnersGuidetoBlogging.com.

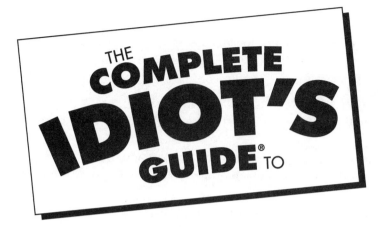

Growing Your Business with Google

by Dave Taylor

ALPHA

A member of Penguin Group (USA) Inc.

For the brightest stars in my firmament, Kiana, Gareth, Ashley, and Linda.

ALPHA BOOKS

Published by the Penguin Group

Penguin Group (USA) Inc., 375 Hudson Street, New York, New York 10014, U.S.A.

Penguin Group (Canada), 10 Alcorn Avenue, Toronto, Ontario, Canada M4V 3B2 (a division of Pearson Penguin Canada Inc.)

Penguin Books Ltd, 80 Strand, London WC2R 0RL, England

Penguin Ireland, 25 St Stephen's Green, Dublin 2, Ireland (a division of Penguin Books Ltd)

Penguin Group (Australia), 250 Camberwell Road, Camberwell, Victoria 3124, Australia (a division of Pearson Australia Group Pty Ltd)

Penguin Books India Pvt Ltd, 11 Community Centre, Panchsheel Park, New Delhi—110 017, India

Penguin Group (NZ), cnr Airborne and Rosedale Roads, Albany, Auckland 1310, New Zealand (a division of Pearson New Zealand Ltd)

Penguin Books (South Africa) (Pty) Ltd, 24 Sturdee Avenue, Rosebank, Johannesburg 2196, South Africa

Penguin Books Ltd, Registered Offices: 80 Strand, London WC2R 0RL, England

Copyright © 2005 by Dave Taylor

International Standard Book Number: 1-59257-396-7
Library of Congress Catalog Card Number: 2005925423

07 06 05   8 7 6 5 4 3 2 1

Interpretation of the printing code: The rightmost number of the first series of numbers is the year of the book's printing; the rightmost number of the second series of numbers is the number of the book's printing. For example, a printing code of 05-1 shows that the first printing occurred in 2005.

Printed in the United States of America

Note: This publication contains the opinions and ideas of its author. It is intended to provide helpful and informative material on the subject matter covered. It is sold with the understanding that the author and publisher are not engaged in rendering professional services in the book. If the reader requires personal assistance or advice, a competent professional should be consulted.

The author and publisher specifically disclaim any responsibility for any liability, loss, or risk, personal or otherwise, which is incurred as a consequence, directly or indirectly, of the use and application of any of the contents of this book.

Most Alpha books are available at special quantity discounts for bulk purchases for sales promotions, premiums, fund-raising, or educational use. Special books, or book excerpts, can also be created to fit specific needs.

For details, write: Special Markets, Alpha Books, 375 Hudson Street, New York, NY 10014.

Publisher: *Marie Butler-Knight*
Product Manager: *Phil Kitchel*
Senior Managing Editor: *Jennifer Bowles*
Senior Acquisitions Editor: *Renee Wilmeth*
Development Editor: *Michael Koch*
Production Editor: *Megan Douglass*
Copy Editor: *Ross Patty*
Cartoonist: *Shannon Wheeler*
Cover/Book Designer: *Trina Wurst*
Indexer: *Angie Bess*
Layout: *Ayanna Lacey*
Proofreading: *Donna Martin*

Contents at a Glance

Part 1:   **The Business Case for Google**   1

1   Increasing Your Business Visibility   3
You need more customers, here's how you get them.

2   The Benefits of Increasing Your Visibility with Google   13
If you build it right, they will find you.

3   What Is Google Anyway?   23
Advertising, shopping, weblogs, and a search engine, too.

4   Learning About Google Search   35
To understand your customers, you have to search like them.

5   Disassembling the Google Search Engine   47
Lifting the veil on PageRank, relevance scores, and all the other critical mysteries of Google.

Part 2:   **Building Your Google Plan**   59

6   What's Your Core Business?   61
You can't improve your web presence until you identify your core business.

7   Living in an Online World   71
The subtle nuances of business names, domain names, and the rest of the Internet.

8   Your Business Website   81
Time to assess the state of your current site and identify areas for improvement.

9   Assessing Your Competitors   95
Think you don't have any competition? Think again.

10   Keeping Track of Customers   109
The best businesses are always one step ahead, because of their intimate knowledge of their customers. Here's how they do that.

Part 3:   **Improving Your Online Business Site**   119

11   The Basics of Building a Good Business Site   121
Read this chapter and you'll find out what makes a great business website, and it isn't particularly similar to a personal site.

12 Developing Online and Offline Content   137
It's all about content, whether in print or digital.

13 Stretching Your Marketing Dollars   151
*Smart, low-cost ways to exploit web technologies to minimize
your expenditures and maximize the effect of every dollar
spent.*

14 Secrets of the Online Marketing Masters   161
*Insider tips on how to change your website to improve your
search engine ranking, and more!*

Part 4:   **Promoting and Growing Your Online Business**   **171**

15 Content, Content, Content!   173
*If each web page is a hook trying to lure customers, it's time
to learn how to throw out more hooks.*

16 Becoming a More Popular Site   185
*Simple ways to increase your PageRank and increase your
web page findability.*

17 Becoming an Online Expert   199
*Promote yourself as an expert, share your knowledge, and
you'll be promoting your business, too.*

18 Advertising Your Business with Google AdWords   213
*An innovative method of promoting your site through simple
text ads, often at remarkably little cost.*

19 Making Money with Google AdSense   235
*Turn your website from a cost center into a profit center with
Google AdSense.*

20 The Advantages of Affiliate Programs   249
*You already promote related products, why not make a small
commission on each sale?*

21 Avoiding Dumb Online Promotional Mistakes   261
*There are snakes in the search engine optimization grass that
you must avoid, and here's how to do so.*

Part 5:   **What's Next on Your To-Do List?**   **275**

22   Growing and Expanding Your Content   277
Ingenious ways to attain content for your site, for far less than you expect.

23   The Future of Findability   291
What happens when Google isn't #1? It's not too early to start planning for the future.

Appendixes

A   Websites Worth Exploring   301

B   Glossary   307

Index   313

Contents

Part 1: The Business Case for Google   **1**

1 Increasing Your Business Visibility   **3**

The Importance of Visibility...4

What Is Your Current Business?...6

Your Current Internet Strategy...8

    E-mail and One-to-One Communication *8*

    Newsletters and Other Publishing Venues *9*

    Your Website *10*

    Your Online Store *10*

    Your Brand Identity *11*

You Need More Customers! 12

2 The Benefits of Increasing Your Visibility with Google   **13**

You Want Customers, Not Traffic 15

Driving Customers to Your Website.....................................17

Driving Customers to the Products in Your Store....................18

Build Buzz about a Product, Service, or Idea.........................19

Maximize the Value of Your Marketing and PR......................22

3 What Is Google Anyway?   **23**

It's a Search Engine with More! 25

Google Labs...25

Google Mail 26

Paid Advertising with Google AdWords 28

    Ads that Appear on Specific Searches Only *29*

    Three Different Types of AdWords Accounts *29*

AdSense: The Networked Ad Distribution System 30

Weblogs Help Keep Your Website Fresh...............................32

Froogle and Catalog Shopping with Google 33

4 Learning About Google Search   **35**

The Genius of Google 36

A Basic Approach to Searching..38

This Is How Your Customers Find You 39

Advanced Search Techniques, a.k.a. Punctuation Soup 40

The Importance of Quoting 43

Special Search Notations...43

The Surprising Importance of Word Order in Queries 45

5 Disassembling the Google Search Engine 47

Why You Need to Care How Google Works 48

The Magic of PageRank 50

Why You Want Spiders to Visit Your Site 52

How Spiders Work *53*

How Often Will Googlebot Visit? *53*

Relevance Scoring 54

Inbound Links *54*

Link Text...*54*

The Content and Layout of the Web Page *57*

The Key Ramification of Relevance Scoring *57*

Yahoo!, MSN, and Other Search Sites 58

Part 2: Building Your Google Plan 59

6 What's Your Core Business? 61

The Importance of Staying Focused..................................62

When Diversification Works...*62*

Think Strategy, Not Tactics *63*

Focus on What Customers Want......................................*64*

Differentiators and Sustainable Differentiators 64

Dare to Be Different *65*

Find Your Long-Term Niche *66*

Competition Is Good 67

Markets Evolve *68*

Watch and Learn *68*

Setting Goals for Your Company 69

7 Living in an Online World 71

How the Domain Name System Works...............................72

Internet-Friendly Business Names and Slogans.......................74

Search Terms and Keywords 75

Domain Names and How to Get Them..............................77

8 Your Business Website 81

Online Curb Appeal 82

The State of Your Existing Site 83

How Functional Are Your Secondary Pages? *83*

What's the Best Content to Include? 86
   Core Content for a Good Business Website............................*87*
   Findability Is About Content! *89*
   What Can You Add to Your Site? *90*
How Often to Update Your Information 92
Creating Two Websites, Not One 93

9 Assessing Your Competitors   **95**
Identifying Competitors 96
   Finding Local Businesses............................*96*
   Businesses with Global Competition............................*99*
   After You've Identified Competitors *100*
Tracking New Competitors............................101
   Using Google News Alerts and Usenet *101*
   Combing Through the Blogosphere *104*
Watching Job Listings............................105
Participating in Discussion Boards 106

10 Keeping Track of Customers   **109**
Understanding the Elusive Customer............................110
Learning What Customers Seek............................111
   Exploring Wordtracker............................*111*
   Capturing Queries from Your Own Search Service *115*
What Are Customers Talking About?............................116
   Discussion Boards *116*
   Weblogs and Individual Websites............................*117*
   Mailing Lists *118*

Part 3: Improving Your Online Business Site   **119**

11 The Basics of Building a Good Business Site   **121**
The Key Elements of a Good Website............................122
   Keep Your Website on Topic............................*122*
   Remember that It's Your Site *124*
   Limit the Complexity of Your Site............................*124*
   Don't Get Caught Up with Design Fads............................*125*
   Design a Search Engine–Friendly Site *127*
Business Website Considerations 127
   It's All About Trust *127*
   Use the Right Technologies *129*
   Have Calls To Action *129*

Sell Your Company to the Visitor *130*
Don't Send Your Visitors Away..*131*
Be Responsive to Your Customers...*132*
Think Globally, Not Locally *133*
Five Ideas to Remember 134

12   Developing Online and Offline Content   **137**
Tying Your Collateral into Your Website 138
Have Visual Consistency Across Media *138*
Don't Be Shy About Your URL *140*
Answer Customer Questions on Your Site 142
Question and Answer Formats *142*
Weblogs as Q&A Alternatives...*146*
What Other Content Do You Have? 148
How Can You Serve Your Customers Better? 149

13   Stretching Your Marketing Dollars   **151**
The Marketing Expenditure Conundrum 152
Product-Based Websites 153
Turning Your Press Releases into Content................................155
Newsletters and Customer Communications.............................156
Writing Style *157*
Too Much Design, Too Little Content *158*
Sponsoring Other Newsletters and Sites 159

14   Secrets of the Online Marketing Masters   **161**
Search Engine–Friendly Page Design 162
Skip the Fancy Applets and Navigation Toolbars........................*163*
Too Much Design Detracts from the Content...............................*163*
The Importance of Page Titles...164
The Diminishing Relevance of Meta Tags 165
The Skinny About Keyword Density 166
Naming Links and Pages Effectively 167
Requesting Thematically Related Inbound Links 168
The Pitfalls of Trading Links 169

Part 4:   Promoting and Growing Your Online Business   **171**

15   Content, Content, Content!   **173**
Update Your Site Frequently 174
Adding Discussion Forums 176

Surveys and Games 177
Finding Content for Your Site 178
Weblogs as Content Management Systems 178
   Incorporating a Weblog into Your Site........................180
   The Value of RSS, Really Simple Syndication 181
   Writing for a Weblog 184

16 Becoming a More Popular Site   185

Submitting Your Site to Search Engines 186
   Yahoo! Directory........................186
   The Open Directory Project 187
   About.com 188
   Topical Web Directories and Search Engines 189
Submitting Your Weblog to Blog Indices.................191
Requesting Inbound Links 192
Creating Mini-Stores........................193
   Opening an eBay Store........................194
   Joining the Yahoo! Shopping Program 195
   Joining the Froogle Merchant Program 197

17 Becoming an Online Expert   199

Information Wants to Be Free 200
   Who Are These Experts? 201
   The Secret Benefits of Being an Online Expert 202
Mailing Lists 202
   E-mail as Advertisements........................203
   The Importance of Signatures........................204
   Mailing List Do's and Don'ts 206
   Finding Good Mailing Lists 206
Hanging Around Discussion Boards........................207
Weblogs and Weblog Comments 209
Usenet Groups........................210

18 Advertising Your Business with Google AdWords   213

Understanding How AdWords Works 214
Finding the Best Keywords 215
   Picking Good Keywords 216
   Working with WordTracker 216
   Keyword Research with Google AdWords........................219

Creating an Ad Campaign 220
Step 1: Language and Location Targeting 221
Step 2: Create AdGroups 221
Step 3a: Choose Keywords and Maximum Cost-Per-Click 223
Step 3b: Specify Your Daily Budget 225
Editing and Modifying Your Campaign Settings 225
Setting Per Keyword Maximum Cost-Per-Click 228
Monitoring Your AdWords Campaign 231
Writing Good Ad Copy 232

19 Making Money with Google AdSense   235

Understanding How AdSense Works 236
Configuring an AdSense Ad Block 237
Maximizing Click-Through Rates 240
How Much Money Can You Make? 241
Stay Focused on Your Business 243
Figuring Out Where to Include AdSense Ads 244
AdSense for Search 245
Avoiding Ads from Direct Competitors 245
Some Additional Thoughts About AdSense 247

20 The Advantages of Affiliate Programs   249

Affiliate Programs in a Nutshell 250
How Affiliate Programs Work 250
Sophisticated Affiliate Management Systems 251
The Affiliate Terms of Service Agreement 252
Acceptable Sites 253
Ownership of Intellectual Property 254
Acceptable Promotional Techniques 255
Commission Structure and Payment 256
What to Require on an Affiliate Application 257
When to Add Affiliate Products or Services to Your Site 257
A Sampling of Affiliates 258
Signing Up 259

21 Avoiding Dumb Online Promotional Mistakes   261

How to Recognize Pay-for-Placement Scams 262
Managing a Link Farm 264
Ranking for Obscure Keywords 264

Ten Dumb Tricks to Avoid on Your Website 265
    Hidden or Cloaked Text 266
    Keyword Stuffing 266
    Doorway Pages 267
    Different Pages for Different Visitors 267
    Refresh Pages 268
    SEO "Content" Pages 269
    Too Darn Many Links 269
    Duplicate Content 270
    ALT Text and META Keywords 270
    TITLE Tags 271
What Tools to Avoid 271
    Position Analysis Tools 271
    Backlink Farming Tools 271
The Smart Alternative 272

Part 5:   **What's Next on Your To-Do List?**   **275**

22   **Growing and Expanding Your Content**   **277**
The Importance of Copyright Law 278
Licensing Content 280
    Republishing Magazine Articles 280
    Finding Authors to Republish 281
    Excerpting Articles on Your Site 282
    Working with a Writer's Syndicate 282
    Hiring a Writer 283
Syndicating Your Own Content 284
Publishing Your Own E-mail Newsletter 286
Including Content in Your Store 288
    Provide a User-Friendly Shopping Cart 288
    Content, Even During the Shopping Experience 288

23   **The Future of Findability**   **291**
It's All About Content! 293
    Companies Don't Leverage Their Content Online 293
    Tapping into the Zeitgeist 294
Optimizing the Organic Way 295
Through the Looking Glass: The Future of Google 296
    The Problem of Affiliate Websites 296
    How Affiliates Corrupt AdWords 298

Facing the Competition..*298*

Don't Write Off Google Yet *300*

Appendixes

   A Websites Worth Exploring   **301**

   B Glossary   **307**

       Index   **313**

Foreword

One of Steve Jobs's most quotable lines is, "There must be a better way." He was, of course, referring to a better way of interacting with a personal computer.

Steve's line is applicable time and again to the game-changing impact of Google:

- There must be a better way to advertise my goods and services.
- There must be a better way to search for information.
- There must be a better way to use the Internet as a marketing weapon.
- There must be a better way to use Google to grow my business.

This book explains these better ways, and it does this in such an insanely great manner that I felt compelled to get off my complacent butt and write the foreword.

This book is not a simple compilation of tips and tricks. Instead, it provides two of the most important things you can get from a book:

- A conceptual framework that shows you how to holistically approach, analyze, and alter your business to increase sales. Call this "doing the right thing."
- A down-and-dirty tactical approach to optimizing a dozen little things in your business and on your website that differentiate you from your competition. Call this "doing it the right way."

I disagree with only one aspect of the book: the title. It's totally inaccurate because the idiot is the person who doesn't read this book, not the one who does.

Guy Kawasaki
Managing director, Garage Technology Ventures
Author of *The Art of the Start*

Introduction

When you started to think about moving your business online, even if just as a digital billboard advertising your retail outlet or professional service, you were doubtless inundated with expert advice. Your site was likely built by one of these ostensible experts and today serves as a lonely outpost, producing the occasional customer.

Here's the unfortunate reality: odds are very good that your web designer has led you astray. Not through any fault of their own, but because web designers and developers have a bad habit of being focused on how things look rather than on how things actually work.

Worrying about pretty graphics was a fine strategy a few years ago, but as Google and other sophisticated search engines have grown in importance, the need for websites that are built around content, about *what* rather than *how*, has become critical. In a nutshell, your business website needs to be focused on *what you're selling*.

Think of the World Wide Web as a vast information ocean, with millions of hooks floating just under the surface, waiting for your potential customer to seek your product or service. Successful business sites are based upon maximizing both the value of their hooks and the number of hooks, to have optimal page design for findability and as many pages with legitimate, relevant content as possible.

If you aren't already viewing your site as an information resource, then chances are very good that every time a customer searches for your product, your competitor is closing the deal and leaving you out in the cold.

The good news is that it's not about spending money. Solving this problem isn't about splashy and expensive advertising campaigns or signs on Fifth Avenue and along Rodeo Drive. It's about rethinking what it means to be an online business in the twenty-first century, and that's exactly what *The Complete Idiot's Guide to Growing Your Business with Google* will help you do, in great detail.

Don't just flip to the chapters that sound good, however. Read through all the material; study this as if there's an exam at the end. In fact, there is a test, the test of what results your business sees after applying the hundreds of smart ideas found in this book.

Like any competitive field, there are dangers lurking and unscrupulous consultants and self-appointed experts who will offer you help in this regard, too. Beware! Their help can end up with your site quite literally vanishing from the major search engines *forever*. I don't need to tell you the consequences of that happening and its impact on your business!

While reading this book, I hope you will rethink your business web presence. I include extensive and widely varied examples for just that purpose, demonstrating time and again how literally any business, from a plumbing business to a gas station, can reap significant benefits from a thoughtful, findable, content-centric online presence.

And I bet you'll have fun in the process, too!

Oh, let me tell you a secret, shall I? I understand your reticence about buying a book called *The Complete Idiot's Guide*, but it's really your competitors who are going to feel like idiots when they see the changes you've made to your online presence and the remarkable benefits you'll be reaping.

Trust me, by the very fact that you've picked up this book, you're far from being any sort of idiot. You're just starting a journey into the next era of business, an era when online and offline will blur, an era where *findability* will be more important than branding, than even marketing.

Enough introduction. Time's a wasting, so let's get started.

How This Book Is Organized

This book is divided into five parts. The sequence is designed to lead you through the process of learning how Google works, why it's the leader in the market, what is and isn't working on your website, and how to change and improve things to grow your business with Google.

Part 1, "The Business Case for Google," asks you to take a hard look at your current Internet strategy and the results you're seeing with your website. It explains how successful sites attract customers, not visitors, gives an in-depth tour of Google's iconic search engine, and then visits some other valuable Google properties. Perhaps most critical, Part 1 introduces you to the importance of content on your site and explains weblogs as a method of managing your content.

Part 2, "Building your Google Plan," starts by requiring more introspection on your part, this time requiring you to identify your core business, your value proposition, and how your business fundamentally differs—if it does—from your competition. Time is spent talking about the importance of domain names and the state of your current business website, wrapping up with an introduction to competitive research and customer research on the web.

By the time you've completed these first two parts, you should have a very good sense of your business, whether it's been translated to your business website accurately and the strengths and weaknesses of your existing site.

Part 3, "Improving Your Online Business Site," offers an extensive checklist of smart strategies to expand your presence online, improve your business website, integrate your online and offline communications, and stretch your marketing dollars. Part 3 wraps up with one of the most important chapters in the book, "Secrets of the Online Marketing Masters," a must-read for everyone associated with your website, especially any of the developers.

Part 4, "Promoting and Growing Your Online Business," picks up on the importance of adding content to your website and turns the melody into a full-blown symphony. It's the cornerstone of this entire book, that websites need to focus on findability, and that the single best way to increase your findability is by adding more content to your site. Part 4 also explores important methods whereby you can generate revenue from your website and change your website from a cost center into a profit center.

Chapter 21 is another must-read chapter, because you learn exactly how *not to* improve the findability of your site. There are lots of consultants pitching magic techniques to improve your search engine ranking, but it's all snake oil or worse, and this chapter explains all their dastardly tricks and why *you must avoid them at all costs.*

Part 5, "What's Next on Your To-Do List?" addresses a common failing in business help books by focusing on the future of the web and findability. Building the best possible site today, just to find out that it's worse than useless tomorrow, is not only frustrating, but can be devastating for your business. Instead, this last section explores ways to set up your site for long-term success and details exactly what will be important in the next generation of search engines and beyond.

There's an appendix that has a glossary of jargon and buzzwords that are tossed around in the web and marketing business, but you won't need to reference it as you go through the book; I've put lots of effort forth to avoid acronyms and computer jargon. Because I'm frequently writing about my own experiences, you'll get to chuckle along, too.

Extras

As you go through the pages of this book, you'll see special boxes that will help you avoid problems, understand technical lingo, gain a leg up, and learn something new and helpful.

BizTips

These boxes contain tips that can help you do things better or easier.

Memo

These boxes contain general notes or comments.

Buzzwords

These boxes contain definitions of terms and expressions that may be new or confusing to you.

Beware

These boxes contain warnings about things you should avoid if you want to stay out of trouble.

Acknowledgments

It's taken me years to gain the knowledge and insight needed to write this book in an informed and coherent manner. Many people and groups have helped me on this journey, but none more than The International Society of Online Entrepreneurs (known informally as "Internet Hotshots"), an invitation-only group of top-notch businesspeople who have taken the leap into the online world and carved out completely new businesses for themselves.

I've also had lots of wonderful advice on the content of this book as I've proceeded, including invaluable feedback on AdWords from Dan Murray, search engine optimization insight from Brad Fallon, and affiliate marketing tips from Shawn Collins. The following other entrepreneurs also offered their time generously to improve the content and presentation: Adam Boettiger, Chuck Eglinton, Janet Attard, John Locke, Jon Trelfa, Judi Wellnitz, Steve Loyola, Tara Calishain, Tim Carter, Tom Novak, and Werner Klauser. Having listed them all, however, I'm still the man in the middle of the production whirlwind and any mistakes herein are purely my responsibility.

Google Corporation has also helped with the content of this book, ensuring the accuracy of Chapters 18 and 19. Google also granted me the rare privilege of violating the AdWords and AdSense terms of service agreements so that I could share real figures and real results. Thank you for your help, and thank you, Larry and Sergey, for your brilliant insights into what makes a good search result in the first place!

WordTracker Corporation was also generous with a complimentary account and thoughtful feedback on the material that discusses their valuable keyword research tools.

Finally, my most heartfelt acknowledgements go to my family for putting up with yet another book project and for letting me vanish for extended periods of time to research and write. There wouldn't be much point to these projects without the wonderful reward of knowing my wife and children are ready to play and celebrate.

Special Thanks to the Technical Reviewer

The Complete Idiot's Guide to Growing Your Business with Google has also been reviewed by an expert who double-checked the accuracy of what you'll learn here, to help us ensure that this book gives you everything you need to know about Google and online business ventures without leading you astray. Special thanks are extended to Werner Klauser.

Trademarks

All terms mentioned in this book that are known to be or are suspected of being trademarks or service marks have been appropriately capitalized. Alpha Books and Penguin Group (USA) Inc. cannot attest to the accuracy of this information. Use of a term in this book should not be regarded as affecting the validity of any trademark or service mark.

Part  The Business Case for Google

You're reading this book because you aren't happy with the status quo and you want to see your business grow significantly in the next few months. To accomplish this goal, you'll need to rethink your business presence and, most critically, learn how to use Google the same way as your customers.

This part explains all of these foundational ideas, discussing why the concept of findability is the new business strategy and how Google factors into that goal. You'll then learn all about Google search and the many other facets of the company (and how they can all help your business grow).

Most critically, you'll also learn about PageRank and how the Google search engine figures out what pages should be listed first for any given search query. Vital information for any online business!

Increasing Your Business Visibility

In This Chapter

- ◆ Why visibility is critically important
- ◆ How to identify the essence of your business
- ◆ How to gauge your current Internet strategy

As recently as a decade ago it was an unusual business that was accessible to customers online. Maybe if you were running a computer repair business or sold high-end HAM radio gear, but mostly there was the business world and the quite separate online world. Indeed, most of the online world was still corralled in tightly controlled and managed content offered by a few large companies like America Online, CompuServe, and the Microsoft Network.

The Internet changes everything, however, and if you're still thinking about your business as separate from the online world, then you're missing out on the chance to grow, expand, improve your offerings, learn more about your competition, keep more up-to-date on industry trends, and, most importantly, find new customers and retain more of your existing customers.

Not only does the Internet change everything, but Google changes the Internet, too. It wasn't more than a few years ago that the most important thing you could do for your business was make sure you were listed in topical website directories, that you found out about competitors from print publications or word of mouth. With its billion-page index and lightning-fast search engine, Google has redefined the Age of Information, in a way that has profound implications for your business. It's the realization of the promise of vast amounts of information, freely accessible, for those who are willing to swim in the information sea.

And why Google? As I write this book, Google is the clear industry leader, the "go-to source" for any information needed. Whether I'm searching for a manual for my new toaster, updating an application on my Treo, or even trying to find a fellow writer to have a digital tête-à-tête, much of what defines the modern web starts on Google's simple search page.

In five years, there'll be meaningful and valuable competitors, other search engines that will offer capabilities not available in Google, better search results, more geo-mapping, a personalized search history, tightly integrated web and desktop search, and myriad other possible features. Prime contenders for the new crown as king of search engines are Yahoo! and the Microsoft MSN Search teams (both of which are discussed throughout the book).

And it doesn't matter what kind of business you have. Whether you are trying to sell your first novel, balancing the books as a freelance accountant, introducing an environmentally friendly dry-cleaning system to your neighborhood, or selling used cars, there's not a business around that can't benefit from being online and making savvy use of Google and the entire Internet.

The Importance of Visibility

Pick up a book that professes to lead you through the challenges of evaluating a possible franchise opportunity and you'll encounter one of the most enduring clichés of business, that success for a retail establishment is all about *location, location, location.*

I'm not going to deny the wisdom of that, because for some businesses that have a prime location with a lot of foot traffic and a lot of potential customers already in the mood for your product, it can make a significant difference in whether the business is successful or not. Two examples of this are a florist who leases space adjacent to a large hospital, and a fast-food restaurant built across the street from a busy high school.

I'll bet that there's at least one restaurant in your town that has a terrible location, no viable and related businesses near it, and somehow it manages to win awards and always be busy, though. For that business, location isn't the cornerstone of their success, or perhaps they've just turned the entire concept on its head and recognized that they can compete by having lower overhead by being away from the prime rent areas and leveraging the savings with advertising and better staff.

Memo
Location, location, location: How does that translate in a digital world? *Findability.* If you can't be found, you don't exist.

Whether the business owner has opted to pay the premium to be located in a critical spot or has chosen to locate outside of the mainstream and apply the savings to marketing or a more easily attained profit point, what they have in common is an awareness of *visibility*.

That's ultimately what this book is all about: visibility, or, in Internet parlance, findability. Can people find you, find your products, and learn enough about your business to become customers? And just as importantly, can existing customers communicate quickly and effectively with you so that you can maximize your customer retention, because another business maxim is that it always costs less to retain an existing customer than to find a new one.

Visibility is the most fundamental yardstick against which to measure how well your company and products are known to both your existing customer base and your potential customer base. Companies with high visibility invariably are more successful than those with low visibility. But that makes sense, doesn't it? The restaurant four blocks from your office, the one tucked into the strip mall and too poor to afford a nice sign or display ad in the Yellow Pages, is never going to compete with the chic eatery downtown that sends out coupons to local businesses and is active in Chamber of Commerce events.

On the Internet, visibility revolves around the question of *when people search for your product or service, do they find you or your competitors?* It's what I call *findability*.

That's the essence of this book, in one sentence, and I'll come back to it again and again as I take you through the spiral of Google services, online business, and the Internet.

What Is Your Current Business?

Before I get too excited about the many wonderful opportunities to increase your findability, let's start at the beginning, and the beginning of any business is to figure out exactly what your business *is*, and what your business *isn't*.

One hallmark of a successful small business is focus. Every expert will give you the same advice, to narrow your vision, not to try to be everything to everyone, but to pick one specific product or service and strive to be the very best.

When I work with start-up executives, here's how I address the never-ending challenge of staying on focus. I give them a folder with the word "tomorrow" written upon it in big, bold letters. Then each time a great new business idea pops up, I encourage the exec to write it down in as much detail as possible, then put the paper into the folder and the folder back in the drawer. Tomorrow, that is, when they're a success and are ready to move in a new direction or expand their offerings, they can pull the folder out, read through all the brilliant ideas, and identify one or two that still seem like a good idea.

As you begin this journey of learning how to grow your business online using Google and other Internet technologies, therefore, a good starting point is to isolate the key *differentiators* that make your company what it is.

To do this, pull out some paper and try to answer the following questions.

- What is your key service or product offering?

- How much competition do you have in your segment?

- How does your company differentiate itself from the competition?

- How would your customers explain what differentiates your company from your competition?

◆ What kind of barriers to entry are there in your segment?

◆ How *sustainable* are your differentiators?

A lot of entrepreneurs are surprised when they begin to analyze their business and find out that they're one of a thousand fish in a small pond, perhaps, or have the opposite situation, with very little competition because they've already established themselves as the leader in their segment.

Whichever place you might be in, having a firm grasp of your business and its *sustainable differentiators* is of critical importance, because it is the foundation for everything else we explore in this book. If you're not sure of your business focus, then try explaining your business to an uninterested bystander. In ninety seconds.

Buzzwords _____

A differentiator is something that enables customers to see how you are different from your competitors, and a **sustainable differentiator** is a differentiator that you continue to leverage even after your competitors realize how smart your differentiator is and seek to use it themselves.

It's much harder to have a sustainable differentiator. Consider how other airlines now have low-cost shuttle services with seating similar to Southwest Airlines, and how Apple's design success has spawned dozens of look-alike PC manufacturers.

I won't go so far as to say that if you can't describe your business in less than 10 words you haven't yet distilled your business down to its essence, but I do think that focus and clarity are critical to growth and success.

Another effective strategy is to frame your product or service in terms of a problem/ solution pair. For example, a mobile auto mechanic might think of her business in terms of customers being too busy. In this case, the problem is that people whose cars aren't working properly don't have the time to get their car to a mechanic. The business opportunity is the solution, bringing the tools and expertise to them, either at their home or their office, and fixing their car on location.

That's a good start for a business focus, though it's still too broad because the expertise needed to fix the brakes on a Hummer is quite different from the expertise required to debug a recurring electrical problem on an old Mustang. In this case,

I'd suggest that the mechanic might take inspiration from auto repair facilities and specialize in a particular brand or type of car, offering a ninety-second pitch:

> Porsche owners are busy, successful people who don't have the time to get their car repaired. As a certified Porsche mechanic, I bring my garage to you and fix your car wherever is most convenient for you.

That sounds like a good business, doesn't it?

Your Current Internet Strategy

If you are that mobile mechanic, your greatest challenge isn't learning more about Porsche engines or figuring out how to manage your time; it's how to gain customers in the first place.

The fundamental challenge of all business is to identify your ideal customers and then find them. Or, in the Age of Information, to ensure that they can find you.

To identify and find potential customers, businesses must have visibility in their target community. Without potential customers knowing about your business, you can have the best service or product in the world and you'll still fail. This is, of course, the better mousetrap conundrum.

The Internet is quite a bit more than just the World Wide Web, so when you assess the state of your Internet strategy, it's imperative that you consider all of the following:

- ♦ E-mail and one-to-one communication
- ♦ Newsletters and other publishing venues
- ♦ Your website
- ♦ Your online store
- ♦ Your brand identity

Let's go through these one by one.

E-mail and One-to-One Communication

If I had a nickel for each time I've visited a website and sent an e-mail to tech support, sales, or marketing, and that e-mail was never answered, I'd be able to pay for a very nice holiday for my family. The problem isn't that these companies aren't making it easy for you to find their e-mail addresses; it's that they aren't answering the messages.

When you get an e-mail from a customer or potential customer, do you *always, 100 percent of the time*, answer it promptly? Can customers even find your e-mail address or contact form?

This seems so obvious, but if you're going to have a contact capability on your website, make sure you answer all inquiries, and if you don't want to spend your time that way, hire someone who will. You need to think of it as every unanswered message being a lost sale.

Memo
Even entrepreneurs should be responsive via e-mail, and you can test me in this regard! Pop over to the book's website— www.findability.info—and send me a question just to see how quickly I respond.

Newsletters and Other Publishing Venues

Printing and distributing a glossy full-color magazine is prohibitively expensive for all but the largest of companies. With the Internet, however, you can publish a regular or infrequent newsletter, updating both existing and potential customers of specials, new products, and industry news.

While some companies hire a designer and send out newsletters with fancy formatting that includes graphics, logos, and other sophisticated elements, there's no reason you can't send out a simple text message that looks much more like a personal e-mail message from you than a formal communiqué from the marketing department. Frankly, the personal touch is probably a lot more effective in terms of establishing a strong relationship with your customers anyway.

As an example, I have a newsletter I send out to my readers every few months. The total cost is the time it takes for me to decide what I want to talk about and write the actual message. A minimal effort, yet it lets me establish a relationship with my customers, cross-market my products, and even pre-sell new projects, leveraging an already successful relationship.

Doesn't sound like a major effort, but I get 20 to 50 new subscribers to my newsletter every single month, whether I remember to send out an issue or not. No one ever unsubscribes. These are my very favorite customers because they're fans; they're devotees; they're exactly the kind of customer every business wants to foster.

This is another key concept of online marketing: the Internet is working for you even when you're not doing anything. Online entrepreneurs like to refer to this as "making money while you sleep," and it really happens once you have everything set up properly for your online business.

Are you using a newsletter to spread the good news about your company?

Another facet of online publishing is joining and sharing your expertise in online forums and discussion lists. I'll talk about that more in Chapter 17.

Your Website

You do have a website, right? And it quickly and accurately conveys the essence of your business, detailing your products or services while conveying your sustainable differentiators?

Being able to say yes to those questions doesn't mean you're done, however, because you should be exploiting the dynamic nature of the web and maximizing your findability. One way to accomplish this is to view your website not as an electronic billboard, to be built and ignored, but as a stall in a bazaar, having to constantly change to reflect the latest needs and interests of your customers.

It's also critical to recognize that thinking of your website as a dynamic facet of your business is important regardless of whether you have something you can sell online or not.

Your Online Store

One of the greatest mistakes I see in the world of online business is that companies with products believe that their products are all that count, and companies that don't have tangible products don't think that they're selling anything.

If you have products, then you should ask yourself: How am I selling my *company* to customers, establishing our expertise, and demonstrating why they should buy from us rather than our competitors?

Memo
A great entrepreneurial question: What can I sell that would create an additional income stream?

If you have a service, then it's likely that your website is focused on demonstrating your expertise. But ask yourself: What could I sell that would create an additional income stream and let potential customers "sample" my expertise without having to engage my services directly?

Scale is important, too, because as a service provider you can only work a certain number of hours in a day, so you're constrained to a maximum income of your hourly wage times the number of hours you can work in a year. Or are you? I'll explore this question as we proceed through the book together.

Your Brand Identity

Ultimately all successful businesses need to create a brand, to become a known name, to be "China Gourmet" and not "that Chinese place, whatchamacallit, off Broadway." The mobile Porsche mechanic I discussed earlier also needs to create a brand and thereby gain that all-important visibility.

Even as an author, creating a brand is quite important. Consider Tom Clancy, who has leveraged his considerable talent in writing fictional thrillers into a quite profitable sideline as a consultant to computer and video game developers.

I've done the same thing with one of my websites. Look at Figure 1.1 and notice that it's not a boring, mostly static self-aggrandizing author site, but rather a *branded* Ask Dave Taylor! site where you're invited to let me help you answer your questions and solve your technical and business problems.

Figure 1.1: Why call tech support when you can ask Dave Taylor? Just pop over to www.AskDaveTaylor.com.

I won't say that it's *all* about branding, but there's a definite and important connection between thinking of your company as a brand and gaining top visibility in your market segment.

You Need More Customers!

The bottom line is for your business to grow, and for you to be more successful, you need to find, engage, and retain more customers and successively better customers. You might need to start out with prices that are lower than your competitors, but as you establish a brand and gain visibility in your market, you won't stay there for long. Before long you'll be commanding premium prices and turning away customers.

But remember, this is the age of the Internet, so success is about making your business *findable*, because in the twenty-first century your customers will find you, not vice versa. And that's what this book is all about.

The Least You Need to Know

- All businesses need to have a comprehensive Internet business and marketing strategy.

- In the business world, visibility is key, but in the online world, findability is the new mantra for success.

- You need to identify both your differentiators and your sustainable differentiators to proceed.

- There are many ways to market your business online. Stopping with just a website misses out on many opportunities to establish a strong relationship with your customers, community, and industry.

The Benefits of Increasing Your Visibility with Google

In This Chapter

♦ The critical difference between traffic and customers

♦ How to build buzz

♦ How to maximize your PR and marketing dollars

If you spend any time around Internet aficionados, you've probably heard again and again why having a website is cool, but "cool" doesn't easily translate into the bottom line. Often missing from books on the subject is an explanation of *why* it's a good idea for your business to be online.

Let me relate the story of a current client and her web woes. She has a successful conference business and seeks to supplement her income by selling recordings from the conferences. She'd hired a web developer to build a site and while it offered some rudimentary information on the conferences and a conference registration form, it wasn't helping her business. Worse, because of how the site had been designed, you could search for her conferences in Google and never find them, which meant that potential conference attendees weren't able to find out about the event and register.

To solve this problem, we completely rethought her web and Internet presence to address the question of what she was trying to accomplish online and how to best achieve her goals. Her goals are probably quite similar to yours:

- Establish a better rapport with her existing customers

- Help potential customers find her site

- Sell products—and her conference—to visitors

- Offer useful information resources to the community of which she's a visible member

A web designer or graphics firm would seek to achieve these goals by having an attractive, graphically complex site and paying for targeted advertisements on popular topical websites and portals.

But that's not how we solved this problem. Instead, we realized that a conference shouldn't be something that's created behind the scenes and then promoted in glossy brochures that can be downloaded by visitors, but rather a conference is an event that evolves and takes shape over quite a period of time. Now, as speakers are signed up and venues are selected, each news item becomes an update on the website, an online article online within the framework of her *weblog*.

Buzzwords

Weblogs, also known as blogs, started out as informal online diaries. However, weblog management tools have since evolved to where they now offer an ingenious method of managing a website where the *content* is separated from the *underlying technology*. The tremendous upside is that weblog authors can write a few paragraphs of text as if they were composing an e-mail message and have the tools automatically turn their message into attractive and cross-linked material on the website.

Weblogs embody many important concepts that help you learn how to grow your business with Google, and they'll be addressed in detail in Chapter 15 and throughout the book. In fact, go back to Chapter 1 and look at Figure 1.1 again. Ask Dave Taylor is a weblog.

The value of this approach, where the content is separated from the web technologies, is that her business has evolved beyond "how do I make a page that looks nice" to the much more important "how do I create a site that attracts and engages my customers?"

Findability is about thinking like your potential customer, asking yourself what they need to know about you, your company, and your product line.

My client has moved into the realm of findability and the benefits are obvious, including a more active site, more opportunities to promote her products and events, and a much easier method of creating new content that helps grow her customer base and net sales.

You Want Customers, Not Traffic

One of my underlying precepts is that you need to rethink your website and Internet presence to gain customers, not gain traffic. If you just want to have lots and lots and lots of people visit your site, for example, you can simply give something away. But is giving away a Nintendo game system or Amazon.com gift certificate a strategy that's going to drive *potential customers* to your site, visitors who will subsequently buy your products or engage your services? I doubt it.

Yet much of the counsel of so-called Internet experts amounts to methods you can use to generate traffic that you don't want, and that will *actually cost you money, not generate any additional income.*

How does having lots of traffic cost money? Because your website lives on a computer that also hosts other websites, and your monthly charge is partially based on how busy your site is. The more traffic you get, the more *bandwidth* you use, and the more your hosting bill will cost you each month. Remember, lots of traffic to your website is bad. Qualified traffic is what you seek: every visitor should be a potential customer.

In the technical world, the crushing and expensive effect of a massive burst of traffic is known as the "Slashdot effect." This is named

Buzzwords

Bandwidth is the amount of traffic your site sees. Think of it as water flowing through a pipe: To be able to have more water go through the pipe, you need to enlarge the pipe. If you receive sufficient traffic to require a bigger pipe (that is, more bandwidth to your server) you can easily end up paying hundreds or thousands more each month.

after a tremendously popular tech website slashdot.org, which is famous for crushing websites with a tsunami of incoming traffic through a simple link on their home page.

In a classic example of net entrepreneurism, you can even buy T-shirts emblazoned with various witty comments about the Slashdot effect!

The key to attracting new customers is to offer enticements that are thematically relevant to your business, enticements that would be appealing to potential customers, but not someone who isn't a likely customer. If you are a musician, for example, you might give away a previously unreleased musical track for people who come to your site. If you are selling earrings, you might have a new customer special where new customers can receive an additional 20 percent off their purchases if they haven't previously purchased anything from your store.

Even better is to tie promotions to desirable behaviors. Rather than "visit our site, download a new song," a much smarter approach would be to offer the free download *after they've signed up for your newsletter*. Now you're starting to think like someone who is growing his or her business with Google! Instead of enticing visitors, you're signing up potential customers. Better yet, you have a captive audience to whom you can promote new products, highlight an older product that needs a boost, and even offer previews of upcoming products and begin to build buzz in your community.

One company that does a brilliant job of this is *The Teaching Company*. TTC sells audio and video recordings of top college professors lecturing on a wide variety of topics, and they have a loyal customer base. Visit their site at www.teach12.com, shown in Figure 2.1, and sign up for their mailing list, and you'll find that about once every quarter they offer a free lecture through their newsletter. These lectures all begin with a minute or two of advertising for the full lecture series, and I would be unsurprised to find that whatever lectures are promoted in that manner enjoy a significant upswing in sales. Figure 2.1 shows the TTC website.

Figure 2.1: The Teaching Company uses enticements to turn visitors into customers.

Driving Customers to Your Website

What's so appealing about these smart and relevant website enticements is that they don't cost anything and can be very effective at drawing in customers. If you're a musician, you doubtless have hundreds of recordings that never made it onto a CD, and if you're selling jewelry, then your pricing is already structured such that a 20 percent discount for new customers still leaves you with a healthy profit and a potential customer for life.

> CAUTION
>
> **Beware** _____
>
> Many managers believe that they need to retain tight control over promotions and, for example, are afraid of being ripped off by customers who trick the system and get the new customer discount more than once. I think they're missing the forest for the trees, however, because the real question is whether the net benefit of gaining new customers outweighs the possible cost of a small percentage of customers exploiting the system for a small discount.
>
> Remember, customers who "trick" the system are still buying products or services, which they might well not have otherwise purchased.

Driving Customers to the Products in Your Store

What if your business doesn't lend itself to turning website visitors into customers? Perhaps you run an art gallery and have already recognized that people don't buy fine art from websites, but need to see it in person before they can make a purchase decision.

Memo
This isn't to say that you can't sell art online, however! There are some interesting examples worth visiting if you're interested in this business segment, including www.nextmonet.com and www.art.com.

Even the most enthused web zealot will suggest that some businesses aren't suited to the Internet. But that's because they're trying to solve the wrong problem. The criterion for success shouldn't be whether you can *sell* your product through your website—after all, most products and almost all services can't be delivered digitally—but whether you can *sell your customer on visiting your place of business*.

Going back to the example of the art gallery, what buyers have in common is both a love of art and the concurrent challenge of knowing what art is available at any given gallery. Yet isn't it puzzling that art gallery websites don't offer news of interest to art lovers, information on what artists are featured at other galleries in town, and new and noteworthy artists that aren't currently featured at the gallery? Instead, the websites are much more likely to offer a photo gallery of currently available art work, a sentence or two about each piece, and "buy" buttons that never seem to generate any actual sales.

The key concept these businesses are missing is that if you have a product or service that requires the customer to interact with you in person or otherwise cannot be delivered electronically, the goals of your site need to be building awareness and convincing visitors why they should visit your place of business and become customers.

If you can't easily figure out how the web can help your business, neither can your competitors. This suggests that there's a tremendous opportunity for you to create the definitive go-to site for your customer community. This is thinking outside the web box!

> **Memo**
>
> Sometimes having to stretch your thinking to figure out an online tie-in is good. If it isn't easy, your competitors have probably already given up!

Build Buzz about a Product, Service, or Idea

Automotive manufacturers used to think of their product line as a collection, where each vehicle needed to be promoted within the context of a coherent and unified marketing campaign. If you were to visit their website, you'd find as much about the car company as about a given car. Now it's common to find that individual products are promoted on their own websites with their own campaigns that have almost nothing in common with the rest of the company marketing efforts.

The Toyota Scion is an interesting example of this phenomenon. It's a visually distinct car aimed at college-age buyers, with specific options and a price point that their target demographic finds very appealing. But you won't find much about the Scion at the Toyota website or in Toyota ads. Instead, the Scion is its own brand within the company and even Toyota dealerships commonly have a separate Scion area, with visually distinct architecture, completely different brochures, and even different sales people. The Scion website (www.scion.com) makes it quite clear that it's not Toyota's business as usual, as shown in Figure 2.2.

Buzz, or word of mouth, can be about more than a car or any specific product. Google itself uses the web to build buzz and experiment with different ideas through the public face of its Google Labs.

> **BizTips**
>
> Build buzz for your own products by thinking of them as separate, discrete projects, not as simply another entry in your catalog.

Figure 2.2: The Toyota Scion website builds brand identity and helps increase the buzz surrounding this successful car.

As a public speaker, I also use the Internet to build buzz for my upcoming talks. If I'm going to be talking about maximizing brand identity online, for example, articles on my weblog and in my newsletter will explore this topic, offering opportunities to create interest in my talk and draw more attendees to the event itself. The more Google-friendly I can make these articles, the more findable I can make them, the greater visibility they'll have, and the more effective they'll be at attaining my goals. ("Google-friendly" is a key concept later in the book. Don't miss it or all your find-ability efforts might be in vain.)

The Internet offers many opportunities to spread the word about a new product or service through word of mouth. With traditional publishing, for example, only publishers can produce magazines with national distribution, but on the web your customer's website can enjoy just as much visibility—or more!—than your own site.

This isn't something to fear, however, but rather something to recognize and exploit: If you can identify and excite a core set of customers, then they'll do your marketing for you! A simple example of this might be when someone stays at a bed-and-breakfast and has a particularly good experience. They write about it in their weblog or e-mail it to some of their friends and it's quite foreseeable that bookings at the B&B could see an up-surge without any specific B&B marketing efforts or expenditure.

BizTips

Always try to establish a relationship with your visitor so you can go back to them with important and helpful news later. Not spam, mind you, but legitimate marketing efforts.

That's why it's so important to capture your customer information when they visit, so you can share good news and invite your customers to become, in essence, part of your marketing, public relations, and quality assurance team. Remember, when one person has something positive to say, that's exactly what you should be including in your customer newsletter, letting positive feed upon positive. Further, one great tool for marketing is customer testimonials, so whether they're letters written to you or articles in discussion groups or on someone else's website, you should be leveraging them.

I had an example pop up while writing this chapter, actually. A chap who purchased one of my more technical books wrote me a remarkably positive e-mail message lauding the title, so I promptly sought, and received, his permission to highlight his message on my website for marketing purposes. A quick glance at my reviews page for that book at www.intuitive.com/wicked will demonstrate how positive buzz can feed upon itself and help expand into the greater community.

The potential downside of someone having a bad experience and spreading that feeling among your possible customer community might seem daunting, but you should already be seeking to maximize your customer satisfaction anyway. Further, this way, if you're keeping track of your own company mentions online, you should quickly be made aware of the negative PR and be able to contact that customer directly, offering them some sort of compensation package to help alleviate their distress.

Maximize the Value of Your Marketing and PR

One of the key themes in this chapter is that by spending your energy and resources wisely, by creatively thinking about your customer community and how you can appeal to its needs and wants, you can spend less money on marketing, advertising, and public relations and see an *increase* in your revenues.

> **Memo**
>
> Imagine! A business book that helps you spend *less* and see better results because it's not about "how much" but "how smart."

> **Memo**
>
> Google AdWords is the program Google uses to match text advertising with the search results on the site. Yahoo!, MSN Search, AOL Search, and other search engines all have similar programs and all are important avenues for promoting your business online.

The purpose of spending money on these traditional business methods of gaining customers is to increase the visibility of your company. But in the online world, it's not about visibility, but about findability, since, as we've discussed earlier, your customers are going to find you, not vice versa. In this world, having highly targeted ads that show up only for those people most likely to be customers is going to be more cost effective and generate better results than the typical scattershot approach of display advertising or other methods built upon crude demographic slices.

Let's go back to the mobile Porsche mechanic to illustrate this point. If she is based in, say, Chicago, Illinois, then paying to advertise on national Porsche owner sites or in Porsche magazines would be less effective than using Google AdWords to have their ad displayed when people search for both "Porsche" and the name of any of the cities that comprise greater Chicago. (Chapter 18 focuses exclusively on the AdWords program.)

Ultimately, making your website and online business more findable will directly benefit your revenue stream. Whether or not you opt to pursue other marketing and public relations options, knowing how Google works, how people search, and how to create a website that helps your potential customers find you will produce tangible benefits.

The Least You Need to Know

- ◆ Your customers will search you out. Will they find your website?
- ◆ Fresh and constantly updated content is what makes a site compelling and engaging.
- ◆ Promotions should always be tied directly to desirable customer behaviors.
- ◆ Capture customer data because you can't market to people you can't reach.

Chapter 3

What Is Google Anyway?

In This Chapter

- ◆ The many different sides of Google
- ◆ Paying for ads with Google AdWords
- ◆ Being paid to include ads on your site through Google AdSense
- ◆ How weblogs help you update your site frequently
- ◆ Froogle and catalog shopping with Google

With so many search engines on the web, why am I so obsessed with Google? There's MSN Search, Yahoo!, Alta Vista, and hundreds—if not thousands—of other search engines, all of which offer various capabilities and can help your business garner traffic and customers. So why be so intimately tied to Google?

The answer is that, as I write this book, Google is the king of the hill, the top dog, the online search engine that more people use than any other, and as such, it's vital that you be findable therein. Yes, you should make sure your site and business are part of Yahoo!, are found in MSN Search, and so on, but here's the secret scoop: If you're building a site and working on an online promotional campaign aimed at improving your traffic and, simultaneously, your rank in Google, you're doing all the right things to be well-ranked on these other search engines, too.

Google changed how Internet users thought about searching by creating a system where the results for a given search are not just based upon the web page content, but also factor in how popular those pages are on the web. Providing dramatically better results, Google quickly rose to its leadership position, and now MSN, Yahoo!, America Online, and other search companies are trying to catch up, building search systems that use approximately similar methods of sifting through the web to find the best matches.

One thing that all of these search companies do have in common with Google is that everyone is trying different diversification strategies, hoping to turn a great search engine into a great online business. Google has added an e-mail service, a social networking service, a busy advertising network, a catalog shopping feature, a news consolidator for information junkies, and much more.

This chapter will give you a guided tour of the Google empire, talk about some of the most interesting facets of Google the search engine, and also mention some of its additional capabilities that can directly affect your bottom line.

Think of this chapter as a roadmap for more detailed chapters later in the book. If nothing here whets your appetite, you need to pinch yourself, wake up, and read it again. If you're like me, you'll have a highlighter in hand, ready to begin improving your website traffic, selling more goods or services, and turning your *cost center* into a *profit center*.

It's a Search Engine with More!

The first thing to realize about Google is that it's much more than just a search engine. In fact, even as a search engine, Google offers a lot more capability than just "type in a few words, and I'll show you a list of matching websites." Chapter 4 covers a lot of the hidden capabilities of the Google search box, but Google is really building an online empire, staking out territory in areas as diverse as social networking, weblog creation, geographic information systems, advertising, and even mapping and location-specific searches.

The best way to learn about what they're willing to share with the unwashed masses (read "people who haven't promised their firstborn in return for a chance to see the secret research projects") is to point your browser to www.google.com and click the "more" link.

The current set of tools and technologies is shown in Figure 3.1.

There are lots of options, most notably Answers, Catalogs, Froogle, Groups, and Google Labs. Notice that some very interesting capabilities are shown on the lower section, Google Tools, including a language translation tool, a photo organizer, Google's desktop search capability, and Keyhole, a very interesting satellite and geographic data search tool that enables you to fly around your city and zoom in on specific streets and neighborhoods.

BizTips

If you have a few minutes to spare, download and try Keyhole. It's an amazing example of the fabulous capabilities of modern computers and network technology.

Google Labs

Rather than get hopelessly sidetracked by all these cool features, I'd like to keep our little tour bus on the main avenue by visiting Google Labs, which you can reach by typing in the website address http://labs.google.com.

Here in the Google Labs, you can see what's new and get a good sense of how the team at Google is solving your information retrieval problems and experimenting with other ideas to create an even more useful site. Sometimes there's nothing particularly related to commerce, but other times the features shown are terrific!

Figure 3.1: There are plenty of tools lurking behind the simple Google home page.

Google Mail

What I find most interesting, however, is that many of the best features of Google aren't linked off any of these pages. They're not part of Google Labs, per se, and they aren't listed as a tool or service either.

Google's free web-based mail utility Gmail is a good example of this: *there's no overt link from Google's site to Gmail,* but if you go to http://gmail.google.com, you'll find the most sophisticated web-based e-mail system online, shown in Figure 3.2.

Figure 3.2: With its typically sparse design and 2GB mailbox, Gmail is one hard-to-beat web-based e-mail solution.

The one wrinkle with Gmail is that you have to be invited by an existing member to get a Gmail account, so it's not like Yahoo! Mail or Hotmail where you can just sign up and immediately begin using it. This is actually the Gmail approach to minimizing bogus, temporary, and so-called throwaway accounts that are the bane of both Hotmail and Yahoo! Mail.

If you want to get involved with Gmail, the greatest challenge is to find an existing Gmail customer to e-mail you an invite. You can send me a message—to d1taylor@gmail.com—but

---

Memo

Google is demonstrating another brilliant marketing strategy with the invitation-only Gmail program with something called *perceived scarcity*. There's no reason that they couldn't add a million new users per hour for the next year, but by creating unfulfilled demand, they create buzz and publicity. Very smart.

I can't invite everyone since there's a set limit of 50 invitations per week. You can also go to eBay and bid on invitations. Most of them sell for about $0.50 to $1.00. Another option is to ask your techie friends, IT personnel, or web developer.

Paid Advertising with Google AdWords

From a business perspective, one of the most exciting and engaging features Google offers is AdWords. Every time you search on Google and notice the small, boxed advertisements on the right side of the page, you're seeing ads placed through the AdWords system.

What makes AdWords so exciting from a business perspective is that it's a completely different advertising model than anything you've ever seen. Print advertising is priced based on circulation, and if 10,000 people would see the ad, it'll typically cost you 10 times what a 1,000-subscriber publication would charge. This translates directly online with the CPM (cost per thousand) pricing of banner ads, animated ads, pop-up ads, and so on.

All of this traditional advertising, online and off, suffers from the same fundamental problem: an inability to ensure that the advertisement has some meaningful relationship to the content on the page. If I visit a web page about troubleshooting Microsoft Windows XP, ads selling me a carbonated beverage or vacation in Hawaii are pointless, off-target, and a waste of advertiser money. No one clicks on them. Contextless advertising is dead. It's a numbers game and the numbers are stacked against you.

Buzzwords

Heuristics are the set of evaluatory formulas that Google applies when it analyzes a web page to figure out the main subject or theme of the page.

By contrast, Google can already analyze and deduce the subject of any web page, a *heuristic* that's the basis of the Google search tool. Apply that to advertising and Google AdWords ensures that you only have ads displayed on searches that are from customers who are interested in your products or services. What's astonishing is that having your ads displayed on the search results pages is *free*. You only pay for anyone who actually clicks the ad and comes to your website.

Relevance is a big deal because the goal of online advertising is to *get visitors to click on your ad and get to your site*. The better targeted your ad, the more likely your firm will appeal to the searcher and the more likely they'll click on your ad, come to your site, and purchase your product. The measure of success, after all, isn't how many people clicked, but how many sales were closed. That's the real bottom line.

Ads that Appear on Specific Searches Only

Google AdWords is the "buy" side of the Google advertising network, where you, as an advertiser and business owner, can pay for each visitor that Google brings to your site. Notice I didn't say "pay for each thousand displays of your banner," which is the old, dead model of online advertising! This is much more sophisticated.

Three Different Types of AdWords Accounts

Still not convinced that AdWords offers a completely different, and more intelligent, way to advertise online? Consider that when you sign up for the program—at http://adwords.google.com—you can select from one of the following three types of accounts:

♦ Global or nationwide

♦ Regions and cities

♦ Customized

With global or nationwide, your ads will appear to searchers anywhere in the country or countries you select. This is best for global or specific country–focused businesses. Regions and cities only shows your ads to searchers located in the specified regions or cities you choose, and customized limits the ad display to searchers who are within a specified distance from the location you choose. Both of the latter options are for regional businesses.

> **Memo**
>
> Most AdWords advertisers have global or nationwide accounts, as explained in Chapter 18.

Since the web frees you from the constraints of a limited regional customer base, many online business sites are happy to gain customers from anywhere in the world. For them, the default global or nationwide option is the smart choice. After you've signed up, purchasing an ad is as easy as specifying the text, associating it with a few search terms that people would type in, and indicating a maximum per-day fee you're willing to pay for your ads (see Figure 3.3).

Since this is just an introduction to whet your appetite, I'll defer more discussion of AdWords until Chapter 18, when you'll really dig your teeth into this important and exciting topic. Stay tuned but don't flip ahead: The other half of the Google ad network is also critical to learn about.

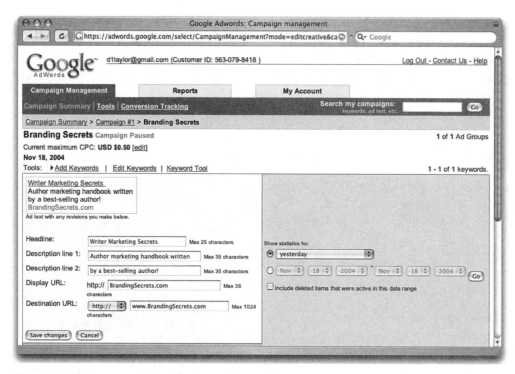

Figure 3.3: Buying a targeted ad placement with AdWords.

AdSense: The Networked Ad Distribution System

AdWords is the yin to AdSense's yang with Google advertising. As an advertiser, you buy ad placement through AdWords, and ads are not only placed automatically on the Google search results page (which is nice) but they're also placed on any other web page on the net that's both relevant and hooked into the AdSense network.

What's really fabulous about AdSense, though, is that in addition to offering you more potential venues for your advertising, AdSense offers you the opportunity to *make money from your own website, too*. It's free to join AdSense, and your earnings are based purely on how many people clicked the ads you displayed on your website.

BizTips

I have colleagues who have created dozens of websites that utilize AdSense to generate meaningful revenue streams (daily income of hundreds of dollars). They're the digital equivalent of magazines that are published purely to generate advertiser revenue for the company, and they work!

The AdSense program—at www.google.com/adsense—is straightforward to join: You need a website that actually has some content and has been indexed by Google, but I'll bet you already have that. Then they give you a snippet of code that you just cut and paste into the pages that you want to include their advertising, and *poof* you're part of the AdSense network. With any luck, some percentage of your visitors will find one of the ads interesting, click on it to learn more, and you'll see a small percentage of the amount that advertiser pays Google for the traffic.

Figure 3.4 shows a page of mine with some AdSense ads included. Notice that they're integrated into the very design of the page, too: You certainly don't need to do that if you'd prefer to be more low-key, but it's a trade-off. The more visible the advertising block, the more likely visitors are going to see what's advertised and click on one of the ads, netting you some income from their visit.

Figure 3.4: The "Scan Disk" links in the middle of the article are Google AdSense and this page generates revenue every time an ad is clicked.

There's a lot more to AdSense than just this brief introduction, but your brain should already be awhirl with ideas and opportunities. Could your customer newsletter be a set of pages on your site, seeded with AdSense ads to offset the cost of hosting the site? Could the questions you answer in an e-mail be put on a Q&A page that not only offers information but some related ads, too?

Companies that understand the value of AdSense and AdWords as a targeted pair find that producing web pages with great information for their target customer can generate sufficient revenue via AdSense to more than pay for targeted advertising on the AdWords network, allowing their marketing efforts to essentially be cost-free.

Weblogs Help Keep Your Website Fresh

When you go to a website and see that the content hasn't been updated since 1998, do you think, "Ah, great stuff! This was so well written that it's just as true today as it was in 1998"? I bet you don't! Instead, you probably think that it's obsolete and useless information and quickly move to a different page with fresher, more up-to-date material.

The Google site-matching heuristic works in a surprisingly similar way, preferring sites that have been updated in the last few weeks to those that have similar information but haven't been touched in years. Google likes weblogs so much it purchased one of the largest weblog-hosting companies, Blogger, and made it part of the Google network.

You can constantly tweak and fiddle with your site, rewriting your introductory paragraph, rephrasing product descriptions, and otherwise making mundane changes so that your site stays fresh, but the best and easiest way to keep your site content fresh is to utilize a content management system that lets you constantly add nuggets of useful and interesting information. A content management system enables you to focus on *what* without having to worry about *how*: you type in an article or essay, then the content management system translates that into a properly formatted web page that's consistent in design with all the other pages on your site. Weblogs or blogs are a particular variety of content management systems.

Originally, weblogs were created to allow people to have electronic diaries that they shared with friends, but in a short period of time, business professionals realized that weblog technology offered a flexible and powerful infrastructure. Further, having a weblog as part of a business site allows you to personalize the site and put a face on the company, making the business seem more friendly.

Weblogs allow you to add a sentence or two or a ten-page essay on business competition, a new product, or a nice testimonial from a customer. (I'll bet you've just been filing those away, or even deleting them, haven't you?)

> **Memo**
>
> One great use of a business weblog: sharing customer testimonials with potential customers. There's nothing like knowing that other people love a product to convince you to give it a second look.

Blogger helped pioneer the entire technology and offers hosted weblogs for thousands of customers. Blogger is online at www.blogger.com. Even if you are planning on hosting your weblog in-house, it's still worth visiting Blogger to see what people are writing about, what's popular, and, most of all, to get a sense of what excites Google about this technology.

Froogle and Catalog Shopping with Google

The final facet of Google that's important to explore as an entrepreneur and marketing maven is Froogle. The best way to understand Froogle is to consider the value of a search system you could ask to only show you products for sale. Instead of a general query for "nike air jordan" that produces millions of matches that have nothing to do with buying shoes, you can use Froogle to find shoes that are for sale.

That's nice if you're shopping, but if you're selling products through your website, it's crucial that your products be in the Froogle database, so that when potential customers search, they find your products, and you have yet another valuable marketing venue.

Hooking into the Froogle system isn't easy, for a variety of reasons. In Chapter 16, I'll talk more about how to get involved with Froogle, but if you're eager for knowledge, pop over to www.google.com/froogle/merchants to learn more.

It's worth noting that it's free to have your products included in Froogle, and you can keep the information fresh and accurate without their intervention. To do so, though, you need to create a data feed of your products and product information so that they can have the most accurate information possible about your products.

BizTips _____

It's free to include your product line in the Froogle shopping engine so there's no reason not to be there.

If you're getting excited about the many opportunities available to promote your business and products through Google and related companies, then you're probably ready to flip to the next chapter. If you're still not sure, then ask yourself: "Am I willing to invest some time and a bit of money to double, triple, or even quadruple my sales online?"

In this chapter, I've offered you a guided tour of some of the most interesting Google-related properties. There are plenty of others, including their Scholar Search for academics, the Google-sponsored social network Orkut, and more. However, from a business perspective, these properties are considerably less interesting.

The Least You Need to Know

♦ Keep up-to-date with future Google products and offerings—and scoop your online competitors by reacting quickly—by watching Google Labs and Google Tools on their site.

♦ Google AdWords offers a great venue for advertising your site and products. You bid on specific keywords to ensure that customers searching Google find out about your products when it's most relevant.

♦ You can join Google AdSense and earn money on advertising that Google adds on your web pages, turning your website into a potential profit center.

♦ Frequently updated websites are more interesting to both search engines and potential customers. One of the easiest ways to keep your site fresh is to incorporate a weblog. Originally created for online diaries, weblogs offer many compelling benefits for an online entrepreneur.

Learning About Google Search

In This Chapter

- The secret world of Google search
- How your customers find you
- Advanced Google search techniques
- The surprising importance of word order

To compete effectively you need to know how your customers think, who your competitors are, and how they are courting and servicing those customers. Expanding into new business areas requires the same research, so it's no surprise that successful businesses spend millions of dollars on research and competitive intelligence.

Knowing how to appeal to your current and future customers can help you identify an effective strategy for improving your visibility, but the challenge of findability, of being able to anticipate how these customers are going to look for your business, is something else entirely. Remember,

---

> **Memo**
>
> Don't panic! You might not control your potential customers, but you can certainly influence them.

your customers are out of your control and rather than lead them to your business, you need to create the best possible online business presence and wait for them to arrive.

Before you get anxious about that last sentence, having your customers find you online isn't quite as out of your control as you may think. As an example, you can learn a lot by studying how more successful competitors appear online, what kind of information they offer to their potential customers, and what services they make available to existing customers.

Ultimately, though, knowing your customer comes from *being your own customer*. In the world of business, you'll hear this as "eating your own dog food" and it's an idea best embodied by two Stanford engineers, Bill Hewlett and David Packard, co-founders of HP. The foundation of Hewlett-Packard is the concept of "the next bench", where employees were told to build products for their colleagues. The net result? Every HP employee was also an HP customer and the company has grown into one of the largest tech firms in the world. There are a lot of business books that suggest you should view your customer as a different breed, as a group of people that you can never be a part of, but can only study and analyze. I find this entire philosophy baffling and suggest instead that you can and should always be your customer, at least in a sufficiently meaningful way to help you improve your business.

The focus of this chapter is to show you how to use Google to search for information online, information from the more than *eight billion* pages of information that Google indexes. As you proceed with this hands-on technical chapter, you'll want to have a computer hooked up to the Internet and a web browser so you can try out different types of searches on Google. After all, if *you* can't find your site and product or service information online, how are your customers going to find you?

The Genius of Google

As the World Wide Web has grown exponentially, searching has come to occupy more and more of people's time. That shouldn't be a surprise given the vast size of the web.

When your library is one bookcase you can just browse to find a good book, and even when your library spreads across three or four rooms, it's manageable to put books on the shelves randomly, knowing that you can find them later without too much fuss.

But if you imagine that your library sprawls across hundreds of square miles, even an organizational taxonomy like the Dewey Decimal System fails.

The solution is not to rely on organizational hierarchies, but to create tools that enable you to look at all of the books simultaneously. This lets you find "books that discuss the rise and fall of the Aztec culture" or "books written by Jack London that mention Oakland".

A straightforward solution would be based on an enormous index of all words used in the books, but that wouldn't work. A straight match on word occurrence would suggest that this very book is about Aztec culture because this phrase appears twice in the manuscript.

> **Memo**
>
> When a collection becomes too big, even the most organized hierarchy breaks down and a mechanized search system becomes critical. For the Internet, it's Google.

Solving this puzzle is where the genius of Google co-founders Larry Page and Sergey Brin appeared. While grad students, Page and Brin recognized that the "best" matches for a given query depend not just on the appearance of the search words, but upon a variety of other factors, including frequency, proximity of words, where in the document the words appear, and how many other documents point to this document.

In fact, the calculation of the best match is one of the most important concepts we'll discuss in this book. It's a bit tricky, though, because *PageRank* refers to the importance of the page on the Web, while a different concept that I call Page Relevance Score measures how relevant a given page is for a specific search query. Page Relevance Score is affected by PageRank, but they're not the same measure.

Prior to Google, search engines were more typified by the website directory Yahoo!. When it started, Yahoo! was essentially a catalog of sites, each with a ten- to thirty-word description submitted by the site owner. That wasn't a good approach and the Yahoo! directory became increasingly irrelevant as the World Wide Web grew.

> **Buzzwords**
>
> All web pages in the Google database are assigned a **PageRank**, a measure of their relative importance on the web. PageRank measures how many other pages on the web point to the given page. PageRank is an important topic, and I explore it in Chapter 5.

Instead of a database of thousands of site descriptions, Google lets people search through each and every page of all of those sites, expanding into millions, then billions of different documents.

When you're searching the World Wide Web using Google, you aren't searching *sites* but are instead searching *all the pages on those sites*. Even superficially, this should highlight the importance of ensuring that each and every page of your website is designed for findability, not just the increasingly obsolete home page.

A Basic Approach to Searching

Having been inspired by the previous chapters, you'd really like to reinvent your art gallery website to encompass news of the art world, listings of showings at all galleries in your region, and articles interesting to your customers. You'll need to think like your customer to accomplish this, to find the best possible information sources and the other galleries in your area.

A typical approach to searching with Google is just to type in a word or two, and that's how we'll start. The first search is for news of the art world, and a logical first search is for "art news".

This isn't a good approach to finding information. In fact, our Google search is producing over 23.3 million results that have some sort of relevance to the two search terms "art" and "news".

It doesn't take long to realize that one- or two-word searches aren't very helpful because they match too many pages. It's akin to knowing the book you seek is on the third or fourth floor of the library, but still being left with miles of shelves to navigate.

Go to the *New York Times* website at www.nytimes.com and you'll see that the title in the window frame of your web browser shows "The New York Times > Breaking News, World News & Multimedia." Move to www.samsung.com and you'll find out you've entered "SAMSUNG's Digital World".

These are the *titles* of the respective web pages, and as I'll discuss a bit further into the book, the words in the title are of critical importance to the findability of your website. For now, as you learn more about Google search strategies, try to also pay attention to the titles of the different matches.

A better search approach than wading through 23.5 million matches is to type in more words to further constrain the results and find better, more relevant pages. Instead of just searching for art news, let's narrow the search down to "art news about painting and artists in Maine". You can type in that entire phrase if you'd like,

then see that Google ignores the common words "about", "in", and "and". A more succinct search query that produces the same results is "art news painting artists Maine". This search produces a more easily explored 139,000 matching pages.

One final refinement is that we should be searching for painting or painter. But instead of producing more matches, adding "painter" to the search narrows the results down to 113,000 matches. All key-word searches have an implicit AND, so the search for "art news painting painter artists Maine" is interpreted as "art and news and painting and painter and artists and Maine".

BizTips

All words in a search have an implied "AND" between them. Specify more words and you'll get fewer matches.

What we'd really like is to search for "painting or painter" and "art news or artist" and "Maine". These more sophisticated searches are possible, as you'll see in just a moment, but the question you should be asking is not *can it be done,* but *do my customers really know this much about searching Google?*

This Is How Your Customers Find You

Fortunately we don't have to guess about how people use Google to find specific information, because all web servers keep a running record of how people found the site, including the specific search phrases used.

Typical searches that people are using to find pages on my site, for example, include the following:

♦ firefox import bookmarks safari

♦ internet safe colors

♦ script to unscramble words

♦ play films on ipod

- starbucks history

- funny questions about prius

These searches are all written the same way you've already seen, terse three- to five-word descriptions of the results sought.

If you're looking for a Porsche mechanic in Chicago, you might search for "Porsche mechanic Chicago". If you're launching your mobile Porsche repair service, therefore, it's this type of search that you need to keep in mind as you develop your website.

Before we leave the topic of searching to learn the many ways that Google can help you grow your business, let's delve into some sophisticated search techniques. As you research your customers, identify and explore your competitors, and recognize the tremendous value of Google and the Internet for competitive intelligence and new product and service inspiration, it's helpful for you to be a power Google searcher!

Advanced Search Techniques, a.k.a. Punctuation Soup

The fastest way to learn how to improve search results is to learn about the alphabet soup of advanced Google searches. The two most important punctuation characters in this regard are "+" and "-". Add a plus sign to a word and it means that every match *must* have that word even if Google otherwise wants to discard it as too common. If you want pages that match "cost of living" rather than the normalized "cost living", use "cost +of living".

Preface a keyword with a minus sign, by contrast, and *no* matches can contain the specified word. The search "art news" also matches sites that actually have news about art museums. To eliminate these spurious matches, change the search to "art news –museum" and you'll shave off *a million pages* from the earlier 23.5 million results.

Let's switch research topics and try and identify which ski supply stores in Aspen, Colorado, have a web presence. The default connector for a multiword search pattern is "and", so a search for "ski boots gloves goggles Aspen" is really a search for "ski and boots and gloves and goggles and Aspen", which actually narrows down the search too much.

> **Memo**
>
> On most keyboards, the "|" symbol is located on the same key as the backslash "\". Some keyboards actually show it as two small vertical lines, one above the other, and it can be difficult to distinguish from a colon. Also, you'll find that geeky types call this the "pipe" symbol.

To connect words with a logical "or" instead, either use the word "OR" or use the "|" symbol on your keyboard.

Using the "|" notation requires a grouping mechanism, however, or things won't be interpreted correctly. If I just searched for "ski | boots | gloves | goggles | Aspen" then I'll be shown pages that match *any* of these words, which is quite a bit more than desired. Logically, I should be able to use "ski boots | gloves | goggles Aspen" but Google doesn't interpret that query the same way we do: It sees "ski boots" or "gloves" or "goggles Aspen".

To group search terms together, use parentheses. Now, finally, we can create a good search query:

> ski (boots | gloves | goggles) Aspen

The results of this search are shown in Figure 4.1.

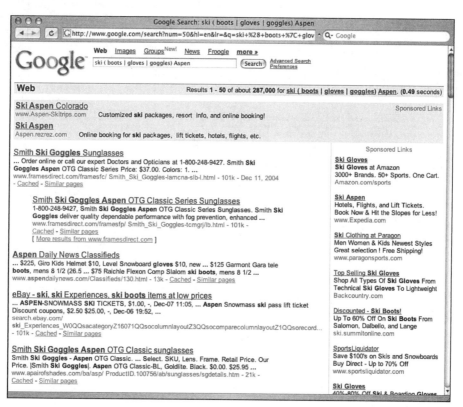

Figure 4.1: Sophisticated search techniques enable you to use Google to zero in accurately on the specific information you seek.

When I started building this particular search, my goal was to do competitive research on ski supply stores in the Aspen, Colorado, area, but we've ended up matching much more. To narrow the results down to stores in that area, add "Colorado" and the additional pattern "(store|buy)" to identify stores rather than informational sites.

This pattern is quite complex, but should be understandable:

> ski (boots | gloves | goggles) Aspen Colorado (store | buy)

The results of this search are shown in Figure 4.2.

Figure 4.2: A list of stores in Aspen, Colorado, where you can buy skiing gear and equipment.

There's another notation we can use to narrow down the results even further.

The Importance of Quoting

A search for "art news" or "Aspen Colorado" matches documents that have both the words within, but not necessarily adjacent. A web page that included the phrase "News from the band 'Art of Noise'" would match "art news", and "Buy Colorado state maps at any store in Winter Park, Aspen, or Vail" would match "Aspen, Colorado".

To turn a set of keywords into a *key phrase* you need to surround it with quotes. Simply adding quotes to group Aspen and Colorado together on the previous search, for example, cuts down the results from 49,000 to 5,020.

Let's go back to the art gallery site and see how these additional search capabilities can help narrow down the results. Your goal is to find sources of news about the art world with a focus on painters and painting in the state of Maine.

Memo
Quotation marks are the secret weapon of power Google searchers!

Here's how I'd accomplish this search now:

"art news" (painting OR painter) Maine

The result is a manageable 3,700 matches, including the news page of the Maine Arts Commission and some bios and news from galleries in Maine, all of which are excellent, highly relevant matches.

Special Search Notations

There's one more type of special search notation that is worth learning before you're finished with this admittedly technical chapter. This time, though, it's not punctuation characters, but special words that you can use to tightly constrain the results.

The notation takes the form of a word followed by a colon followed by the information you specify to limit the search results.

BizTips

You can easily search all indexed pages of your own site on Google by using the site: notation in the Google search box. I do this quite frequently.

The easiest and most useful of these notations is "site:" which constrains results based on the domain name of the system upon which the page is located.

If you add "site:org" to a search, the only results you'll see are from websites that have a ".org" domain name. Matches on pages with a ".com", ".net", ".edu", or even ".co.uk" are all filtered out of the results.

There are some very powerful searches you can now do using this notation. For example, to search all U.S. Government sites for 1040 tax forms, you could use:

site:gov 1040 tax

To search all educational sites for research on what colors work best in a retail environment, you could use:

site:edu affect color retail sales research

Don't stop with the last three letters of the domain name in a "site:" search, though, because you can also use this very same technique to search quickly and easily all known pages on a specific website.

Looking for the marketing contact at Kodak? Use this search:

site:kodak.com marketing contact phone

Want to find out if Porsche lists any mechanics or garages on the company's site? Try this notation:

site:porsche.com (mechanic OR garage)

BizTips

Later in the book you'll see that one of the interesting capabilities of the Google AdSense program is that you can add site search to your own site and be paid for any ads in the search results page that visitors click. That's discussed in Chapter 19.

You can also use this notation to search your own site. In fact, there are many websites that use Google itself as their site search engine.

If you want to get highly sophisticated in your searches, there are a number of other notations to learn. A sampling includes the ability to search within document titles (intitle:), within URLs (inurl:), within actual anchor tags, that is, the words that web developers have made clickable, with "inanchor:", and even search just pages that point to a specified web page ("link:").

A few quick examples. The following notation shows all web pages that have a direct link to my Ask Dave Taylor website:

link:askdavetaylor.com

The following notation matches all documents that have both the words Aspen and Colorado in the title:

intitle:Aspen intitle:Colorado

There's an easier way to do multiword title searches, too: start your query pattern with allintitle: instead. The following is functionally identical to the previous search query:

allintitle: Aspen Colorado

To search for all pages that contain a specific word in the URL (that is, the full address of the page, not just the domain name) you can use:

inurl:aspen

This will match both www.AspenCountry.com and the Weather Underground forecast page www.wunderground.com/US/CO/Aspen.html.

The Surprising Importance of Word Order in Queries

Before closing my overview of sophisticated Google searches, there's one more facet of searching that I want to discuss—the importance of word order in searches.

When Google shows the search results, your query has gone through some very sophisticated analysis and the pages shown are presented in rank order from most relevant to least. This should be pretty obvious by the fact that there's almost always a good match within the first five or ten matches shown.

BizTips

Change the order of words in your search query and you'll often change the order of pages shown in the result.

The way that the ranking is calculated is based not just on what words and patterns you have specified, but also the order in which they appear in the search. This can be quickly verified by comparing the first five matches for the search "results franchise car wash investment" and "car wash franchise investment results".

When I run these two searches on Google, the first generates 39,400 matches, while the second generates 38,400 results. You read that correctly: one thousand matches were eliminated by changing the order of the query words. In addition, while the top result is the same for both queries, the second match on the first pattern is "Automotive Franchise Opportunities: Franchise Business Directory", while the second match on the second pattern is a completely different page entitled "Start and Grow your Small Business".

One ramification of this is that you should order your search terms in most important to least important order. To really learn more about the financial reality of car wash franchises, a better search would be:

> "car wash" franchise investment results

which produces 4,940 results, many of which are directories of franchise opportunities. A few more minutes researching and you should be quite a bit more knowledgeable about the opportunities available to you in the car wash franchise business.

The Least You Need to Know

- To increase your site's findability, you must learn to search like your customers search.

- Google's search language includes a variety of special notations to help refine your results, including "-" to omit words, "|" to indicate a logical OR between keywords, and parentheses to group multiple keywords in an OR pattern.

- Google also enables you to search only specific domains (such as ".au" for Australian sites) by using the "site:" notation.

Disassembling the Google Search Engine

In This Chapter

♦ Why you should care how Google works

♦ The importance of PageRank

♦ Why you want spiders visiting your site

♦ Understanding relevance scoring

♦ Google versus Yahoo! Search and MSN Search

The previous chapters included many examples of Google searches that produce thousands or even millions of matches, but the question of *how* Google figures out which matches are relevant hasn't been addressed. There are actually two topics here, because Google uses a formula they call PageRank to calculate the relative importance of a site—and the pages within the site—to the overall web, and uses a different calculation that I call a Relevance Score to calculate the relevance of a page to a given search.

Let's start with a caveat, though: the exact details of the PageRank and relevance score calculations are the crown jewels of Google's intellectual property. There are some early academic papers by the founders that explain an early version of the PageRank formula, but no one outside the company really knows how it works today. There are so-called "search engine optimization" (or SEO) experts who claim they have the secret to Google's calculations, but the assumptions they make are based on guesses from the community, not specific details from Google.

> **Memo**
>
> This chapter contains the most accurate information possible, but Google doesn't disclose the details of its search engine, so you'll want to pop over to www.findability.info to check for updates or news.

As a result, the information in this chapter might well be wrong.

If it is wrong, it's only going to be wrong in the nuances, however, so the basic concept of PageRank being based on inbound links and relevance being based on a formula that calculates keyword frequency and keyword usage will still steer you right, and, most importantly, will still indicate how to restructure and rethink your online presence to maximize your findability.

Google isn't the only online search engine either. I'll talk briefly about the Yahoo! and MSN search engines, competitors that obviously aren't using the Google internal PageRank formula.

The basic concepts that underlie Google's formulas are elegant, logical, and ingenious, so these other sites must be using similar calculations. If you're using proper and legitimate methods to increase the quality of your pages, the layout of your site, and the value of your site to the online community, you'll be gaining relevance points on all three search engines, not just Google.

Why You Need to Care How Google Works

You're reading this book because you want to grow your business, to become more findable. You can spend all your marketing dollars building and promoting your website, ignoring the details of how Google works internally. It's just not efficient or cost effective.

When you think of a few key phrases that should describe your product or service offering and use them as a search query, does your site bubble to the top of the results? Probably not. In fact, odds are good that there are more than a million matches to the query.

I have a site called Real Life Debt, and one key phrase that should lead searchers to my site is "personal finances". A search for those two keywords on Google doesn't have me listed at the top, however, and there are over five million matches, as shown in Figure 5.1.

 **Beware** _____

Some self-styled "search engine experts" offer #1 placement for keywords. They're all con artists and should be avoided. In fact, no one can guarantee placement on the Google search engine results page.

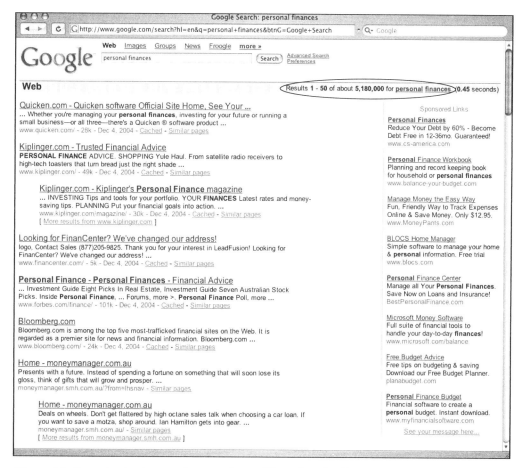

Figure 5.1: Even the simplest search can produce millions of results. Does your site even make it into the first thousand matches?

BizTips _____

Chapter 4 demonstrates a variety of sophisticated Google search techniques, one of which is exactly what I need here. To ensure that my site's pages are in the results, I can search for "site:reallifedebt.com personal finances". The result shows that Google knows about 163 separate pages from my site.

Why are some pages granted the top slots while other pages that seem just as relevant, valuable, and interesting to a searcher end up relegated to the 207th page of matches, or worse?

The answer to this question is at the heart of this book, and one of the reasons you picked up *The Complete Idiot's Guide to Growing Your Business with Google* in the first place. That's good, because I promise that if you apply the simple techniques and concepts presented to modify and improve your online presence, you *will* move your way up in the results. You can imagine how valuable it would be for *your* site to be listed on that first page of results.

Beware _____

I receive well over a thousand unsolicited e-mail messages daily, of which 10 to 20 are from search engine placement consultants who promise me the #1 slot. They can't possibly deliver what they're promising, and some of them use sufficiently unorthodox techniques that they can actually result in your being banned from the Google index completely. Even results page 207 sounds a lot better than being completely eliminated. Don't fall for these scam artists. Just delete these messages and proceed with more traditional, legitimate means of creating a more valuable site. Your rank will improve as a result.

The Magic of PageRank

The heart of the Google system is a concept called *PageRank*. It was the PageRank equation that Google co-founders Larry Page and Sergey Brin developed while graduate students at Stanford University. The best way to think about PageRank is to consider it a popularity vote. When an existing site points to your site, your site gains in PageRank based on the importance of that other page on the Internet.

Memo

PageRank has nothing to do with how relevant your page is for a given search query.

This is quite logical. A pointer to your website from the Whitehouse.gov home page should be worth more, that is, should mean your page is more important to the overall web community, than a pointer to your site from your sister's personal hobby page.

PageRank has nothing to do with the relevance of your pages to specific keywords or searches, however. It's the foundation of the Google calculations, so for a few minutes, forget about search results and let's instead just consider the method by which Google ranks the billions of pages on the web to identify which are most important.

A second factor for the PageRank formula is the number of pages that point to a page. This is the whole voting concept I mentioned earlier. If you have 108 different pages pointing to your page, that's going to be more valuable than if you have 4.

The third important factor is how many other links are found on the pages that point to your site. That is, if a site points to you and only has three other site links on the page, that's more valuable than if you are one of hundreds of links off a great big list.

Take a deep breath and let's jump in.

The PageRank for a given page is the sum of the calculated PageRank of all linking pages divided by the number of links on each page. Here's a formula to show this:

$$PR(a) = PR(b)/links(b) + PR(c)/links(c) \ldots PR(n)/links(n)$$

This isn't the actual formula used by Google since there's really no way to know exactly how things work inside the massive Google search engine, but for purposes of our discussion, this will work fine.

There are some important conclusions to be drawn:

1. Getting more sites to link to your site is an excellent way to increase your PageRank.

2. Links from pages that have lots and lots of other links aren't particularly valuable.

Linking doesn't drain PageRank from your pages, so it pays to be generous in linking to other relevant sites. The trade-off with pointing to other sites, though, is a strategic business issue because when you invite your visitors to go elsewhere, it's likely that they won't come back. If you have a storefront, you don't have coupons from

BizTips

PageRank is shared so as your own site gains in PageRank, remember to offer links to other sites that help your customers solve problems or identify compatible products and services.

neighboring merchants piled up by your sale rack, inviting customers to go elsewhere instead of purchasing your products!

The PageRank concept proves confusing because there's a summary PageRank calculation shown with the Google Toolbar that indicates the relative importance of a given web page to the overall web community. You can download the Google Toolbar for yourself by going to http://toolbar.google.com.

The toolbar PageRank value is an approximately logarithmic scale of 1 to 10. A PageRank of zero means that the page isn't in the Google database. Generally, sites with a PageRank of 1 to 4 are considered unimportant, PageRank of 5 to 7 are strong content sites, and PageRank of 8 to 10 are the top sites on the Internet.

BizTips

PageRank is important, but you should devote your attention to Relevance Score for better results.

To give you an idea of the relative PageRank (PR) of some sites, Google. com and Whitehouse.gov are a PR10; Yahoo.com, IBM.com, and IRS.gov are a PR9; Unicef.org, Army.mil, and Colorado.edu are a PR8; and my own site, Intuitive.com, is a PR6.

The Google Toolbar is seductive and there are plenty of people who become obsessed with their PageRank. You'll do best to consider it a curiosity, because it's much more important to be findable for the specific keywords your customers use in searches.

Why You Want Spiders to Visit Your Site

The first generation of World Wide Web directories, Yahoo! and the like, were fundamentally limited by the fact that website owners had to manually submit information about their sites to be included. Yahoo! was helpful, but it wasn't until websites like Lycos (now Terra/Lycos) introduced the concept of *spidering*, where their system actively explored the known web and added new sites and pages as encountered, that the foundations for Google were in place.

BizTips

A crawler and a spider are the same thing, software applications that travel and explore the web, looking for new content to analyze and index.

When you consider that thousands of new web pages are added to the World Wide Web every minute of the day, the job of finding all those pages is incredibly complex.

How Spiders Work

Spiders work by building a list of all other pages referenced by a given page, and cross-checking against a database of known pages to eliminate duplicates. Multiply that by a billion and you can see that it's a phenomenally difficult task to actually keep track of the web as it continues to evolve.

But that's exactly what Google, Yahoo! Search, MSN, Lycos, and other spider-based search engines do. Somehow. Fortunately it doesn't really matter how spiders work, just that you want them to visit your site frequently and find all your new and updated pages so that they can be added to the database and found by people searching the web. One simple tip in this regard is that the discovery of new pages can be hastened by ensuring that existing pages point to the new pages. It's better to link to all the new pages from your home page than to point to one, have that point to a second, and so forth.

How Often Will Googlebot Visit?

The other important facet you should know about the Google spider, called the Googlebot, is how it determines how frequently it needs to visit your site. If Googlebot only visits your site every 90 days, a typical starting point for the 'bot, then the new material you add, the new product announcements, and even the announcement of expansion into new business segments could be missing from the Google database for up to three months.

The frequency calculations are simple and smart: If the page changes a lot, we should visit it a lot, but if it rarely changes, we can delay our visits for weeks or even months.

Let me restate that: *If the page changes a lot, Googlebot will visit it frequently. If it rarely changes, Googlebot won't visit anywhere near as often.*

In practice, this is a very good reason to change your content with some frequency. If Googlebot visits your page and finds that it's changed since the previous visit, the next visit will occur on a more timely basis. If you have daily content additions, it shouldn't take more than a month or two for Google to be analyzing that particular page daily. This is one of the core reasons for having a weblog or blog as a cornerstone of your business website.

There's a tremendous benefit you can gain from frequent visits because your new content can't be found until Google knows about it. Google also seems to visit high PageRank pages more frequently than low PageRank pages.

Relevance Scoring

I've been talking about how Google finds and indexes your site, but not what is perhaps the most important and critical topic of all: How does Google figure out the topic of your web page and determine how relevant—or how good a match—your page is to a given search query?

Since the relevance scoring formula is the crown jewel of Google, there's no way to know how relevance is *really* calculated. Based on experimentation, analysis, and the consensus of the search community, however, we can make some very good guesses at the mechanism.

Inbound Links

I've already discussed the importance of other sites pointing to your site. That's "inbound linking" in Google parlance, and everything else being equal, sites that have lots of inbound links are a better match for a given search query than those that have very few inbound links.

Encouraging your customers, suppliers, partners, and associates to link to your site is a winning strategy in this regard, and I'll explore how to encourage that in Chapter 14.

BizTips

You can see how many inbound links you have by searching for your domain name with the special link: operator. Want to see how many sites point to intuitive.com, as an example? Search for "link:www.intuitive.com".

Link Text

What isn't immediately obvious when you think about relevance scoring is that *how* the other sites point to your pages is also important. To explain this, I'm going to have to get a bit technical, so bear with me.

Memo

The word or words used to point to your site are of paramount importance, which is why it's smart to encourage good linking, as discussed in Chapter 14.

There are two basic ways one page can point to another, with either a graphical link or a text link. A graphical link is a picture, photograph, or other graphical element that, if clicked by a visitor, takes them to another page. The graphic can be anything from a company logo to a picture of an office building. A text link, by contrast, is one or more words, typically in blue and underlined, that, if clicked, take the visitor to another page. These are the more common links on the web.

From Google's perspective, there's quite a bit of difference between these two links, because the text that's made clickable—the words shown in blue and underlined (depending on the design of the site)—is considered a great indicator of the content of the linked page.

To illustrate, let me show you how a text link looks in *hypertext markup language* (HTML), the page layout language of the web:

```
Dave's a great event photographer (
<a href="http://www.colorado-portraits.com/">
site</a>).
```

When this sentence is received by a web browser, it will be displayed approximately like this: "Dave's a great event photographer (<u>**site**</u>)." Click on the word *site* and the visitor will be whisked to the website.

There are two important items of information here. The link to the website is important and has already been discussed, but the *word that is used as the link text is just as important*. In this illustration, the word *site* is the link text. Google uses these link text phrases as important factors in calculating relevance scores.

If you're thinking, "Hmmm … *site* certainly doesn't seem like good link text!" you're absolutely right. To increase the findability of your web pages, it's critically important to recognize the value of link text and encourage other sites to use key phrases that describe the content of your site. A much better way to point to the photography site is:

```
Dave's a great
<a href="http://www.colorado-portraits.com/">
event photographer</a>.
```

Instead of the useless word *site* being the link text, the key phrase "event photographer" is used instead. This simple change makes the linked page more relevant to searches for "event", "photographer", and, of course, "event photographer".

It's quite surprising how commonly nondescriptive links are featured on web pages. Figure 5.3 shows an example of this type of poor linking strategy.

Memo

Not only does better link text improve the relevance of the target page with Google, it's also just better web design and more friendly, too. Go look at your business site. Are your links characterized by this smart strategy?

The links shown in Figure 5.2 are internal links, that is, links to other pages on the same site, but *Google looks at pages, not sites.* The internal links on a site are just as important as external links for reinforcing the main topic of each page. The FirstGov for Kids site could significantly improve the relevance of its pages by changing "Arts" to "Art Projects", "Computers" to "Learn about Computers", and "Music" to "Music History" throughout the site.

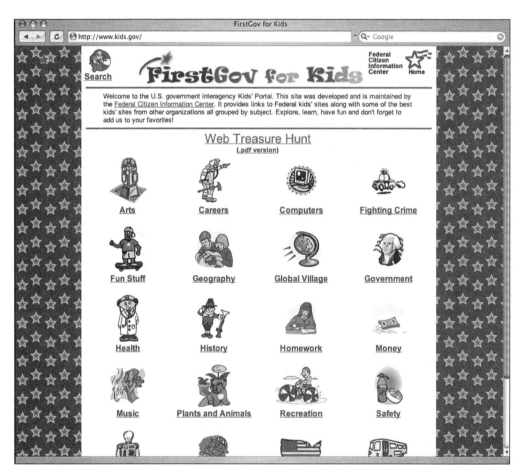

Figure 5.2: The FirstGov for Kids site is visually attractive, but link text like "Arts" and "Computers" can't improve the relevance score of the linked pages.

The Content and Layout of the Web Page

There's a third factor that influences relevance scores, too, and that's the content and structure of the web page itself. In a nutshell, the more frequently a word or phrase is mentioned on a web page and the more importance that is placed on the word or phrase in the design of the page, the higher its relevance score will be.

A page that's entitled "Art Projects for Young Painters" and has "Art Projects" both as the section head and a half-dozen times within the first ten paragraphs is going to produce a high relevance score for "art projects". A similar site that has "Fifty Fun Painting Projects for Children" as the title, "Project #1" as the first section head, and an essay comparing different painting media—"watercolors", "tempura", "oils"—without ever stating the phrase "art projects" on the page will rank much lower.

That doesn't mean that the latter page isn't more relevant for a search that includes the terms "painting projects children watercolors", but if you want to have a page that's highly relevant to searches for "art projects", then you need to incorporate that key phrase multiple times on the page.

BizTips

Reiterate your key words or phrases more than once on your pages, ideally in section headings as well as in prose. It's an easy way to improve your relevance score.

The Key Ramification of Relevance Scoring

Relevance scores for a given search are therefore comprised of three different factors:

- Number of inbound links
- Link text
- Analysis of word and phrase usage on web pages

There are likely other factors, possibly including PageRank, but since the actual relevance score is a closely held proprietary secret of Google, let's just accept that this is a reasonably accurate formula and proceed.

Yahoo!, MSN, and Other Search Sites

I've spent this entire chapter theorizing about how Google calculates PageRank and relevance scores, both of which are important factors to increasing the findability of your site and, ultimately, growing your business with Google.

But Google isn't the only show in town. There are a number of other web search engines built around spidering software analyzing the contents of pages, finding new pages, and creating a massive database that can be searched with remarkably good results. Top among these competitors are Yahoo! Search and MSN Search.

While less is known about how these two sites calculate which of the billions of known pages are likely to be the best matches for a given query, their underlying formula must be quite similar to the Google formula.

The fundamental similarities between the search engines is a relief, actually, since it implies that time spent optimizing a website to make it "Google-friendly" will also pay off in making the site more easily and accurately analyzed by the other engines, too.

Memo

Remember, optimizing your web pages for Google will benefit you with other search engines, too!

This ultimately means that not only will your online business be more findable by potential customers using a Google search, but also by those that opt for Yahoo! or MSN searches.

The Least You Need to Know

- ◆ Google's PageRank is a coarse measure of how important your site is to the overall web.

- ◆ New pages on your site are found through Googlebot, a spider program that searches and analyzes web pages.

- ◆ The more frequently you update content on your pages, the more frequently Googlebot will visit your site.

- ◆ Relevance score is based on the number of inbound links, the link text of those links, and the content and layout of the individual web page.

Part  Building Your Google Plan

It used to be enough to just have a few pages on the web that marked your territory and justified the use of a trendy website address on your receipts. But that's passed and now it's about rethinking, and possibly re-inventing, your business to fit into the new age of information. It's also time to rethink your business website, too, realizing that it plays a much more important role in the future of your business.

The Internet offers many opportunities for interaction and research, ranging from identifying your primary competitors and keeping an eye on new competitors to learning more about your customers and what they're really talking about when there isn't a salesperson in the room.

Think of this part as helping you understand how to write a Google- and web-centric marketing plan for your company.

Chapter 6

What's Your Core Business?

In This Chapter

- The importance of focus
- Differentiators and sustainable differentiators
- Surveying the competitive landscape
- Setting viable growth goals

To grow a business, it's critical to understand not only the business sector, but the strengths and weaknesses of the individual business. Whether you offer a service or product line, failure to grasp the core of your business inevitably leads to wasted development effort, ineffective marketing campaigns, an off-target web presence, and, ultimately, dissatisfied customers.

There are two ways that most entrepreneurial businesses are created. They are either birthed by the passion and enthusiasm of the founders, or they're more methodically created based on a perceived market opportunity. Neither is superior and both face the same fundamental business challenge: turning a good idea into a viable and successful business.

To turn an idea into a business, some companies cast a wide net to see if any fish are caught. Many new consultants do this, too, when they explain their areas of expertise and then add, "but I'll do just about anything that helps pay the bills." That's a bit like walking into a bicycle store just to be surprised when the clerk asks if he can give you a foot massage or serve you a bowl of soup.

> **Memo**
>
> Focus. Success in business is all about focus.

The Importance of Staying Focused

The most important rule for any small business is to stay focused. Identify the unique value proposition of your business or service, then make sure that every idea you have, every inspiration for expansion, is consistent with your unique value proposition and strengthens it.

If you have a hardware store in a small town, expanding into new tool lines or yard equipment is sensible and helps reinforce the customer perception that your business offers a range of products that meet their needs. Imagine adding a small gourmet food area to the store instead. Unless you are in a very unusual town, the hardware customers will ignore the new area, and the potential gourmet food customers never materialize because the local supermarket offers a better selection.

This is just as true for service providers. It would certainly be peculiar if the guy who came out to install your cable television also specialized in custom flower arrangements, and I'm sure you don't want your surgeon to have a sideline as a website developer.

When Diversification Works

As companies grow, they can diversify with less risk. Amazon.com started out selling books, then expanded into DVDs and music CDs. As that business grew, CEO Jeff Bezos and team transformed their business model from online retailer to an e-commerce platform. Today Amazon enables a number of large retailers to sell online using the Amazon platform.

Wal-Mart also shows that diversification can be a successful strategy. Behind the scenes, though, Wal-Mart remains very focused on their value proposition and they'll quickly jettison any business that isn't profitable. In particular, Wal-Mart invests heavily in its inventory management solution and minimizes the complexity of its inventory control system by carrying only the top two or three products in any given category. Wal-Mart offers fewer food choices than a supermarket, and fewer clothing choices than a clothes store, but the Wal-Mart differentiator is that of the old general store: everything under one roof.

> **Memo**
> Just because large companies can diversify doesn't mean that it's a smart strategy for growing your own business, particularly in the online world.

I'm not arguing that you should diversify and try to be all things to every possible customer. Not at all. In fact, that's the sure path to mediocrity in an early stage company because instead of focusing on being the leader in a specific segment, the desire to cover many segments inevitably leads to lack of attention in each. It's the lackluster corner store that never seems to have what you're seeking or the handyman who isn't particularly good at any repair job.

> **Memo**
> Convenience stores in gas stations can be quite profitable, because smart gas station owners recognize that they don't have to offer the best selection of products. Their core value is convenience, and customers will happily take the wrong size milk, the wrong brand of butter, or a soup other than what they wanted, as long as they can go when traditional stores are closed. This was the basis of 7/11, and I'm sure you have a local shop that gets some of your business even though they're more expensive than the supermarket a few miles away.

Think Strategy, Not Tactics

Focus also comes from thinking about business issues strategically, rather than tactically. What's the difference? Strategy is "we need to be a leader in the local automotive market," while tactics are "we should have frequent sales on tires to draw customers into the store." The problem with operating a business tactically is that you can't focus or identify your core business, and even if you do, you'll probably be moving away from it as much as toward it with

> **Memo**
> The problem with tactics is that you never get a chance to lift up your head and survey the industry picture. Businesses succeed because their leaders remain aware of industry trends. I like to think of this as the "lead" in leader, rather than the "err ..."

your growth efforts. It also becomes more likely that your growth plans will be inconsistent with the real value of your business to your customers.

A book publisher that agrees to publish a few titles on topics completely different from their area of specialization runs the risk of diluting their brand identity in exactly the same way, confusing their customers, losing focus on their core business, and diluting the overall value of their organization.

As a business owner, you need to figure out what lies at the heart of your business and then use that as the basis for all your growth decisions, from website design to new product lines and services.

Focus on What Customers Want

One way to pin down the core value proposition of a company is to identify specific customer problems, then state succinctly how the company solves those problems in a unique and interesting way.

As an example, suppose you invented a DVD player that could send the video signal directly to local computers through a wireless connection. The problem being solved is that people with computers and TVs can't simultaneously watch a movie on both units. Your product offers an interesting and compelling solution to that problem.

Doesn't a box that hooks up between an existing DVD player and the television sound like a better solution? It is. Selling a DVD player means that you'd be competing directly with consumer electronics powerhouses like Sony, Toshiba, and Philips, but by identifying the core value proposition and switching to a separate add-on device, you've expanded your possible market and lowered your production cost, too.

An entrepreneur who wasn't focused might start out with the idea of a Wi-Fi DVD player and decide that similar VCRs and stereo receivers would be a good growth direction. Each step on this muddleheaded path makes for a more difficult business, higher overhead costs, and a more challenging competitive environment. Ultimately, this business would likely fail because the cost of developing these products would be greater than any possible sales.

Differentiators and Sustainable Differentiators

In addition to questions of the core value proposition, which help you identify what your business does, it's just as important to know how your business differentiates itself, that is, how you compare yourself to your competitors.

> **Memo**
>
> Differentiators are those facets of your business or service that are unique to your organization. Washing your car is clearly not a differentiator for your local car wash, so they have to create or identify other differentiators to be competitive. In my neighborhood car washes compete on their ecological friendliness (even though they're required to recycle their water anyway) and related automotive services like oil changes, detailing, and superficial body work and repairs.

I've already talked about differentiators earlier in the book, but it's a critical concept because marketing and savvy, successful growth plans come from differentiation. It's only after you've figured out how your company, service, or products differ from those of your competitors that you can begin to see benefit from your marketing efforts.

Dare to Be Different

Before Starbucks popularized fancy coffee beverages at $5 per cup, it would have seemed daft to create an international business focused on selling a hot drink that had previously been relegated to something you bought with your paper or morning doughnut. Starbucks doesn't differentiate based on the cup of coffee itself, though. The success of Starbucks is a combination of the experience, the culture of café that Starbucks has helped popularize, and the standardization of its coffee drinks.

Nordstrom is in a highly competitive business segment, clothing, and has differentiated itself through an emphasis on personalized customer service. By contrast, The Men's Warehouse is also in the clothing business, but their differentiator is that their stores make shopping for a men's suit simple and fast, even if custom tailoring is required.

In the highly competitive, commoditized business of gasoline sales, Chevron Corporation introduced an additive called Techron that they advertised as helping keep car engines cleaner. This is an artificial differentiator because the introduction of Techron didn't solve a *customer* problem but rather a *marketing* problem.

> **Memo**
>
> Remember when gas stations advertised detergent additives as differentiators? Since 1995 all gasoline sold, by law, includes detergent additives.

Techron is particularly interesting because, while it was a differentiator for Chevron, it wasn't a sustainable differentiator in the long run because in 1995 the U.S. government started requiring detergent additives in all commercial gasoline. Now all gas companies have their own additives that promise to help keep car engines clean. ARCO, for example, has a detergent additive called CleanTech, British Petroleum has an additive in their Ultimate premium octane gasoline, Shell has V-Power, and Texaco has CleanSystem.

Find Your Long-Term Niche

Differentiators can help launch a company, but to create and retain a sustainable differentiator is a very different challenge and the basis of much intellectual property law, among other things. After all, if you invent something that helps you to differentiate your business from your competitors, being able to have the differentiator remain a method of distinguishing your company from your competitors is invaluable.

Many businesses are moving towards commoditization, too. Today it may seem like you can differentiate based on service, style, or convenience, but many industries are moving towards a commodity market, where the only meaningful differentiator is price. I don't have to tell you that when the only way you can compete is through price, it's incredibly difficult to grow your company or even stay in business.

In the software business, competitors have moved from promoting individual products to offering suites of tightly integrated applications. Ten years ago, Microsoft promoted Word as a word processing solution and Excel as a spreadsheet, but today Microsoft spends more money advertising the Office suite. Their differentiator is no longer the capabilities of the individual application but the integration of all the tools in the suite. It's likely that won't be sustainable either, and in a few years another differentiator will be featured in the office utility software space.

Another example of a commodity application that has a number of strong competitors seeking to differentiate themselves is anti-virus software. Symantec, McAfee, and Computer Associates all have excellent programs that essentially perform the exact same function. How to differentiate? By including other features and capabilities with the program. McAfee VirusScan can remove viruses from instant messages and "identifies spying and pop-up programs," among other capabilities.

One example of differentiators in the highly commoditized software business is rebates. Seems like half the products for sale at the local CompUSA or other computer outlet have some sort of rebate available from the manufacturer. This is a particularly interesting differentiator because it lets the companies compete on price, but with a constrained time frame. Some day the rebate will end and the price will no longer be competitive.

Of course, rebates are interesting for a completely different reason, too: most people just don't bother to send in the forms. So while they think they're getting a competitively priced product, they end up paying a surcharge, a laziness tax, and the manufacturer has succeeded in differentiating without having to actually differentiate!

Anti-virus software exhibited the cycle of differentiation that occurs time and again in different market segments: differentiation based on capabilities, then based on ease of use, then the quest for new differentiators once all competitors reach parity of offerings.

Sometimes the differentiator can be spun off as a new product, too. Microsoft originally had a free utility customers could download that would let them save Microsoft Word documents in "web format," making Word a rudimentary web page development tool. This proved quite popular and Microsoft shortly thereafter replaced the download with a completely separate application called FrontPage.

Competition Is Good

Underlying the discussion of differentiators is the presumption that you have competitors and are going to continue to have competitors in your market segment. For some business people, competitors are upsetting and the failure of a competitor is cause for celebration, as there's now more opportunity for your own company.

This view presumes that there's a finite market for any given product or service and that the more supply there is, the less demand there will be. But the supply and demand equation only holds true at a given moment in time. Industries mature, evolve, and expand.

BizTips

A business sector only remains without competitors as long as it isn't profitable.

Markets Evolve

Twenty-five years ago you would have been hard-pressed to find a financial planner who would factor in the cost of a daily cup of coffee in a client's personal financial plan, but today there are so many people who purchase a daily latté or cappuccino that annual expenditures of $1000 or more are not uncommon.

Beware

Entrepreneurs with a great idea often say "there's no competition," thinking that investors will find the remark comforting. In fact, it's quite troubling, because it either means that there probably *isn't* a business opportunity or that the entrepreneur is unable to do good competitive research.

When televisions were introduced, companies didn't anticipate homes with a screen in every room—even the bathroom!—let alone portable TVs and DVD players in automobiles. Telephone lines were originally apportioned out so that multiple residences were forced to share a single "party" line. Now a typical household has three or more phone lines, and if you add cell phones and office phone numbers, a typical family of four is probably responsible for 8 to 10 different phone lines.

Competition defines a market segment, often creating an entirely new category. Growing your business in parallel with your competition is proof that there's a viable market and customers.

Watch and Learn

Rather than fear and shun competitors, therefore, it is far smarter to watch them and learn from them. There are companies that do very well letting other firms take the risky first steps into a marketplace, watching every move and analyzing the success or failure of each promotion and product.

In the fast-food industry, companies follow this strategy with remarkable frequency, letting one company introduce a new type of meal and copying them if it proves successful. Television and movie companies are even more infamous for their copycat style. If a movie or TV show taps the public zeitgeist and is a runaway success, it's a sure bet that 12 months later there'll be a half-dozen similar productions on the air.

Memo

There's no shame in copying the success of a competitor!

If you have smart competitors, they'll be watching what you do quite closely, too, which is one good reason to not introduce anything online—or even mention anything in the product pipeline—until you're ready to launch the product.

One area of competitive analysis, just to start you thinking, is job listings. If you run a couch factory, for example, and suddenly start advertising for cabinetmakers, your competitors can quickly conclude that you're about to expand your furniture line.

Setting Goals for Your Company

The purpose of ascertaining your core business, clarifying your differentiators, brainstorming on what can be sustainable differentiators, and understanding your competition is so you can have an unbiased assessment of your company and how it compares to other companies in your market segment.

With a realistic view of your company, you are now in a position to set goals and objectives. But setting goals isn't a matter of stating "We're going to become the largest bookstore in the world." That goal may be inspiring, but it's very difficult to achieve and the ramifications of a never-attained goal might include morale problems, desperation, pure tactical management, and worse.

Better goals are "increase sales by 10 percent in the next six months" or "improve customer retention by 25 percent by the end of the year." Good goals have a specific, measurable outcome and a date by when they should be attained.

BizTips

Always have measurable goals and always figure out how to measure them. And do so!

What are your goals for your business?

One hotly debated topic in business school is whether the fundamental objective of any business is to "make money" or not. According to the basic tenets of capitalism, the exact goal is actually to maximize shareholder value, which isn't quite the same. Whether you have shareholders or it's a one-person operation, your fundamental goal is nonetheless going to be to make more money. That's not a good, attainable goal (are you going to consider yourself successful if you make $10 more this year than you did last?) but it can certainly be transformed into a viable goal. Here's one possibility: "We're going to increase sales so that our earnings after taxes are 20 percent higher than last year."

Spend a few minutes focusing on your business. Identify your core value proposition and what fundamental customer problems you're solving. Now expand to consider how your competitors are solving these same problems for your customers and how you are differentiating yourself. Finally, create a few goals or objectives for your company and write them down. Tape them to the wall by your desk and review them every day, particularly on days when you're considering an expansion into a new business area or marketplace.

The Least You Need to Know

- Successful businesses stay focused on their core value proposition and grow from there as opportunity presents itself.

- Differentiators are what help you stand out from all the solutions in the marketplace and they should be the cornerstone of your marketing and growth plans.

- Competitors should be embraced, not feared. Without competitors, there is no viable market segment.

- Set measurable goals that include specific target dates, then go back each year and ensure you have attained them.

Chapter 7

Living in an Online World

In This Chapter

- ◆ How the domain name system works
- ◆ Internet-friendly business names and slogans
- ◆ Search terms and keywords
- ◆ Domain names and how to get them

In the physical world, location is everything, whether you're opening a restaurant, bookstore, or auto shop. Translating the importance of location into the online world is a bit more tricky, because on the World Wide Web, every website, from the most elaborate to the most humble, is just a few mouse clicks away.

The online version of scarce real estate is unquestionably the ubiquitous little one- or two-word phrases that appear in print ads, on TV and billboards, and even on the cover of this very book. They are domain names, and they're the lingua franca of the online world.

> **BizTips** _____
>
> Short, pronounceable, and memorable are the three key metrics for what makes a good domain name.

A decade ago, when commerce was just starting on the web, domain names were plentiful and companies competed for a coveted dotcom domain. Indeed, the late 1990s investment frenzy and subsequent collapse of thousands of Internet-related start-ups takes its name from this class of domain names: the *dotcom crash*.

Today there are dozens of top-level domains available for online businesses, a growth that's somewhat akin to waking up one morning and finding that there are new shopping malls on every side of the mall you just paid a premium to locate your store within.

But are all domain names the same? How does the domain name system work, anyway? And what can you do if the domain you want is already taken? In this chapter, I will explain how the domain name system works, discuss the evolution of domain names, and talk about what makes a great domain different from a good one. I'll also share with you the type of domain names you want to avoid completely.

How the Domain Name System Works

Without going too far into the technical side of things, the domain name system is built as an upside-down tree, with each domain having a unique namespace. This means that even though you may own *yourbiz.com* it doesn't mean that your competitor can't register and use *yourbiz.net*, *yourbiz.info*, or *yourbiz.org*.

> **Memo**
>
> If you think of domain names as a phone number, you'll miss the point. Customers don't really care if your phone number is 555-1234 or 555-1268, but if you instead consider how companies pay to gain control of mnemonic toll-free numbers (you probably know a half-dozen of them yourself), you'd be getting closer to the scarcity and value of domain names.

Originally there were six major domain name trees (in the industry, the top-level domain name trees are called *top-level domains* or TLDs. Computer people seem inordinately fond of acronyms!) called .com, .net, .org, .mil, .edu, and .gov, for commercial companies, Internet service providers and other network infrastructure companies, nonprofit organizations, military networks, educational institutions, and government agencies, respectively.

In those days, it was critically important to register your dotcom name, because if you were a commercial business, there was no alternative top-level domain you could use: it was .com or nothing.

Companies had to prove that they were legal IRS nonprofits to be granted a .org, and even today .mil, .edu, and .gov domains are restricted.

In the last few years, the entire domain name system has been overhauled and there are now essentially no restrictions on who can register which of the different primary domain names. Your business can just as easily be a .net as a .com. Concurrent with this loosening has been the introduction of dozens of new top-level domains, notably including .biz, .us, and .info.

A good domain name for your business doesn't have to end with .com any more. A good domain name can now be measured by how memorable it is and what I call the *radio ad test*—if a potential customer hears your domain name on the radio, will they get to your website, or end up guessing at odd spellings or cryptic acronyms. If you have to spell out your domain name or write it down so someone will remember it, you've failed the radio ad test.

Identifying a good domain name for your business is a matter of balancing the need for something short and mnemonic against what's still available or for sale at a reasonable cost.

CAUTION

Beware _____

One group of online entrepreneurs that you'll encounter are domain name squatters. These are people who buy up thousands of domain names with the hope of selling them to companies at a dramatic markup. Domain names can cost as little as $6 per year, but domain names with perceived value can sell for thousands or, in some rare cases, millions of dollars. The challenge with buying a domain from a squatter is that domain squatters are opportunists, so any sign of interest will instantly translate into the purchase price increasing.

There are some legal protections if the domain name you seek is held by a squatter and is associated with a registered international trademark, but these cases can be very difficult to win because you need to demonstrate that it either hurts your business or that it creates significant confusion in the market.

Identifying and acquiring a good, memorable domain name is one of the great challenges of the Internet business age and different companies have different strategies.

Internet-Friendly Business Names and Slogans

One of the most common strategies is to name a company based on available domain names. No kidding, there are lots of companies that will change their name or rebrand themselves based on the domain name that they can acquire.

At some level this makes sense, because one method of making a domain name memorable is to incorporate it into the name of the company.

Having a domain name that has nothing to do with your actual business or business name can confuse your customers. However, if you're a bicycle shop called *University Bicycles*, the odds of you obtaining a relevant domain name are slim. There are probably thousands of University Bicycles shops in the United States of America.

One possible solution that doesn't involve renaming your business is to seek a domain name that describes what you do or what your customers seek to do with your products or services. The domain universitybicycles.com might not be available, but BikeSeattle.com might well be a possibility. Of course, it's not perfect, because this domain could just as well be a company specializing in bicycle tours of Seattle and the surrounding area.

BizTips

Memorable is usually better than shorter, if you have to choose between the two. Just make sure it's pronounceable!

There's a general business rule, too: unique, descriptive business names are more memorable than generic names.

Even without any discussion of domain names, companies with unique, memorable, descriptive, and interesting names are more likely to be remembered and discussed by potential customers than generic nondescriptive names.

An example of this is the difficulty most people have remembering the name of their favorite Chinese restaurant; the majority of Chinese restaurants use a similar two-word naming scheme, where one name is either a region of China or a cooking utensil and the other is a positive descriptive attribute. Golden Wok, Peking Palace, Mandarin Gourmet, and China Plate are all very common restaurant names.

Given the frequency of restaurants with these common names, opening up a new Chinese restaurant and having a website that helps introduce new customers to the business could be quite problematic for just this reason. A restaurant called Szechwan Heaven is going to have a difficult time identifying an available domain name.

Search Terms and Keywords

Findability is the foundation of everything I'm discussing, and findability can suggest a certain approach to domain names, too. A findable domain name is one that is based on a common keyword or term that customers are likely to use as a search query when seeking your business.

An example of a findable domain name is Szechwan-of-Portland.net because someone searching for a Chinese restaurant in Portland might well use the query Szechwan Portland. Google highlights words that match a given query, and those words can match a domain name just as easily as they can appear in the title or body of a web page.

The best domain names, however, are a word or two without any hyphens or superfluous words. The domain name penguin.com is excellent, while penguinbooks.com is still pretty good, and penguin-books.com is acceptable, but can cause confusion. In addition, the latter fails the radio test: Would your ad have to say penguin dash books dot com to be clear?

BizTips

Try to avoid hyphenated domain names, especially if you don't also own the nonhyphenated version. Remember, hyphenated domains fail the radio test, too.

Plenty of companies use hyphens in their domain names, however, and it's not an inherently bad strategy *as long as you also own the nonhyphenated domain name, too*. You can just imagine the confusion when a customer goes to penguinbooks.com and finds a completely different website—and company—than they do at penguin-books.com.

Another approach is to make up a word and use that as your company and domain name. Yahoo! did this. Xerox and Kodak predate the Internet, but they also had unique and unusual names that were easily translated into domain names. This is a viable strategy, inventing a name and then using that as your company name. The only problem is figuring out how to ensure your customers remember how to spell it properly—does Exxon have one x or two?

That brings up an interesting note: Some domain squatters buy up common misspellings of domain names and then rely on users typing in domain names incorrectly for traffic. Visit www.goggle.com, www.yahho.com or www.cnnn.com for examples. If this happens to your domain name, there's not much you can do unless you want to pursue a trademark violation suit for "a potentially confusing similarity in name" but that might prove quite expensive.

Memo

A sticky situation in the world of domain names is trademarks. You would think that it's clear cut: If you have a word as a trademark, you should have eminent domain over the domain name and be able to yank it from anyone else. The problem is that trademarks are only valid within a specific category, and though you might own the trademark for the name "Superior Wheels" in the area of transportation, another company can be granted the trademark for Superior Wheels in a completely different business space. Now who owns the trademark and therefore the domain?

Even if you're an uncontested trademark holder, some trademarks are more defensible than others. A trademark on "Tommy" in the clothing space (as Tommy Hilfiger owns) doesn't give them clear ownership rights to the domain "tommy.com" because there are a number of other companies that also have legal claim on the name, including people with the name Tommy.

BizTips

Domain names that are two or three words scrunched together can work well. Just remember to use some capitalization to help people see the multiple words and remember the domain. For example, my domain reallifedebt.com is more easily read as RealLifeDebt.com, isn't it?

What's true of the relationship between domain names and business names is also true for corporate slogans. It may sound odd, but if you're going to come up with a slogan for your business, why not consider that your domain name, too?

Consider the mobile Porsche mechanic in Chicago. Possible domain names could include mobilemechanic.com, porschemechanic.com or, if their slogan is "Your Porsche fixed in your driveway," perhaps drivewaymechanic.com or repairsOnSite.com.

Don't forget that specific product names can be good domain names, too, as the example of the Toyota Scion shows (see Chapter 2). Many companies now release products and have domain names to match, even if those domains funnel you back to the main corporate website.

Domain Names and How to Get Them

How do you find out which domains are available and, once you find a domain that is still available, how do you register it for your own business? Depending on your Internet service provider or web hosting company, there are many different organizations that can search the domain name registration database and register a domain for you. If your ISP has such a service, use that since it'll be automatically set up and ready to go.

Domain registration and the first year of domain ownership should cost roughly $10, though some registrars, the companies that help manage the domain name registration database, charge as little as $6 and others as much as $35 annually.

Note that being able to register a domain doesn't guarantee that you have a permanent legal claim, just as domain squatters can find that they've violated trademark law and be compelled by the courts (or the World Intellectual Property Organization [WIPO]) to transfer the domain to its rightful owner.

If you are just doing research, there are lots of different websites that can check if domains are available or not. The best either check across dozens of top-level domains or offer a raft of suggested, similar domains that are available.

An example of the former is a site I've worked with for years, MyDomain.com. Search there for the word bicycle, and it'll show that the .net, .com, .org, and .biz are all taken, but that bicycle.nu, bicycle.sr, and bicycle.md are available, as shown in Figure 7.1.

Actually, the domain bicycle.md is excellent and would be a terrific domain—and business name—for a bicycle repair shop. That's an example of how searching for a domain can also produce an interesting possibility for a business name.

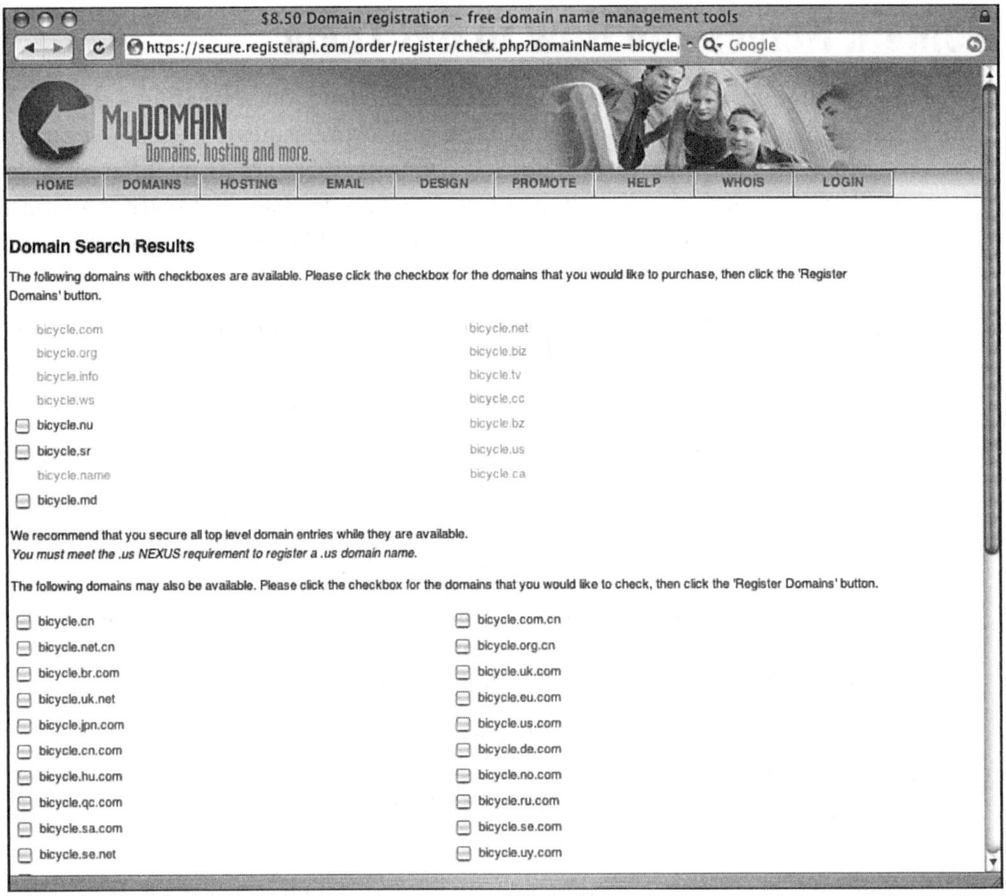

Figure 7.1: MyDomain.com lets you search by keyword or key phrase and shows the availability of the corresponding domain across over 40 different top-level domains.

Buzzwords

The **whois** system is a database of all domain names and their owners. All registrars have whois areas on their sites where you can find out the name, address, and phone number of any domain owner.

An example of a website that offers suggested synonyms or variants of a domain name is Enom.com, as shown in Figure 7.2.

Some domain names are already registered but don't seem to be in use, or at least attempts to bring up a web page on that domain fail. In that case, you can use one of the many *whois* services to identify the owner of the domain and contact them to inquire whether the domain might be for sale. I use Whois.Net to identify this type of information.

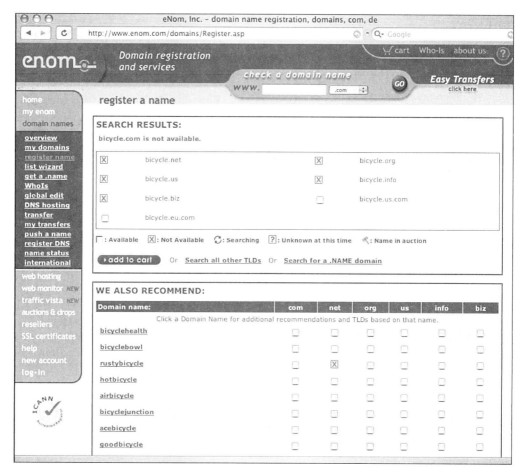

Figure 7.2: Enom offers a valuable synonym search that can help your creativity flow in the search for a domain name.

Buying a domain name can be a tricky business because a domain that might be worth almost nothing suddenly increases in perceived value when someone from a large corporation inquires about its availability. You can imagine if the marketing department of Proctor & Gamble asks about buying a domain name, a few zeroes are hastily added to the price tag!

If you do want to inquire about buying a domain name, you'll do best to keep a low profile and send your query from an AOL, Gmail, or other generic system rather than your corporation. I've purchased domains for as little as $25 and rejected offers of over $200,000 for domain names I own. It's pure capitalism—the value of a given domain name is completely determined by what the market will bear.

Generally, therefore, I recommend that you'll do better to use tools like Enom and a thesaurus to find a really good domain name that's available today. Keep in mind that the more easily your new domain name can be pronounced, the more likely your customers will remember it.

Finally, while dictionary word domains (like bicycle.com or books.com) are highly desirable, they're also the most in demand, the hardest to protect legally, and the most likely to already be in use.

A little creativity can go a long way with domain names.

After all, Google has a peculiar domain name, yet it's quite memorable now that the company is a success, isn't it?

(Google also owns gogle.com, gooogle.com, goooogle.com and so on. However, someone else got to goggle.com and gooooogle.com first, and they're now owned by a spyware sales company and an online gambling site, respectively.)

The Least You Need to Know

♦ Domains with a .com are preferable, but memorable domain names that are easy to spell are best.

♦ Many companies choose business names based on available domain names or create new words so that they can have a domain name that matches their company name.

♦ Internet service providers frequently offer domain name lookup and registration services. Domain names should cost no more than $10 per year.

Chapter 8

Your Business Website

In This Chapter

- ◆ The state of your existing site
- ◆ What content to include
- ◆ How often to update your information
- ◆ The value of multiple websites

Curb appeal is a term that real estate salespeople use to describe how a property appears from the street. Nothing about what it's like inside, nothing about whether the layout and configuration would match the needs of a prospective buyer, just how the property looks upon first glance.

In the world of business, your retail outlet is your curb appeal: If you don't have attractive signage and a pleasant, professional storefront, a significant number of potential customers could be driving past without even slowing down. They don't know that you have the best selection of competitive products, offer superb service, or have a beautifully designed interior.

In this chapter, I'll assess the state of your current business website and help you consider your design to ascertain whether it's doing all it can to help you bring in new customers and drive sales. You'll also be introduced to an important axiom, that findability is about content, thoughtfully deployed.

Online Curb Appeal

Your website is the online world's version of curb appeal, and when the page loads and visitors get their first glimpse of your layout and design, they inevitably make snap judgments about the site and, by extension, the company.

We've all grown up being told not to "judge a book by its cover" because it's the content of the proverbial book that's important. Similarly, making decisions about whether to extend the hand of friendship to someone based purely on their appearance isn't a good way to go through life either. But, you know what? Everyone is judging the elements of their environment all the time anyway. As business guru Tom Peters might say, "Deal with it!"

Designers believe that you have *15 seconds* to capture the attention of someone who has come to your website. If your site doesn't offer them something interesting, compelling, or valuable, they'll back up, choose a bookmarked site, or click away from your site through one of your own external links.

Even if we posit a more rationally paced world, it's a sure bet that if you can't engage your visitor within the first minute or so of them landing on your page, you have a serious efficacy problem with your website.

There's also a very important effect of the ubiquity of Google search that needs to be explored here, too: most visitors to your site *never see your home page*. Almost all website designers miss this critical realization and spend most of their time tuning the home page, the top of your web universe, then spend little or no time on subsequent or secondary pages. *Your home page is irrelevant.*

> **Memo**
>
> You have less than 60 seconds to engage your visitors and turn them into potential customers. They got there because they're interested in something on your site or because of an advertisement or a write-up about your company. Now, can you convert them?

However, if you have actual content on your site—articles relevant to your customers, information about specific products, or explanations of technical specifications—these content pages are inevitably going to end up with a higher relevance score and be visited more often than your home page.

I'm not saying that you shouldn't have a home page, or that you should ignore it in favor of designing beautiful and highly effective secondary pages, but the reality of the twenty-first century World Wide Web is that your *site* is what's important, not your home page.

Print advertising, television, and radio spots all list your website address, leading people to your home page, but the majority of most website visits are from searches and what Internet folk call *deep linking*.

The modern Internet is all about deep links. Think about it: if you want to tell others how to find the users guide for a new LG plasma TV, you want to link directly to the guide, not to the LG home page with some narrative explanation of how to dig through their site to find the page in question. Everyone else building useful sites online holds this same philosophy, so it's beholden on you to create excellent, informative pages throughout your site, and not just rely on a nice home page.

Buzzwords

When one website points to the home page of another site, that's called a link. When one site points to a specific subpage on another site, a page other than the home page, that's considered a **deep link**. The further away from the home page the link points (by number of clicks required to find it), the deeper the link is considered.

One fascinating ramification of all this searching is that your website has secondary pages that see considerably more traffic than the home page. For potential customers who see their first glimpse of your site through one of these secondary pages, what kind of impression do they gain?

The State of Your Existing Site

Most websites are still designed with the assumption that the main pitch, the explanation of who, what, when, where, why, and how, should appear on the home page and needn't be replicated on any other pages on the site. That's a mistake.

How Functional Are Your Secondary Pages?

Your first task in this chapter is to identify a few secondary pages on your site and, with the assumption that each is the *only page* that a visitor will see, ask yourself whether each page:

♦ Tells who you are

♦ Tells what you do, sell, or offer

◆ Indicates how your company differs from your competitors

◆ Invites visitors to learn more about your business

◆ Does all of the above in a compelling, enthusiastic manner

Remarkably few business websites can pass this simple test. Worse, many sites forget all about navigation on secondary pages, relying instead on the user clicking the browser's Back button to return to the home page. If the page has been found through a search engine, though, the Back button simply jumps back to the search engine results page, not another page on the site.

Consider the Artdolls.info site, an artist site focused on soft sculpture and doll making. The top screen shot in Figure 8.1 shows the original design of a secondary page of the Artdolls.info site, about a particular facet of doll production. There are navigational links on this secondary page, but they're far from obvious and won't encourage visitors to explore the rest of the site now that they've made it to this spot. Not even the site logo is clickable. The home page shown on the bottom of Figure 8.1, by contrast, offers many different navigational options and is more engaging.

The need for navigation that engages the visitor and encourages them to visit other parts of the site is a constant requirement through the entire site, even down to the level of financial information or press releases. Consider Figure 8.2 of the otherwise well-designed MassageSpecialists.com website (www.massagespecialists.com/news/ ms-rel-012901.htm).

There's much more to a good website than having clear and logical navigational capabilities, but being able to get around is a critical component of any effective web design. Other components include an attractive design (though it's critical not to have design trump usability). Sites that require long downloads for animated introductions or are so complex that many users see a "broken" version are just not good business websites.

Always assume that potential customers can come into your website at any seemingly random point, on any page, logical or not. Then ask the question: will they be invited to explore the rest of the site, or not?

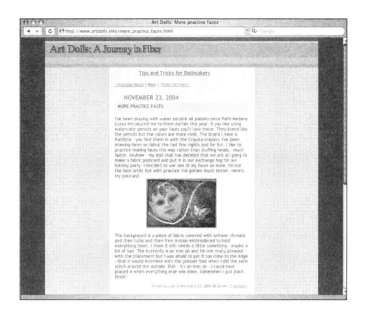

Figure 8.1: (Top) The original design of a Artdolls.info secondary page, about a particular facet of doll production, had no navigational links. (Bottom) The home page offers many different navigational options and is more engaging.

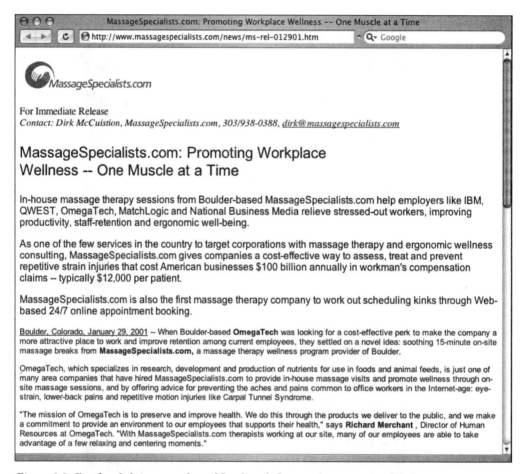

Figure 8.2: *I've found their press release. Now how do I get to the company website?*

What's the Best Content to Include?

A business site should include as much material as helps sell the company and the products, and no more. It's never a benefit for your company and your sales efforts to have a personal weblog, irreverent bio pages for staffers, or links to sites that you may like, but which have nothing to do with your product or service.

Memo
Some business owners think that giving your business a personality and letting your employees be unique online individuals is a positive trait. They might be right, but when I go to a site looking for a service or product to buy, I don't want to be distracted. When I go to a consumer electronics store, for example, I don't really care what movies are the favorites of the sales people. I want to know how *my favorite movie* shows on their screens. When business analysts talk about *frictionless commerce* they're talking about minimizing distractions and obstacles between your customers deciding to purchase your product and the completed transaction. As you go through the purchase sequence on an e-commerce site, ask yourself how much "friction" intervenes. There's a reason that Amazon.com has "one-click purchasing."

Core Content for a Good Business Website

A good business website should be able to answer the basic questions posed earlier (who, what, when, where, why, and how) and should do so in a manner that reinforces your expertise.

The mobile Porsche mechanic website could logically have a directory of all Porsches made, maps helping people locate Porsche auto parts stores in greater Chicago, and even stories about Porsche drivers. Additionally, testimonials are always an excellent addition to any marketing material and should be sprinkled throughout the site.

In a business where training and credentials are important, a detailed list of credentials is obligatory. After all, do medical professionals really like using diplomas and certificates to decorate their office walls? Pop over to my business weblog (www.intuitive.com/blog) and you'll see that I list my credentials at the top of every single page.

Service providers should be similarly focused and their websites should immediately convey professionalism and expertise to the potential customer.

BizTips

An excellent example of how testimonials can be included throughout a site is Randy Cassingham's engaging This is True at www.thisistrue.com. Visit his site and look at both how he reaffirms the value of his information product with extensive testimonials and encourages you to visit his online store and buy one or more of his witty products.

A simple example of this is the website of Cynthia Buxton, an acupuncturist in Seattle, Washington (see Figure 8.3).

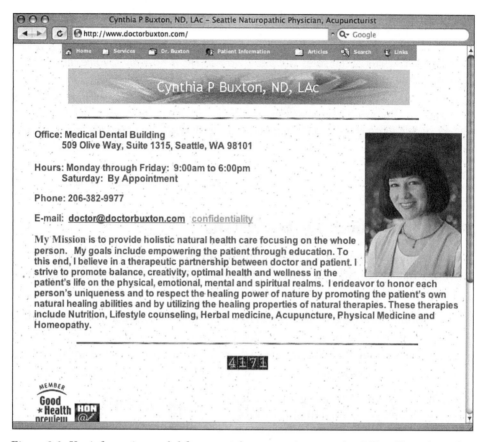

Figure 8.3: Key information needed for potential customers is conveyed quickly, efficiently, and without distracting design elements on Dr. Cynthia Buxton's website.

Her home page, www.doctorbuxton.com, does a good job of directly answering the three key questions that all effective business web pages need to address:

- ◆ Who am I?
- ◆ Why should you care?
- ◆ What can I do for you?

There's still plenty of space for improvement, however. I'd like to see the credentials clickable so visitors can learn more about her training and experience, a map showing how to get to her office would be useful, and an invitation to e-mail the doctor to enquire whether she would be a good healthcare provider would all improve this site.

Additionally, since visitors aren't all going to know about holistic natural care and acupuncture, a few articles would be helpful, and definitions and explanations of her degrees would also help reinforce that she's an expert, yet accessible to her clients.

BizTips

Don't be afraid to use the words "I invite you" or otherwise to make explicit your desire to hear from visitors. Since every visitor is a potential customer, 60 seconds answering a basic question or two can easily translate into not just a sale, but a lifelong customer.

Even better, more content translates directly into better findability. A few well-written articles would unquestionably become the primary entry points for her site and drive a lot more traffic and customers to her service.

Further, Dr. Buxton could then capitalize on the traffic by having relatively short articles on her site, say 800 to 1200 words, with an invitation for visitors to buy a 5000-word or longer electronic book (or e-book) with a much more extensive treatment of the topic. Colleagues of mine have created excellent adjunct revenue streams using just this strategy.

Findability Is About Content!

Findability isn't about having one page that looks good, or even one page that has lots of information. It's about having content, lots of content, that's relevant, interesting, compelling for your potential customers, and is able to lure them in, where you can then sell them on your products or services.

Ask a legitimate search engine optimization specialist the best way to increase traffic and they'll all say the same thing: add more content.

All businesses have some sort of content that can be added to their sites to make it a more interesting destination for potential customers. Even a gas station could have daily price updates, articles on what octane means and how to figure out if your car needs a higher octane gas, articles on gas stations and the environment, special web-only promotions to drive customers into the convenience store, and information on supported community organizations.

Memo

If you can't think of what content you could add to your website to make it more compelling, just consider following major news stories in your industry and republishing summaries with your own brief analysis and commentary.

One criterion for identifying content is that it shouldn't need to be updated too frequently. While having a daily gas price is sufficiently easy that it might take less than 90 seconds to update, having to rewrite and update constantly 10 to 20 articles on a site would be a poor use of time. Eventually the articles would stop being updated and then any value that the business could have garnered from having the additional content is mitigated by the aura of disuse that's conveyed by an old copyright or clearly obsolete information.

What Can You Add to Your Site?

It's time for you to brainstorm and come up with at least 10 different informational articles you could include on your business website:

- What information do your customers need to know to make an educated purchase decision?

- What information do potential business partners need to know about your business?

- What training and experience have you had as a professional, and how can you convey that in an accessible manner?

- What information do you wish your customers knew so that their expectations of your service or products helped them have a positive purchase experience?

- How does your product or service differ from those of your competitors?

Don't discount the value of giving away your expertise. Many service professionals are happy to answer questions from visitors, knowing that their answers frequently produce paying customers. A plumber could have a very effective and informative website detailing step-by-step repairs for ten of the most common plumbing problems, knowing full well that people will search for the solution, see how complex it is, and pick up the phone to schedule a visit instead.

Tim Carter, nationally syndicated home repair expert, demonstrates just this strategy on his Ask The Builder website. Searching his site for tips on mold problems produces dozens of short articles and more extensive e-books, 25- to 60-page reports immediately accessible upon paying a nominal fee. Figure 8.4 shows the result of a search on his site AskTheBuilder.com for "mold".

By leveraging his expertise into a series of short articles, Tim has also created a very powerful environment for upselling his e-books and generating revenue without ever having to come to your door or repair anything.

BizTips

A small but important facet of producing new content is copyright protection. While copyright protects your content even if you omit a "Copyright 2005" notice, there are compelling reasons why you should add this notice anyway.

One of the more frustrating sides of the Internet is that there are many people who take inappropriate shortcuts to attain success, and one of the most common is wholesale copying of content from other sites. Without an explicit copyright mark, you are still legally protected, but it's much more difficult to defend yourself. Instead, I strongly encourage you to add: Copyright 20xx by Your Business Name. To be completely safe, register your article copyright with the United States Office of Copyright. For more details see www.findability.info.

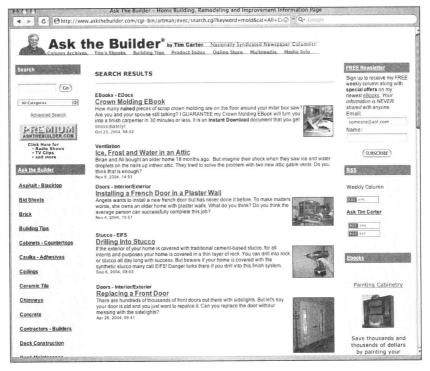

Figure 8.4: AskTheBuilder.com demonstrates in this search result for "mold" how free content can help encourage visitors to become customers and buy more extensive materials.

How Often to Update Your Information

As you add more content to your site, you're improving your findability, but you're also now facing the dilemma of how often should your material be updated?

Most content has a surprisingly long lifespan. An article on the history and effectiveness of acupuncture is going to be just as relevant in five years as it is today. There may be updates worth adding as new research comes out, but it's unlikely to become obsolete. A listing of classic 1960s Porsche vehicles can live forever, with new listings of classic vehicles from other eras added over time. An article on repairing leaky toilets will be just as relevant in 10 years as it is today. (Content that will be just as relevant and current in 24 months as it is today is called *evergreen* in the publishing industry, and it's the best type of material to add to your site.)

Other material will require updates to ensure that the information being conveyed is accurate and up-to-date. A list of merchants in a shopping mall, a directory of authors in a neighborhood, a page featuring popular products from a manufacturer, all will require frequent updates. The trick is to *budget both the time and cost of updates* when putting aside the funds to maintain the website each year.

Also ensure that you pepper your articles with keywords and even consider having a list of keywords or key phrases on each article as well. Have a look at the footer material on my Intuitive Life Business Blog articles (www.intuitive.com/blog/) for an example of how to implement this to maximize findability.

A tangible, specific strategy for maintaining the relevance of your website articles is to print them out and read through them once every three to six months. Anything that seems obsolete or otherwise needing clarification should be rewritten and updated on the site. Remember, too, that after you update an article, Google will automatically see it and index it, updating your relevance score for the page.

Ultimately, the question of how frequently to update content comes down to the obvious: Update your material as frequently as required, and no more.

Instead of spending lots of time on a small number of articles, you will have better results by simply creating more content. I try to add at least one page to my AskDaveTaylor.com website every single day, for

BizTips

Most experts believe that Google prefers web pages that are updated with some frequency. If you had the choice of reading today's newspaper or a newspaper from three weeks ago, you'd also choose the most current. Ensuring that your content is up-to-date might therefore offer an additional findability boost.

example, knowing that a site with hundreds of pages has that many more proverbial hooks in the water for potential customers than a site with 10 articles.

Creating Two Websites, Not One

Because the web is a relatively new medium, it's not surprising that most businesses view their websites as a single entity, as something that serves one purpose, that of promoting their business.

But it costs less than a dollar a month to have a second domain name, and even having a dozen names isn't much of an expense. Setting up more than one website costs more than a single site, but that's a one-time expense and a well-designed site can generate far more value than any expenditure it requires.

If you're thinking "sponsorship," then you understand where I'm heading with this idea. If you have a set of articles ideally suited for your site, why not just push them out to their own site, with its own domain name?

Memo

Don't hide the ownership of the second site and get your user community into a snit, however. A small text link on the bottom of all pages that states "This site content is all copyright 2005 by MechanicOnTheGo.com" suffices to inform curious visitors who owns the material and is responsible for it, without making it so overt that it could alienate visitors and defeat the value of the informational site in the first place.

Our mobile Porsche mechanic could have MechanicOnTheGo.com for her own site, for example, and might also register and build PorscheCountry.info as a separate site that lists the best vehicles from Porsche, allows visitors to add their own reminiscences about the vehicles, and just happens to have a section on tips for maintaining each of the cars. Every page could also include a prominent "Porsche Country is sponsored by Mechanic On The Go, fixing cars onsite in the greater Chicago area since 2003" and, of course, a link to the mechanic site.

I wouldn't have a link to the MechanicOnTheGo home page. However, I'd have a link to a special web page that offers an instant 10 percent discount coupon for new customers!

Don't be afraid to offer discounts to entice new online customers, even if some existing customers might exploit it. You'll still have a net gain in the end and marketing research has long since shown the value of promotional campaigns and the perception of special discounts.

This strategy meets all the basic criteria for an effective business website while significantly boosting findability, improving the reputation of the business in the community, and offering an easy differentiator from other area mechanics. Indeed, other mechanics might well start inquiring about co-sponsoring Porsche Country!

The Least You Need to Know

- Every page of your website should clearly convey your value proposition and invite visitors to explore the rest of the site.

- All business websites should include relevant content, and that content should be updated frequently enough to ensure that it's never obsolete.

- More relevant articles, more content, is always better than a smaller site.

- A successful strategy for expanding content is to create a second, informational site that's sponsored by your business and links to the main business website.

Chapter 9

Assessing Your Competitors

In This Chapter

- Identifying competitors
- Tracking new competitors
- Watching job listings
- Participating in discussion boards

Every business has competitors. That's a fact of business. What the web makes much easier is finding those competitors and analyzing how they're doing business, what successful strategies they're using, and how to leverage that knowledge to improve your own website and online presence.

Gas station owners have an easy job identifying competitors. They need simply drive around the neighborhood and fill up their tank to see price, layout, what's for sale in the convenience store, cleanliness, gauge the friendliness of the employees, and so on.

A service provider has a more difficult task, especially if his competitors might be home-based. It's very difficult to walk down a suburban street and figure out which houses have programmers, marketing consultants, or graphic designers in the basement.

The Internet erases geographic boundaries for many companies, too, so while 20 years ago your competitors were all located within 10 miles of your office, today almost all businesses are global in scope. The programmer who can add a customer database to your website could just as easily live in Bangalore or Thailand as in Oshkosh or West Lafayette.

Retail stores are learning about this change the hard way, as many realize belatedly that the convenience of being located in a busy shopping mall can easily be overcome by an online store with lower prices, free shipping, and no sales tax.

Identifying Competitors

To grow your business, one of your first tasks must be to identify your competitors, assess which are most successful, and identify what features appeal most to their customers. You can then emulate those characteristics while figuring out how to best differentiate yourself from these other firms.

Finding Local Businesses

For a business that is geographically focused, there's no better place to start your research than Google itself. Google offers a very nice geographic search if you type in a zip code or city and state as part of your query. Rather than rely on Google's smart query interpreter, start out with Google Local at www.google.com/lochp. (Google also has a really slick mapping feature that is worth exploring, too. Type in your own street address in the Google search box and you'll be impressed by the results.)

Figure 9.1 shows Google Local where I'm about to search for Porsche mechanics in Chicago, Illinois.

Figure 9.1: Google lets you easily search a specific geographic area for matching sites, a fabulous competitive analysis tool.

Note the "Remember this location" option on the Google Local search page: Check this and the system will remember your city and state in the future (you can always change it if you're casting a wider net to find competitors).

If you ever want to remove your location preference from Google Local, go to the web page http://local.google.com/local?sl=1 and everything will be reset.

The search results are a wonderful hidden capability of Google, as shown in Figure 9.2.

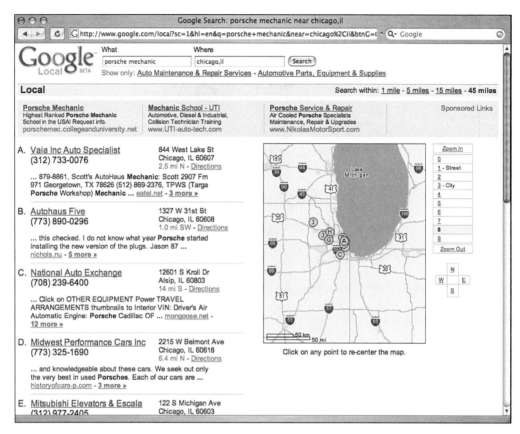

Figure 9.2: Google Local offers alternative search queries, a map locating competitors, and a succinct description of each matching company.

I really like the suggested search queries shown in the Google Local results page because they can help identify competitors more accurately. Some mechanics might not use the word *mechanic* on their websites, for example, so a search for "Porsche mechanic" might not properly identify all your competitors. Instead choose the suggested "Auto Maintenance & Repair Services".

Before you start exploring competitors, look at the paid advertisements shown on the results page, too. If any of these are direct competitors, they're going to be the savviest of the competition and the first to investigate. The search results shown in the previous figure have three ads, two for mechanic schools, and one for Nikolas Motor Sport titled "Porsche Service & Repair."

Beware

Google AdWords matches ads and search results. Advertisers don't pay to have their ads displayed; they pay each time someone clicks on the ad and goes to their site.

If you click on your competitor's advertisement, they'll have to pay Google. It's unethical and unprofessional for you to drive up your competitors' costs, however.

The solution is simple: When you see an advertisement for a site you'd like to visit, type in the address shown instead of clicking the ad. It'll add about ten seconds to your investigation but will be much more ethical. After all, you wouldn't want to be paying for traffic from Google AdWords just to find out it's your competitors investigating your site. The AdWords program is examined in detail in Chapter 18.

Another way to narrow down your results with Google Local is to select a narrower search radius. The default of 45 miles might be unrealistic for your business, because your customers aren't going to drive that far. A pizza parlor would have to serve fabulous pizza to motivate customers to travel 40 miles, and a café would need remarkable ambience to justify a half-hour journey.

You can also search based on proximity to a popular destination rather than your current location. I have a colleague who owns a half-dozen rental properties near Walt Disney World in Florida. When he does competitive research, he uses Walt Disney World as the location, then looks on the map to identify properties the same distance from WDW as his own.

BizTips

Adding your North American business to Google Local's directory is remarkably simple. Just send an e-mail requesting your site be included to local-listings@google.com. You'll want to already have your website online and include the following information in your e-mail to the Google Local team: business name, full business address, telephone number, and URL of your company website.

Businesses with Global Competition

If you sell books online, develop website graphics, or offer marketing expertise to clients worldwide, your competitors aren't within an easy bicycle ride of your office. They're much more likely to be halfway around the globe.

Memo

Since global competitors are often vast in number, it's well worth spending some time studying the advanced Google search techniques discussed in Chapter 4.

Finding these competitors is more difficult because there are lots of them, and because identifying exact competitors requires you to spend a lot of time searching and refining your search queries again and again.

A search for "website graphics design" produces a staggering 16.4 million results. Rather than be overwhelmed, put yourself in the shoes of your potential customer and consider how they might search for a graphics designer. Adding more words might be a good first step, so I'll try "website graphics designer award-winning" which narrows the results down to 243,000. A potential customer faced with that many matches might just jump in to visit the first half-dozen matches, but they might also add a few additional words that describe their business, just to see what comes up.

This is where having your website include descriptions of your clients would be a benefit. Add "stables" to the search and there are less than 600 results. Add "auto mechanic", for a designer that's created websites for auto mechanics, and it's down to 600 again.

After You've Identified Competitors

All the questions that you contemplated for your own business, as discussed in Chapter 8, should now be applied to each and every competitor you can identify. Here are some to start with:

♦ What kind of impression do you get from their websites?

♦ Professional or amateur?

♦ Do they have useful information that appeals to customers, a portfolio of their work, a page of customer testimonials, coupons or other offers for web visitors?

♦ How are they establishing and explaining their credentials?

♦ Do they invite customer queries, and if so, is it easy and fast to fill out their form (or, less enticing, click on their e-mail link) and do they set realistic expectations of how promptly you should expect a response?

Send in a query as if you were a customer to see how long it takes to receive a response and how friendly and inviting it is. The mobile Porsche mechanic might e-mail other Porsche repair centers in the area:

> Hi. I have a '98 Targa 993 C2 and it keeps misfiring when I accelerate. Can you tell me about your experience with this car? Do you have Porsche-specific training? I also travel quite a bit. Do you have any sort of pick-up and delivery service, extended hours, or a loaner vehicle available?

Their responses will not only reveal more about the companies, but also offer you more information about competitive services. Once you've built up an accurate picture of your competitors, you could then call the friendliest of them and schedule a meeting with the shop manager to present your new mobile repair service and explore how your companies could work together.

> **Memo**
>
> There are many examples of competitors who actually end up being partners and finding mutual success in the relationship. You'll encounter your savvy competitors at trade shows, business mixers, and other events anyway, so why not take the proverbial bull by the horns and talk with them directly?

Tracking New Competitors

One challenge on the Internet is identifying new competitors when they start business. To keep track of changes in an industry space, you need to utilize website services that constantly compare search results from the major search sites, sending you notification of changes or new items when found.

Using Google News Alerts and Usenet

Google has a couple of different services in this regard, starting with Google News Alerts. Setting up a few Google News Alerts can help you keep track of industry news, competitors, and even press coverage of your own firm.

Start at the Google News Alerts page at www.google.com/alerts, then type in a specific search pattern that you'd like to track. Figure 9.3 shows a search for news stories that mention Porsche.

Figure 9.3: Google News Alerts makes it easy to keep track of news on a specific topic or within a specific industry.

BizTips

Often the least formal discussion environments host the most interesting discussions. Cast a wide net and spend the time needed to learn about all the nooks and crannies of the Internet, not just the web.

When you set up an alert, notice that you can specify if you want to track news, web page changes, or both. I always pick both to get as much information as possible. To manage your flow of e-mail, it's probably sufficient if you receive reports once a day or once a week. News as it happens could result in a crippling flood of matches and hundreds of e-mail messages if a major story is republished from a wire service by different publications.

The most interesting discussion on the Internet doesn't take place in the formal venue of news media and publications. Two other areas worth exploring in this regard are Usenet, a highly distributed discussion system, and weblogs, individual websites that serve as electronic journals.

Usenet is a sprawling beast with tens of thousands of different topical discussion areas ranging from the most mundane to the most explicit. Reading even a fraction of Usenet would take far more time than you should devote to competitive research, but fortunately Google's got that covered with Google Groups. Go to http://groups.google.com to start. You can enter a word or two and Google Groups will search both group names and individual entries to find matches. Figure 9.4 shows the result of a search for Porsche.

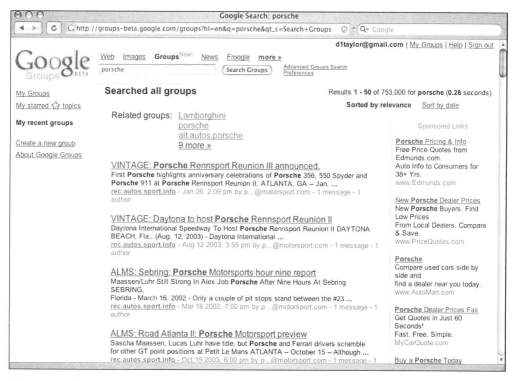

Figure 9.4: Google Groups offers both a door into the sprawling chaos that is Usenet, and a way to navigate through it.

The search matches both Usenet groups—alt.autos.porsche, Lamborghini, and Porsche—and individual postings. 836,000 individual messages. Quite a few! Refining your search to add a few more words might be a smarter strategy, and a search query like "Porsche mechanic Chicago" is more likely to catch just those few articles of interest to you.

After you've settled on a few good search queries that narrow the results down to a dozen or fewer matches, go to Netnews Tracker at www.netnewstracker.com and sign up for a free account.

The system will then execute the specified search for you twice daily, e-mailing a summary of matching articles. This is particularly important as a way of tracking if anyone is talking about your business, so you can enjoy good comments and, if necessary, minimize the impact of criticism.

Combing Through the Blogosphere

The third area where you can find articles and other information about your business, your competitors, and your industry are on weblogs. Fortunately, you don't have to visit each weblog in the so-called *blogosphere* yourself! You can't use Google to keep track this time, however. Instead, another site called Feedster has an e-mail–based Feedster News Alerts service.

> **Buzzwords**
>
> The **blogosphere** is the collective name for all weblogs on the Internet. There are millions of weblogs, but for all practical purposes, there are really only a few thousand worth watching, and those are hooked into Feedster.

Figure 9.5 shows the subscription page for Feedster News Alerts, which you can find at www.feedster.com/alerts.php on the web.

Feedster doesn't have anywhere near as sophisticated a search capability as Google, so you'll get the best results from having multiple searches, one for each keyword or key phrase you'd like to track. As with Google News Alerts, you'll want to track your own company, the names of your major products, the names of your competitors, and a few keywords or phrases from your industry.

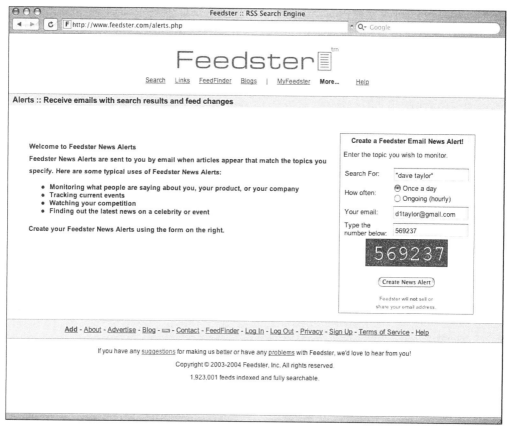

Figure 9.5: Feedster News Alerts lets you keep an eye on discussion topics through the world of weblogs.

Watching Job Listings

The final spot where you can learn more about your competitors, new and existing, is by monitoring the classified ads in your local newspaper. The local paper here in Boulder, Colorado, is the *Daily Camera*, a Scripps Corporation publication. The on-line classified advertising system that the Daily Camera uses is managed by Abracat, which offers AdHound, a service that can automatically monitor the classified ads for specific patterns. Your local paper might not be a Scripps paper, but it's quite likely that it offers a similar classified ad tracking system.

Figure 9.6 shows AdHound set up to search for any employment ads that would indicate new competition for a local house painter.

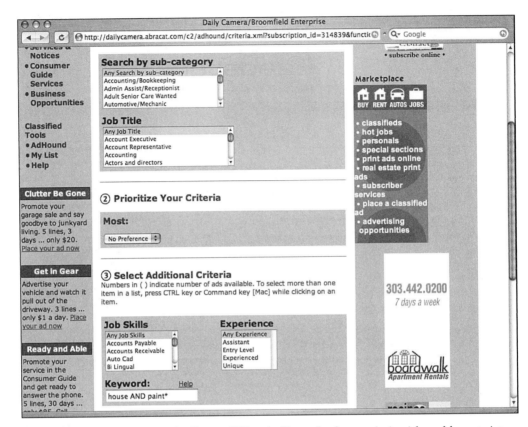

Figure 9.6: A recurring search for "house AND paint" matches house painting jobs and house painters being hired by new and existing competitors.*

Typically, these ad trackers will only run a search for 30 to 60 days, so you'll need to renew the search occasionally, but it's worth it. Having advance warning of new businesses can give you an invaluable competitive edge.

Participating in Discussion Boards

There are many ways to keep up on your competition, but one of the most enjoyable, an approach that will increase your knowledge base, give you terrific insight into your customers, and help you promote your own business or service while you're trolling for nuggets of competitive intelligence, is to participate in popular community discussion forums.

There are two types of discussion forums: those that are e-mail–based and those that are hosted on specific websites with discussion forum software. Both of these will be explored in greater depth later on, in Chapter 17, but for now, just recognize that participating in a community forum is a smart strategy for both customer and competitor information.

To find topical mailing lists, search both http://groups.yahoo.com and http://lists.topica.com for matches. Be prepared to browse for a while. Both sites have weak search engines that typically generate dozens of spurious matches.

To find discussion forums, start at the websites of popular industry magazines and other business publications. In addition, using Google to search for discussion forums can yield good results.

> **BizTips**
>
> When you join a discussion forum or mailing list, just sit back and read the discourse for a week or two before getting involved. This will help you ascertain the discussion style and identify the most thoughtful and knowledgeable participants.

Whatever strategies you opt to use for competitive intelligence, it's critical that you not only identify your competition, but continue to learn from their successes and mistakes.

The Least You Need to Know

- ◆ Google Local is an excellent tool for identifying local competitors.

- ◆ Explore all competitors' websites in detail, and send each company an e-mail query to gauge their responsiveness.

- ◆ New competitors can be identified through Google News, Netnews Tracker, the classified ads tracker at your local newspaper, and similar services.

Chapter 10

Keeping Track of Customers

In This Chapter

- ◆ Understanding customers
- ◆ Knowing how customers look for you
- ◆ Finding out where customers are talking about you

One essential element of a modern business is to learn about your customers by becoming a customer of your own business. You probably think you already know all there is to know about your customer, but think about this conundrum: how can you learn more about the potential customer that never opts to purchase *your* product or service?

Unlike many venues, the online world offers the opportunity for savvy businesspeople to find out what motivates not just their own customers, but their competitors' customers, and even those inevitable browsers and visitors who never actually make a purchase.

This chapter explores some of the many ways that you can glean this information from the web and discuss how to leverage the knowledge to tighten and focus your own marketing efforts.

Understanding the Elusive Customer

Most businesspeople believe that they understand their customers. They know what motivates the purchase decision, what criteria customers consider most important for choosing between products, and why customers pick one business over another. The reality is otherwise, and most companies remain small because their management team doesn't actually understand the wants, needs, and desires of their customer base. More importantly, they don't have a clue about what motivates potential new customers.

A lot of businesses grow from their founder's desire for a specific product or service, just to find that there isn't one in the market. Ergo, create a new business that addresses an unmet market need and success should be guaranteed.

Markets and customers are much more fluid than either of these suggest. Even the most savvy insiders might have an excellent sense of their customer today, but they're gradually going to be more and more out of touch as the market inevitably changes.

> **Memo**
>
> Markets aren't static entities, but it's surprising just how many business people—and business pundits—believe that whatever held true last year should be true next year, too.

Luggage design has changed in ways that were completely unforeseeable at the turn of the millennium. Airport luggage screening has become a lot tougher subsequent to the 9/11 tragedy. A decade ago popular luggage had lots of organizing pockets and an unbreakable lock, but once luggage inspection became a fact of travel, a highly secure piece of luggage became much less desirable.

Fashion is another factor in many businesses. The manufacturer of an LCD display screen for computers might think that having good technical specs are all that's important, but many customers now choose computer equipment based on appearance.

If you're a savvy businessperson—and you are because you're reading this book—then you are already involved with your industry, read the trade publications, attend relevant professional meetings, and otherwise stay current with important business trends. Keeping track of your customers can be a completely different proposition, however, especially if you aren't a customer of your own products or services.

> **Memo**
>
> As products become commodities, fashion becomes an increasingly important differentiator.

The owner of a comic book store might well be an avid comics fan, but the owner of a children's clothing store isn't a child, an OB/GYN could be a man, a funeral home director hasn't actually had a funeral for themselves, a Ferrari mechanic might drive a Saab, and a pharmacist hasn't experienced all the ailments of her customers.

Before the Internet, companies tried to keep track of customers with focus groups, surveys, and other expensive and inaccurate techniques. Keeping your proverbial finger on the pulse of your customer is much easier on the web. Odds are extremely good that your customers, your potential customers, and even your competitors' customers are online chatting away and sharing experiences at this very minute.

The challenge is to find them and learn from them.

Learning What Customers Seek

The first area where Internet research can expand your thinking is found by asking the question: What do my customers search for when they look for my products or services?

If you have a Google AdWords account set up, you can bid on a few keywords that describe your business as if you were going to place an ad on Google (which you'll do in Chapter 17). Bidding on keywords in Google produces a list of suggested synonyms and variations, which indicate popular searches in your business segment.

Exploring Wordtracker

A database of search queries offers the potential for gaining great insight. Not only could you identify full search phrases, but you could also learn how frequently a given word or phrase is used as part of a search query.

For what should be obvious reasons, Google doesn't release that information to the public. Not to worry, though, because Google isn't the only search engine on the web.

BizTips

If you're not having your tech person analyze your website traffic logs to ascertain searches that lead people to you, you're missing out on a critical source of customer information. Generating reports from this traffic information is straightforward and if your IT person can't do it, your web-hosting company certainly can.

BizTips _____

Knowing which words are most commonly used in search queries is a critical element of creating a findable company.

Recognizing the value of a search query database, Wordtracker has obtained ongoing rights to the searches from two search engines, Metacrawler and Dogpile. The Wordtracker website offers customers the ability to search through a 60-day archive of over 350 million different queries.

The Wordtracker service isn't free. A subscription costs about $50 per month, although you can also pay about $8 per day for shorter-term access as needed. Word-tracker also offers a free trial that can still help you ascertain which searches are most popular.

Sign up for a trial account at www.wordtracker.com/trial and enter your name and e-mail address. Read through the introductory material, and then you'll be presented with the initial term entry page shown in Figure 10.1.

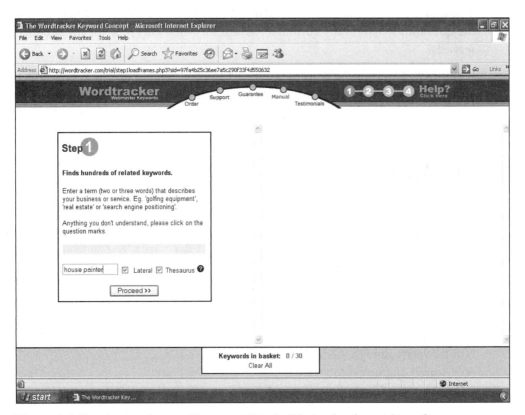

Figure 10.1: Entering search query "fence repair" in the Wordtracker free trial interface.

Note that a good keyword isn't simply one that is searched frequently. The potential value of a keyword must consider both how frequently it's used and how many site matches there are for that search. If you have a web page that matches the search "paris hilton" you'll match lots of searches, but so will 7.2 million other web pages. Instead, it's better to have a less popular keyword and be one of a few hundred matches. Keyword "goodness" as a combination of frequency and popularity is a critical idea, because your business grows most efficiently by accurately identifying and attracting potential customers.

Wordtracker searches for the term you enter and includes *lateral* and thesaurus searches in the results listing.

The results are shown in two categories, related keywords and thesaurus. The related keywords for "fence repair" include "fence", "fences", "home", "fencing", "handyman", "wood fence", and "vinyl fence". There are also a few seemingly unrelated suggestions that I'll summarily discard, including "painting", "roofing", and "drywall". The thesaurus has no useful suggestions for this type of search, but it's worth glancing through nonetheless.

Buzzwords

Lateral searches produce thematically related keywords by identifying the most commonly occurring words or phrases on web pages that also match your specific search term. A lateral search for Coca-cola could produce additional keywords Coke, Pepsi, and soda, for example.

Click on one of the related keywords and Wordtracker shows matching search queries and how often they occur in the search query database. Figure 10.2 shows that "fence repair" is not a popular search term. In 60 days it's only been used 13 times in 352 million search queries.

As you explore the stats shown for each of the related keywords, a pattern of how people search for solutions will appear. For example, "fence" was used 1175 times, while "fences" was used 1102 times and "fencing" was used 2057 times (be careful, though, because fencing doubtless encompasses searches for the sport of fencing along with actual fences).

Also, don't forget to consider alternative meanings for popular keywords: "windows" could be related to home repair, PC operating systems, or even psychiatric jargon.

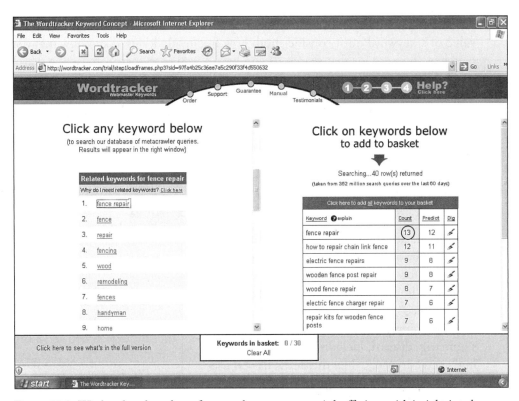

Figure 10.2: Wordtracker shows how often search terms are queried, offering quick insight into how your customers search for your product or service.

Select both general keywords with a high search frequency ("fence") and those that exactly describe your business ("fence repair"). These will be added to your keyword basket. Remember that it's the frequency and the number of matching sites that together will reveal which are actually good keywords.

The third step of the Wordtracker system is to analyze both the frequency and number of matches, assigning an overall score to each of the keywords. To calculate the number of matching sites, Wordtracker searches for each word on the MSN search engine. Figure 10.3 shows the final results.

Notice that one of the results shown at the end of the Wordtracker system is a *KEI Analysis*. While not a critical element, it's worth looking at this single number that pinpoints the best keywords. A KEI of greater than 1.0 is good; one that's greater than 10 is very good; and one that's greater than 50 is excellent. Values that are less than 1.0 are usually considered not worth the effort because they indicate a space that's just too busy, too popular, or too saturated.

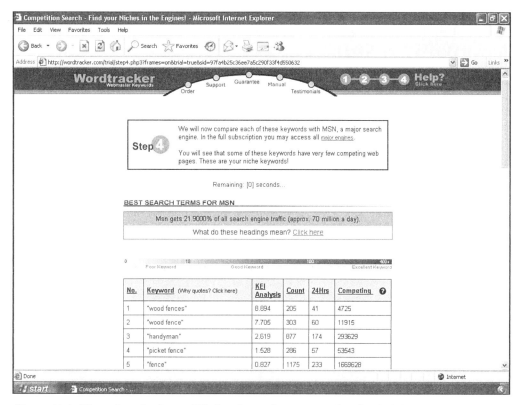

Figure 10.3: The end result of using Wordtracker is that you can identify which keywords have the best combination of search frequency and competing sites, summarized in their KEI Analysis number.

The result of exploring keywords with Wordtracker—and the resultant KEI Analysis—is insight into how people use search engines to find specific information and a list of keywords that should be the cornerstone of your website.

Later in the book you'll learn how to incorporate specific keywords into your web pages to ensure that your pages rank well in Google's relevance scoring system. You've already learned that while "fence repair" isn't used as a search term very often, it also doesn't have many competing sites, and that including words like "handyman" and "picket fence" will help with findability.

Capturing Queries from Your Own Search Service

If Wordtracker is too complex, don't despair. Another way to collect data on what information your customers and potential customers are seeking online is to simply have a search engine on your own site and record each and every query entered.

Capturing and logging search queries from your site, even if you're just pointing customers to the Google search engine, should be an easy task for a website developer, taking no more than an hour of work.

Over time these search queries will produce patterns that should suggest lots of new content for your site—and remember, popular content is the secret to findability—that will appeal to your customers and help reinforce your expertise.

This holds true for an internal search engine, too, of course. Every search done on my Ask Dave Taylor site is logged and I pay close attention to what people are seeking as a way to prioritize what new information to add to the Q&A site to bring more visitors to the site. Then they run searches for the information they seek, which I provide, and over time the site improves and gains further market share and customer-perceived value.

Remember, the value of a website is directly related to whether it helps your customers solve problems or find what they seek.

What Are Customers Talking About?

The other facet of customer intelligence is finding out what your customers, and potential customers, are discussing. There are three different types of discussion venues online: Usenet and other discussion boards, weblogs and individual websites, and electronic mail–based discussion lists.

Discussion Boards

One excellent way to identify discussion groups and Usenet groups that contain articles of interest to your profession, or even discussing your company, is to use Google Groups, at http://groups.google.com. A search on the site for a specific company name or product can yield a surprising number of matches.

BizTips _____

Don't be disheartened if you find a discussion board with almost no postings; just keep looking. For every active discussion board on the web, it seems like there are four or five that are dormant or forgotten.

Your electronics store is considering adding the Philips line of consumer electronics, but wants to check if customers are having problems with the DVD players first. A search for _problem Philips DVD player_ produces 7,000 articles, including entries entitled "DVD compatibility problem", "Philips DVD read problem", and "Philips playback problems". All of them are essential reading for learning more about the Philips DVD players and customers' opinions.

To find discussion boards, start with Google's main search, using the quoted term "bulletin board" to narrow results down to just those that use common discussion management software. A search for *"bulletin board" philips dvd player* produces thousands of matches, including links to The Gadgeteer Bulletin Board, the Radio and Telly Forum, and DVDReview.net. Again, all worth visiting for insight into customer experiences and opinions.

Weblogs and Individual Websites

Weblogs can be searched with tools like Feedster or Technorati, the latter of which is shown in Figure 10.4.

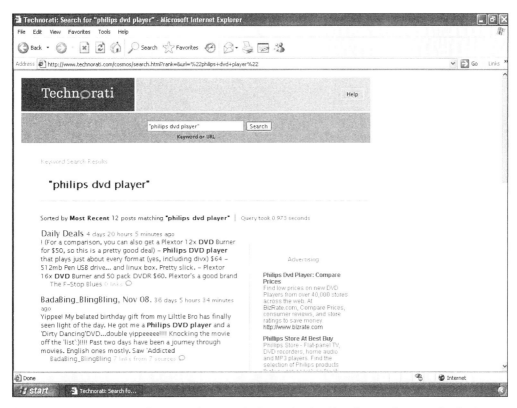

Figure 10.4: Technorati makes it simple to search thousands of weblogs for matching articles. In this case, the search was for "philips dvd player".

To find specific websites that talk about a product or company, go to Google and enter as narrow and constrained a search query as possible. A search for *dvd player* produces 17.5 million matches, while the more sophisticated search *"problem Philips dvd player"* yields 6,000 matches.

Mailing Lists

Google can be used to search for mailing lists, but there are specialized sites that host millions of mailing lists that can be fruitfully searched, too. Start at lists.topica.com, then try groups.yahoo.com.

Remember, the mailing lists that your customers and potential customers frequent are exactly those lists you should be involved with, too, either as just a silent observer or an active participant.

Nothing excites potential customers more than communicating in a public forum with someone from a favorite company. The value of that publicity can be tremendous!

The Least You Need to Know

- Hanging out where your customers hang out is essential to staying up with industry trends.

- Common searches can be identified with the complex but highly informative Wordtracker service.

- Customers can be found online with Google, Google Groups, Technorati, and various other services.

Part  3

Improving Your Online Business Site

Too many web developers and designers are focused on the technology to the exclusion of the message and the capabilities of the medium. In this part, I'll try to repair any damage that well-meaning but uninformed "professionals" have wrought with their talk of web-friendly colors, vertical navigation bars, animated flash content, and the importance of keeping them in control of your site content.

I'll also examine new and savvy methods of tightly integrating your online and offline marketing efforts and ways to stretch your marketing dollar. If your company is like mine, the latter will be particularly sweet music to your ears and spreadsheets!

This part concludes with a discussion of search engine optimization and placement techniques, focused on how you can have your webmaster or IT person make small, simple changes to your site that will improve your findability. And improved findability means more visitors, who can be turned into paying customers.

The Basics of Building a Good Business Site

In This Chapter

- ◆ The stuff good websites are made of
- ◆ The importance of having a search engine–friendly site
- ◆ The do's and don'ts for online businesses
- ◆ Five tips for creating a better online presence

Looking at other websites and analyzing their designs, identifying what on a site is likely to appeal to customers and what you don't like about the site, is easy. What's difficult is making your own site and being happy with the end results.

This book isn't about the nuts and bolts of building a website, though, as there are plenty of those on the market, including my technically oriented *Creating Cool Web Sites with HTML, XHTML and CSS* (Wiley, 2004). We'll never look at the markup language used to create a page or link from one page to another, with just a few small exceptions.

Just as building a house is about a lot more than just figuring out whether the black or white wire should be connected to the "+" terminal on an outlet, building a good business website, a site that helps promote your business in the online world, is about much more important issues than markup and plug-in technologies.

First and foremost, a good business website instantly conveys to the visitor—to your potential customer—what your business is about, how you differentiate yourself from your competitors, what products or services you offer, and how you can help solve the visitor's problems. Some people explore the web for fun, but if someone's seeking out a business-related website, they are in the market to comparison-shop, to learn more about a potential purchase, to find out how to evaluate a specific type of service person, or, ideally, to become your customer.

The Key Elements of a Good Website

There are a lot of stumbling blocks on the way to creating a good business website, many of which are analogous to the challenge of designing and building the house of your dreams.

Keep Your Website on Topic

Every item of information on your website should be directly related to either the exact product or service you sell or should be associated with establishing your credibility. If you sell religious material online, then an adjunct area where you share your own religious beliefs and occasionally add postings with your interpretation of world events makes sense. If you have a bicycle-repair facility, however, an area on your site talking about your stamp-collecting hobby isn't going to grow your business.

Some business sites are quite informal, with links to members of the owner's family, favorite sites, pictures from their last vacation in Jamaica, and various hobbies. A personality-based site can work if you're building an eBay Store or similar informal venue, but most customers seek professionalism over personality.

An interesting example of a simple, very focused website is business coach Paul Lemberg's site (www.paullemberg.com), shown in Figure 11.1.

Figure 11.1: Simple, elegant design and a narrow focus that helps visitors identify what problems Paul can solve.

Remember that It's Your Site

The first challenge in building a good site is that the better the caliber of your team, the more likely you are to butt heads with them and disagree on key design and technology issues. While it's important to listen to advice and suggestions from designers and other experts, they aren't the ones who are footing the bill, and they aren't the ones who are going to be adversely affected if the site fails to perform.

> **Memo**
>
> Website design is a collaboration between business thinking and technologists, with a sprinkling of public relations and marketing. Remember, websites change and evolve over time, too. So launch sooner, not later, and refine as you proceed.

You don't have the UPS delivery person telling you how to redesign your loading dock, your phone service provider doesn't call up and tell you to buy new handsets, and your Internet service provider isn't telling you what type of computer to purchase. They're all decisions you make on your own for your business. Designing your website is the same type of decision.

Having said that, some of the best websites are produced because the business owner knew when to stop complaining and listen to the expert. An example of this is that you may have deep religious beliefs and want to sprinkle scripture or sayings from the Koran throughout your site. A consultant will advise you that, unless it's vital to your business identity, it's a bad idea because it could needlessly alienate potential customers who don't share your religious views.

Limit the Complexity of Your Site

Some business sites end up being so complex, with so many choices and options, that they can be completely overwhelming to visitors and cause them to leave. Simplicity should be your design mantra. Google is a splendid example of the power and value of simplicity. Compare the Google home page with the Yahoo! home page, shown in Figure 11.2, to see what I mean.

Figure 11.2: The Yahoo! web design team eschews simplicity in their page design, offering so many options that visitors inevitably get confused.

Don't Get Caught Up with Design Fads

Your business isn't about website design, so you don't want to get on a design tread-mill where you'll have to redesign and rebuild the site annually. To avoid that, eschew the latest faddish website design elements, elements that can make your site look beautiful but be harder to navigate, harder for search engines like Google to under-stand, and ultimately degrade your findability.

There are two technologies that are quite popular with designers today that are both inappropriate for business websites, with a few notable exceptions: any plug-in and Macromedia Flash.

Plug-ins are little programs that visitors have to download onto their computers before they can see all of your content. This is a bad idea because it instantly puts up a barrier between the potential customer and the sale, and should be avoided at all costs.

Macromedia Flash started out as a plug-in application but is now quite commonly included with web browsers. Flash offers some remarkable capabilities and I've seen some sites that were gorgeous demonstrations of fun and exciting Flash-based design. The problem is, having all your content, your pitch, your product descriptions, and your customer testimonials buried within a Flash "movie" does nothing to help your findability. I won't say that you should never use Flash on a site, but I will strongly discourage you from having a pure Flash site. Use Flash technology to animate one or two small elements, but your content, the real draw of your site, still needs to be just plain web content.

Flash forces you to decide between *usability* and *findability*. My advice: always err on the side of findability, because a wonderfully friendly and usable site that doesn't get traffic does a business no good whatsoever.

Memo
I'm not saying that Flash can *never* be a useful addition to a website. An excellent example of how Flash can be incorporated into a site without adversely affecting its findability is Ask The Builder. Go to the site—www.askthebuilder.com—and you'll see that the two small photographs on the top of the home page fade and are replaced by other pictures. That's done with Flash.

Here are some other reasons why Flash might not be the right choice for your *findable* website:

- You can't jump inside a site or deep link, which discourages others from linking to your content.

- You can't bookmark a favorite page or content area in a Flash site.

- You can't easily print a specific page of information in a Flash-based site unless the site includes printing capabilities.

Other technologies that web designers will encourage you to include are animated graphics (which are just annoying to most visitors), any sort of audio or video that plays automatically upon loading the page, and pop-up windows, automatically resizing browser windows, and other programmatic trickery.

Simple, clean, and attractive always wins out over fancy technology. The goal of your site is to sell your business, to get visitors enthused about your products or services. They should *never* wonder who designed the site or even really be aware of the design in the first place.

Design a Search Engine–Friendly Site

Search engines rank keywords and content that appears earlier on a page as more important than information appearing nearer the end. This is an excellent reason to have your main navigational material on the *right side* of your page, rather than the left. Material to the left of the main content of your site is almost always earlier in the actual source page (which is what a search engine reads to ascertain what the page is about).

Figure 11.3 shows the attractive and professional design of the online magazine *A List Apart* (www.alistapart.com). Notice in particular how all the navigational elements are on the right, ensuring that the content on the page is high up and more SEO-friendly.

> **BizTips**
>
> The *Cascading Style Sheet* web design technology allows your designer to have the navigational elements on the left side, while still reaping the benefit of having the main content appear at the top of your page source. If your designer doesn't know how to do this trick, you might need a more sophisticated web designer on your team.

Business Website Considerations

Business websites are more difficult to create because, in addition to all the considerations necessary for any good website design, there are unique challenges for online businesses.

It's All About Trust

One question I always ask when I land on a new business website is "Does this convey a message of trustworthiness to me?" If I'm going to be purchasing products or services from a business and the only thing I know about it is what I can glean from the website, the site must be very professional, very well-designed, use the right technologies, and be clear and understandable. If the site doesn't give me a high degree of confidence, it's a matter of 60 seconds before I'll be visiting the competition and perhaps giving them my business instead.

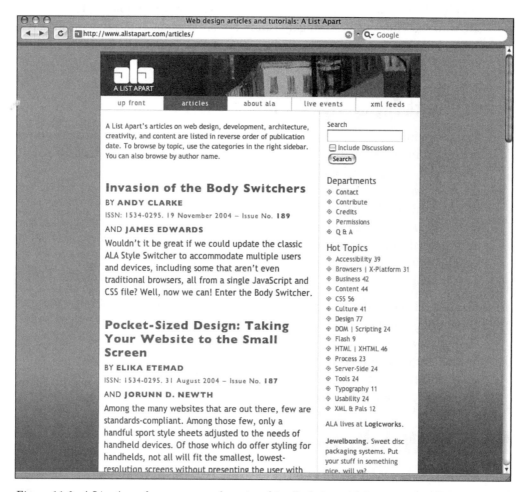

Figure 11.3: A List Apart has a very search engine–friendly design with its navigational elements all appearing after the content on the page, not before.

Here's one way to instill trust: show a photograph of the company president or customer relations director with a very brief bio and a link that enables visitors to send messages directly to this individual.

Use the Right Technologies

Online customers are a savvy bunch, and if you plan on collecting any information from them, you'll want to have a *secure server*. If you plan on transacting business online, processing purchase orders, or accepting credit cards for product or service purchases, you must have a secure server.

In addition to establishing credibility with your customers, using a secure server also alleviates potential liability problems. You've read about banks and state governments that have been hacked and thousands of personal records stolen. You don't want to be put in a position where you need to contact your own customers and relate that you've lost their data!

Buzzwords

Web browsers communicate with remote web servers using a simple protocol called *hypertext transport protocol* (http). It's not secure, and any information sent that way can theoretically be intercepted en route. The **secure server** alternative is called SSL, the secure socket layer. You're using SSL every time a website address changes from an http: prefix to https:.

Beware

While a secure server connection is an important step toward creating a secure and trustworthy system, that's only part of the puzzle. Once the information is received by the server, where does it go? How is that information secured from prying eyes? How do you send the information to your desktop computer so you can process the transactions or record them in your customer-tracking database? All of these questions must be clearly answered by your designer before you proceed with any online transactions.

Have Calls To Action

All effective print advertisements have one element in common, a *call to action*. A call to action is when you tell the visitor or reader what they should do next, and it's often as simple as "Pick up the phone and call …," "Come on in to our showroom for a free test drive," or the late-night staple, "Call now, operators are standing by!"

The general sequence is to catch the visitor's attention, relate a problem that he has, explain your unique solution, then have a call to action that gets him involved.

A house painter might have a humorous photograph of a poorly painted house, followed by the text "Time for a better house painter?" and a clear problem and solution statement:

> Most house painters think it's about slapping paint on your walls and getting to the next job. At Ace Superpainting, we're not done until you tell us you love the new paint job, and we start all jobs with our exclusive six-step preparation to ensure the best possible and longest-lasting result.

The "exclusive six-step preparation" might be what other painters do, too, but you've created a differentiator and are educating your customer about painting in a manner that helps you close business. You could also come up with a memorable name for this preparation process and trademark it; then you could highlight that you're the only house painter in town with the Ace SuperPrep method.

The final step for the house painter's site is to have a nice, clear call for action:

> Click here to get a free Ace Superpainting quote today!

BizTips

All good marketing has a call to action!

Generally, web designers try to avoid phrases like "click here," but when you want the potential customer to *do something*, it's best to tell them what to do. This is particularly true if you have a site design where links to other content aren't displayed in the customary blue with an underline.

Sell Your Company to the Visitor

Too many business websites talk about the business sector and solutions to customer problems without ever *selling the respective company's business to the visitor*. It's difficult to get qualified visitors to your site, so when one does visit, you need to tell them why your company has such a great product line, why your services far outshine those of your competitors, and why your company is uniquely qualified to solve their problems today.

To some extent this is the transition from marketing to sales. Marketing is all about bringing traffic in the door (or to the site), while sales is about turning visitors into customers.

Automobile dealers offer insight into the difference between these two tasks. The balloons tied to the cars in the lot and the advertisements in the newspaper, those are marketing. They're the equivalent of buying an ad through Google AdWords and asking that other sites link to your site.

BizTips

Quiz your own employees: What's the difference between marketing and sales? You'll be surprised by the answers.

Walk into a car showroom, and the very first thing that you see is a beautiful new car, lit as if it were a piece of art, beckoning you to sit behind the steering wheel and imagine it in your own driveway. Not long after, a salesperson shows up and begins his or her sales pitch (often the person says something like "Isn't she a beauty?" or "Are you ready to take this home?" to further encourage you to sell yourself on the vehicle).

Your website needs to be both that shiny new car and the salesperson who lets visitors sell themselves on your products or services. That's why testimonials are so powerful, because they not only convey that other people have had good experiences with your business, but that everyone can be happy with your product or service.

An example of a good business website, from design to copywriting to the inclusion of testimonials, is Digital Ocean (www.digitalocean.cc). They offer an online newsletter, shown in Figure 11.4, and upsell individual information products to their subscribers.

Don't Send Your Visitors Away

While it's customary for websites to point to other sites, a business website should have minimal—if any—links pointing off-site. In particular, any page that's likely to be found through a search engine like Google should be focused on your business, with links to other areas of your site, and nowhere else. If you can't resist having your site point to other sites, then at least put all those other links on a separate page.

BizTips

Each visitor is a precious commodity. Keep him or her on your site by offering compelling content. Don't send them away with links to other sites.

This same logic explains why you shouldn't have flashy ads on your site, too. You have just a few seconds to engage your visitor and try to turn them into a customer. Don't waste that time by encouraging them to go elsewhere!

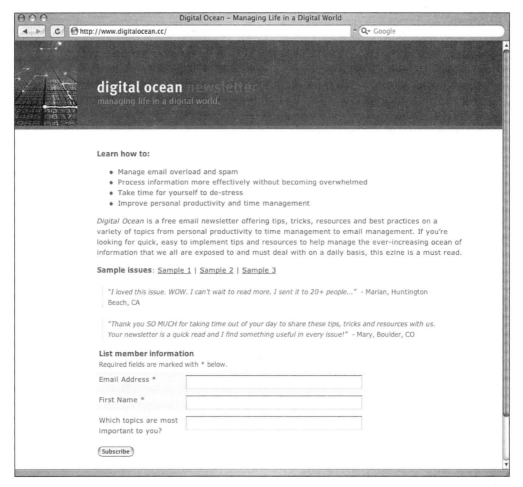

Figure 11.4: A simple design conveys professionalism at Digital Ocean. Notice the testimonial and the multiple calls to action included on the site, too.

Be Responsive to Your Customers

One of the most frustrating facets of business websites is the cheery "contact us" that secretly leads to the black hole of nonresponsiveness. From the very largest companies down to individual service providers, I constantly have the experience of sending queries without ever receiving a response.

If you don't have the capacity to answer e-mail from customers on a daily basis, don't have a link on your site inviting them to contact you.

If you find that most of the queries are asking the same questions, then it's time to update your web pages so that the site answers their questions. If you are still seeing too much mail, then have a categorization system as part of your input form that enables customers to select a priority level or specific product or service. This will let you quickly prioritize which queries should be answered first.

Beware

One of the unfortunate facts of life online is that there are entrepreneurs who believe that sending out millions of unsolicited e-mail advertisements and getting a few positive responses is good business. It's not, and you certainly don't ever want to garner any possible ill will with your customer community by spamming them.

Spammers are a wily lot, though, and they use spiders, programs similar to Google's Googlebot, to visit websites in search of e-mail addresses. When they find one, they sell it and that address begins to see unsolicited messages in an ever-increasing volume. Never include your e-mail address anywhere on your website. Use a contact form instead, like www.paintedsnapshot.com/pub/sample-prints. It also looks more professional.

Think Globally, Not Locally

The Internet is a global phenomenon, so there's no excuse for designing a site that is *ethnocentric*. You don't necessarily need to have Spanish, Chinese, and Russian versions of your web pages, but designs that use American sports metaphors can prove to be completely baffling to someone overseas, and sites that are too closely tied to American politics or celebrities can miss the mark completely in other countries.

In a similar vein, unless your products are on a list of banned exports, why not offer foreign sales for those overseas customers who might pay extra for your particular product? You can add a surcharge to offset the time it'll take for you to fill in customs forms. Just as you wouldn't turn away a retail customer because of his haircut, why turn away an overseas customer because shipping is more complex?

Buzzwords

An **ethnocentric** site is one that is built upon your own cultural, language, and societal perspective. Your customers might not share this perspective, however, so savvy business sites are more neutral in the interest of appealing to the greatest number of potential customers.

Five Ideas to Remember

There's quite a lot to consider when you're building a business website, just as there's a lot to think about when building a retail storefront. It's easy to forget the basics when you're mired in the details, and some web designers love those details and are constantly trying to pull you to their levels even if you are doing your best to only consider the big picture.

Here are five simple ideas that you should keep in mind as you progress with your business website development project:

- **Pages should load quickly.** A bad side effect of complex designs with lots of graphics is that they load slowly. If they load too slowly, then your visitors—your potential customers—are going to become impatient and go somewhere else. This is also a very strong argument against including audio, video, or animation.

- **Your business is the most important element.** Web page designs where the graphical elements are more visually attractive than the information about the company do not engage the attention of potential customers. You only have a few seconds between when the page loads and when they decide to stay or not. Make sure that whatever the design, attention is inexorably drawn to *your message* about *your business*.

- **Identify your business.** It's a business website, so the most important element on every page should be an introduction to your business, products, or service. Articles are excellent additions to the site, but the top of each article should offer visitors a way to learn more about the company, and that link should be duplicated at the end of each article, too.

- **Don't link to other sites.** Many websites will offer you a link exchange; they will point to your website if you'll point to theirs. That's not necessarily a bad thing, but don't give them prime real estate on your site. Every link you have to another site siphons off some of those precious potential customers. If you want to link to other sites, create a separate "other useful sites on the web" page. If you do link to other sites, make sure those new links open up in a new browser window. Your website developer will know how to do this using the target attribute in links.

◆ **Keep it fun and attractive.** Attractive layout and design is subjective, so we're not going to agree on the exact criteria, but sites that try to cram too much onto their pages are harder to understand—and therefore less inviting—than sites with more open designs. There's lots you'd like to say on your website, but it doesn't all have to be in the first paragraph!

Building a great business website isn't rocket science and doesn't involve large investments or state-of-the-art technology. It's like any other facet of your business; it's about clear thinking, focusing on the needs of your customer, and eschewing tricky and fancy for informative and useful.

The Least You Need to Know

◆ The best business websites are focused on selling the product or service.

◆ A simple, fast site design is much more appealing to customers than a highly complex site with lots of different technologies.

◆ Sites that transact business must be secure both in how they receive customer information and how they store it afterward.

◆ Use calls to action to tell visitors what they need to do to become customers.

Developing Online and Offline Content

In This Chapter

◆ Tying your collateral and your website together

◆ Answer customer questions on your site

◆ What other content do you have?

◆ How can you serve your customers better?

Whether you work out of your house or have a storefront in the local mall, there's more to your business than a website. If you have a retail store or office, it's quite possible that the majority of your customers come from the physical world rather than the online world. That means all those online customers who are seeking your product or service haven't yet found you.

You want these potential customers to find you, and to do that, you need to integrate both your online and offline marketing efforts into a single, coherent vision. A mistake that many companies make is to have their online and offline efforts completely separate. An antiques store that sells its best items through eBay auctions typically has no information about eBay in its store. An art gallery rarely points customers to its website to learn about upcoming showings or view additional works from the artists.

Part of growing your business with Google is integrating all of your marketing and sales efforts, so that every online visitor knows that you have a retail outlet or office, and so that every visitor to your store knows that you also have a website, how to find it, and why it's worth a visit.

BizTips

Don't think of your online efforts as separate from your other marketing and publicity efforts. They're all facets of a coherent, considered whole.

There are many different facets to this integration, from including your website address on your business cards to having a virtual tour of your facility on the website.

Tying Your Collateral into Your Website

Look at your business cards, your invoices, your store signage, and your stationary. Do they include your website address? When people call your business line after hours, does the message invite them to visit the company website to get their questions answered and learn more about your products? When you give a talk to the local Chamber of Commerce or get quoted in the newspaper, do listeners and readers find out about your website in addition to your store?

BizTips

One excellent reason to have a short, memorable domain name for your online presence is that it can enhance your collateral rather than clutter it up.

If you're working at home, do you have cards to distribute to colleagues and neighbors, cards that encourage people to visit your website? Does your advertisement in the Yellow Pages include your website address? Do you have fliers posted on community bulletin boards that highlight your web presence?

Even the smallest business produces collateral material. Growing, aggressive companies may produce brochures, one-sheet informational handouts, postcards, co-op marketing materials, coupons in local mailers, and even small advertisements in the back of school yearbooks and other community venues.

Have Visual Consistency Across Media

While having your website address included on everything should be an obvious tip, a more subtle issue is the visual consistency of your collateral. Your website should look the same as your storefront, and your business cards should be reminiscent of your web page design.

Many companies achieve this goal by considering their website as part of the overall collateral package and assign development and maintenance of the website to the marketing department. That might not be a good idea, however, as explored in the following section.

Should Marketing Own Your Website?

Most big companies assign the responsibility for the website to the marketing department, which ensures that all the information on the site is appropriate for public dissemination. Given that your competitors watch your website to gain clues about your strategic plans, vetting material prior to publication is a good idea.

There's a downside to this approach, however, because marketing teams don't always think about expanding the content on the site, and as a result, the majority of business websites are small and static. They have a list of products and a list of press releases. That's it. With few pages and no adjunct content to attract customers, it should be no surprise that those sites aren't very findable.

This isn't to say that marketing shouldn't own the website, but smart companies are starting to encourage other people in the organization to write articles and other material for the site, too. Microsoft's search-engine team maintains a weblog, HP promotes weblogs from some of its engineers, and various smaller companies have "thoughts from the president," letters to customers, or similar material that's added with some frequency. A trend that will grow in the future is companies hiring bloggers to write a daily weblog on behalf of the firm, too.

Visual Consistency, Redux

Visual consistency is all about whether the logo on your receipt is the same as the logo on your website, whether the typeface that you use to print invoices is consistent with the type treatment of elements on your home page, and so on. Ideally, everything should tie in together thematically so that you're creating a distinct visual brand which helps establish you—and make your business seem larger—in the mind of your customers.

The alternative is that the website appears to be an afterthought, something done by a different group in the company with a different agenda and a different set of goals, and that's definitely not conducive to creating a good customer experience. It can also create dissonance in the customer's mind, making him wonder if he's really found the right website when you really want him to be thinking about buying, not design.

Don't Be Shy About Your URL

Website addresses are all around us nowadays, from the tags sewn into clothing and the stickers on consumer electronics to the covers of magazines and highway billboards. That's smart.

The question you should ask is where *isn't* there a website address? Look at magazines on the newsstand: Which ones don't have a website address on the cover? Walk around the local shopping mall and see which stores don't have a stack of cards inviting customers to visit the company website. Collect tchotchkes at a trade show and compare how many include the company's website address and how many do not.

I realize that I'm evangelizing about the immeasurable value of having a website for business, but that's genuinely how I feel about the matter. There isn't a business around that can't garner value and gain potential customers from having a good website.

Some service professionals say that they already have all the business they can handle. That's why they don't worry about having a website, or why they don't pay attention to their site. But they've got it wrong. For all businesses, success comes from growth.

Growth doesn't necessarily mean more customers. However, it can also refer to a higher caliber of customers, or, to put that another way, growth in revenue without adding customers. The top service providers understand this intuitively: when you're too busy, raise your rates.

> **BizTips**
>
> Don't make the mistake of automatically equating growth with more customers. There are other, smarter ways to grow, too, depending on your business.

Other companies believe that their business is completely based in the physical world and that there just aren't potential customers online. Again, a bit of creative thought can show that thinking to be wrong and limiting.

When a retail store is closed potential customers go elsewhere, either finding someone who is open, or deferring their purchase until the next day. Why not have a website address included on the "CLOSED" sign? Real world customers can then find new opportunities for purchasing your products through your site, generating more revenue. Imagine, instead of the negative stop message of "closed," you could have "closed here, open online!"

> **Memo**
>
> A shoeshine man who works in the lobby of a major hotel, for example, could keep a running log of famous people he's encountered on his website and even offer tips on shining your own shoes for when you can't get to the hotel. His business cards—with his website address, of course—could then be stacked in front of the stand. He would soon find that customers are lining up for a shine and secretly hoping to appear on his famous people list.

Even the most banal of places can be advertising venues and drive customers to your website. A restaurant owner could offer special discounts to customers who visit the restaurant's website. Notices could be hung in the restaurant bathrooms with pithy sayings like, "If you'd visited our website this morning, you'd have saved 10 percent on your bill!" and "A click in time saves nine: Visit our website for special 9 percent discount coupons," along with the address of the restaurant website.

Customers would be intrigued, visit the site, then inevitably send their friends to the site, too. The cost of the discount would more than be offset by the additional traffic that the promotion drives to the restaurant.

Even better, collect their e-mail addresses before they can get to the coupon—tell them that they'll receive your monthly newsletter—and now you're building a list of customers to whom you can market new products and services.

What all of these ideas have in common is that promoting your website in the physical world is more about creative thinking than spending lots of money.

In very much the same way, building an attractive, engaging, highly findable website isn't about spending large amounts of money or hiring teams of programmers. It's about understanding how the web works, how search engines work, and then leveraging that knowledge to produce the best possible marketing collateral, online and offline.

BizTips

Promoting your business is always more about creative thinking than spending lots of money.

Answer Customer Questions on Your Site

One tangible area where your website can benefit your efforts to improve your customers' experience and attract new customers is by answering questions. Many websites refer to these question lists as FAQs, *frequently asked questions*.

BizTips

Ask yourself, "Have I answered this question before?" and then think about how you could leverage your answers into new content for your site.

Someone who specializes in hanging wallpaper can quickly rattle off the 20 questions that customers always ask him. A photographer knows what questions potential clients are going to ask, and a muffler repair shop answers the same dozen questions from customers every day.

Businesses that sell products have even more questions from customers, questions on the specifications of the product, its availability, whether it's compatible with other products, how it compares to other, similar products on the market, and much, much more.

These questions should all be captured, written down, and answered once and for all on your website.

Question and Answer Formats

To help with your findability, however, phrase the questions as generally as possible. A question like "Who owns the negatives after a photo shoot?" is far superior to "Ownership of negatives" or "Does the customer own the negatives after a Colorado Portraits photo shoot?" Why? Because the chance of someone searching Google for information about ownership of negatives in the world of photography is much higher than them searching for the name of a specific studio. This is a splendid example of how adding content to your site can help potential customers find you online. (Don't forget that tools like Wordtracker can help you identify common search phrases, too, as detailed in Chapter 11.)

The United States Copyright Office has an excellent FAQ area on its website (www.copyright.gov/help/faq), shown in Figure 12.1, that should serve as a model for how you should structure your own frequently-asked-questions area.

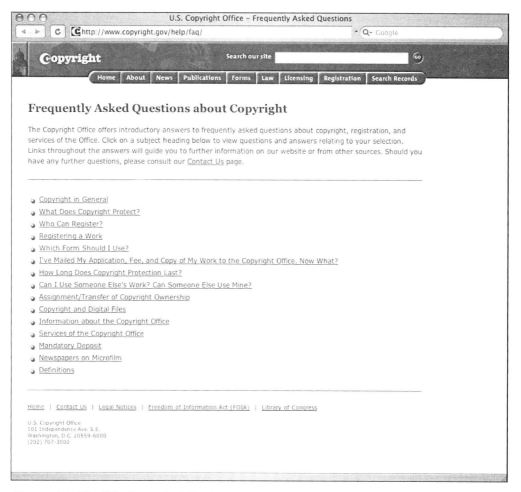

Figure 12.1: The U.S. Copyright Office has a terrific FAQ area with well-phrased questions and many pages of useful information.

One thing that I particularly like about the copyright FAQ is that it's not all one enormous page. While it may seem that having all the questions and answers on a single page is the best strategy, it's actually quite beneficial to have the information split out onto multiple pages. More pages directly equate to more opportunities for you to match a given search query, after all.

By contrast with the Copyright Office page, consider the main FAQ page on the TiVo site (www.tivo.com/1.6.asp) shown in Figure 12.2. The site is focused on selling the popular digital television recording device, yet this particular page is extremely search engine–unfriendly.

Figure 12.2: TiVo's FAQ page doesn't list a single question, missing out on the opportunity to create more search engine–friendly content.

BizTips

My bias for informational sites is to have them in the form of questions and answers. People search for questions or answers, they don't search for neutral information. Solve their problems and you'll turn your visitors into customers by the drove.

You should also ensure that your FAQ information is written in the form of questions and answers. Most people search for information by thinking of either the question they want to ask or the answer that they expect to receive. To find the population of Des Moines, for example, common search queries would be "what is the population of Des Moines" (which is rewritten as "population Des Moines" by Google, but that's okay) or the answer to the question "the population of des moines is" (which, again, is rewritten "population des moines").

Care should be taken in how the questions and answers are phrased, because you don't want to turn off a potential customer who might not know much about the industry, service, or product.

Here's an example of how not to write an FAQ entry, from Ford Motor Company's Ford GT website:

> **Why did you choose the name Ford GT?**
>
> To most car enthusiasts the name Ford GT, which was the name of the original car, evokes memories of Ford's miraculous 1-2-3 victory in the 1966 24 hours of Le Mans.

This answer could easily make some potential car buyers feel excluded from the cult of the new Ford GT because they didn't know about the Le Mans victory and the resultant connotations of the name. Instead, I'd suggest that an answer of the following form would work better:

> The Ford GT is the direct successor of the winner of the miraculous 1-2-3 victory in the 1966 24 hours of Le Mans.

A link to a page about the race written by a Ford car designer would be both fun and informative, too, and would mean that Ford had yet another hook dangling in the sea of information trying to lure customers to their website.

Savvy marketing people also see the FAQ as one facet of an information jewel, where online customer queries are saved as possible additions to the FAQ and where the most common of the queries are turned into an informational pamphlet. The "Common Questions for Photographers" or "Ten Questions About Wallpaper" or "Everything You Wanted to Know About Business Coaches" handout can then be distributed at events where there are potential customers and could even be licensed to competitors that agree to retain your business name and website address in the material.

BizTips

An FAQ search tool lets you capture and record the topics people seek on your site, allowing you to refine your FAQ over time to offer more and more useful information.

Weblogs as Q&A Alternatives

Perhaps having a set of pages that address common questions isn't appealing to you, doesn't fit your business vision, or is too hard to produce from scratch. An alternative is to essentially build the frequently-asked-questions archive one question at a time, as a Q&A forum.

This idea was the genesis of my popular Ask Dave Taylor website, actually. Two years ago I was getting questions from readers and would dutifully answer each one, never leveraging what I'd written and never duplicating answers when the same question came in a second time. I recognized that for every person who asked a specific question, there were five others who had the same question but didn't ask it, or asked it on Google instead of on my site.

As a result, I created a website that was built around content inspired by specific reader questions. Each question would have a two- to five-paragraph response (sometimes I have to ramble a bit to generate that much content) and each would have its own page on the site and link to the product page for the specific book.

The result is that thousands of people are now reading my Q&A, learning about my products and services, and spending their money to purchase my books. In addition, I now see anywhere from 5 to 20 new questions every day, each of which then lets me create yet another page of content, another chance to capture a potential customer and bring him or her to my site. Figure 12.3 shows a typical book-related Q&A on Ask Dave Taylor.

A search on Google for "ask question" reveals that there are a surprising number of websites with a Q&A theme, and within a given business sector, there are magazine columns or even syndicated newspaper columns in the Q&A format. Examples abound, including Dear Abby, Miss Manners, and The Straight Dope.

BizTips _____

Never underestimate the value of laziness as a business motivator! What are you doing the hard way that could be rethought, reinvented, or recast to be easier and more beneficial for your business?

BizTips _____

Your customers are already familiar with Q&A information presentation, so don't write stiff, formal documents, manuals, or web pages. Create witty, engaging Q&A materials instead.

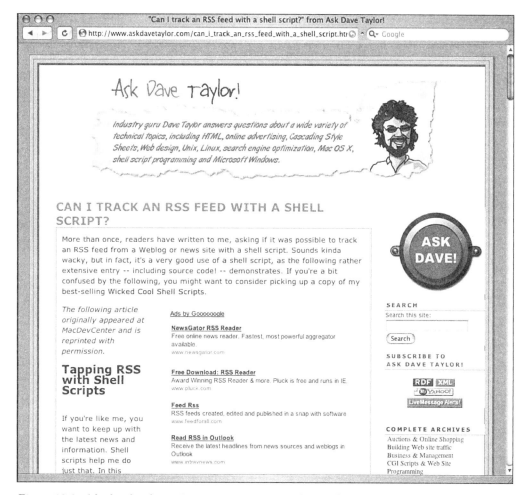

Figure 12.3: A book-related question turns into its own web page, helps drive traffic to the site, and ultimately helps sell more books to the online community.

From the reader's perspective, Q&A is easy to read and is conducive to skimming for content, and from the writer's perspective (and this is a secret) there's no format that's easier to write than a Q&A column. Here's another secret, too: there's no rule that says you can't make up questions or rephrase questions so that you can write the answer you want to include.

If someone writes in to your online shoe store with the question "Why are Italian shoes so overpriced?" it's perfectly reasonable for you to answer instead the question "What makes Italian shoes so much more expensive?" As with the Ford GT example

Memo
The purpose of all question-and-answer areas on a website is to both help the customer solve his or her problems and demonstrate your thought and expertise in your industry segment.

earlier, you don't want to insult your reader, but you also don't want to put yourself in an awkward situation where you can't convey the highest professionalism and give your visitor the greatest confidence in your expertise.

At the end of the day, it's all about generating content that's going to sell your expertise and your product or services.

What Other Content Do You Have?

Customer questions are a wonderful source of content for your site however you organize it, but there are plenty of other information sources you have available.

Product literature is a good example. If you sell products, you have to create one-sheet summaries of these products for your sales team and suppliers, along with a catalog of all your products and, most likely, a comparison chart of how the individual products fit into your overall product line. All of those should be turned into content for your website, even if you don't plan on selling any of the products online.

You don't just want to put a bunch of spec sheets on your site, however; you want to make them into sales collateral.

BizTips
If you're offering PDF documents that are more than 3 to 4 pages long, consider having someone turn it into a multi-page web document instead. A 50-page document could easily turn into 20 to 30 new pages of content on your site.

A lot of companies also have white papers, position articles, letters from customers, industry awards, and other material that they include in their marketing package and media kit. All of this should also appear on the website, along with every single press release, copies of every single magazine or newspaper article that's ever mentioned the company (in a favorable way, of course) or any of its principal employees, and anything else that can offer useful information to visitors.

Additionally, nonprofit organizations in your industry sector might have background and industry material that's suitable for your website, too. There's certainly no harm in asking for permission to duplicate the material—with credit, of course—to add yet more material to your own site.

CAUTION

Beware

I strongly discourage you from getting so excited about adding content to the point that you start stealing material from other sites without permission. It's easy to find stolen content and it's illegal, even if they don't have a copyright notice on their pages. Worse, it'll present you in a very negative light to your future customers.

How Can You Serve Your Customers Better?

It may seem that I've spent much of this chapter talking about how to create content because it's search engine–friendly and increases your findability with potential customers. I have certainly been espousing that perspective, but the real goal for adding content to your site, and for integrating your online and offline marketing in general, is to best serve the needs of your customers.

Memo

Great customer service is an important differentiator between a mediocre company waiting to be overtaken by a new competitor and a market leader, a company that instills great brand loyalty in its customer community.

The decision of what material is suitable for adding to your site, and for determining what online material could become printed collateral for your business, revolves around your customer, the cornerstone of your business.

This is where the web offers great benefits. In the physical world, it can be difficult to ascertain the top questions that possible customers have if they never ask them and never become actual customers. If you never interact with these potential customers, you might never know that your lack of a clear return policy alienates them, or that there's a gaping hole in your product line that sends them to your biggest rival.

Online, by contrast, it's much easier to close the loop on this feedback, using the techniques explored earlier to identify the most popular query terms and turn them into answers on your site. Additionally, a feedback form encourages customers and potential customers to ask new questions, and those can be poured back into a frequently-asked-questions document or Q&A area on your site.

It's a big self-replicating cycle, and savvy online marketers know that their FAQ can grow without bounds, making them appear increasingly savvy about their market space and responsive to their customers.

The Least You Need to Know

- Your website address should be on every item of collateral, from shopping bags to invoices.

- Customer queries can become the basis of an ever-growing frequently-asked-questions area on your site or Q&A weblog.

- The best online content can also be brought back into the physical world as informational pamphlets and brochures.

13

Stretching Your Marketing Dollars

In This Chapter

◆ Product-based websites

◆ Press material as additional content

◆ Newsletters and customer communications

◆ Sponsoring other newsletters and sites

If you have a marketing person on staff or work with a marketing agency, you've already learned that most marketers have a simple formula that looks like this: spending = results. The more you spend on your marketing efforts, from Superbowl ads to full-page solicitations in the *Wall Street Journal*, the more success you'll have in attaining the desired sales goals.

However, this just isn't true anymore, if it ever was. Today, marketing is about being ingenious, smart, entertaining, and meeting the needs of your customer community. In this chapter, I'll look at a bunch of ways that you can leverage the capabilities of the Internet to travel down this low-cost, highly effective marketing road.

The Marketing Expenditure Conundrum

During the heyday of the dotcom era, startups would gamble a significant percentage of their entire marketing budget on a PR stunt, a 30-second ad during the Superbowl, a party featuring a nationally known band, or similar ideas. Invariably they'd reap the benefit of the publicity for a short period of time, and then vanish completely, often never to be heard from again.

The problem with that approach is the same problem with large companies that throw millions or tens of millions of dollars into their marketing efforts: successful marketing is more about being *smart* with your marketing efforts than it is about being splashy. When you go through the mail at home, how many full-color multi-page advertisements do you throw away unread?

BizTips

Marketing isn't about numbers, because your goal should never be *more*. It should be *better*: better visitors, more qualified potential customers, and better conversion of visitor to customer.

The traditional approach to marketing has always been a numbers game. Advertise in a magazine with 100,000 readers and 4 percent will care about your message. Of those 4 percent, 10 percent might be actual prospective customers, and half of those might then actually call your firm or visit your establishment. For the cost of 100,000 eyeballs, you see 200 new customers. Traditional marketing people would say that's a good ratio, a 0.4 percent conversion rate.

Once you start thinking about online marketing, however, particularly Google AdWords and similar pay for performance models, your conversion rates increase dramatically. One reason is that you're no longer paying for viewings, you're paying for clicks, for people who actually respond to your advertisement. Using the above numbers, you're paying for 4,000 visitors to your site, not the 96,000 people who aren't interested in your offer. The advertising probably costs less and the conversion rate is much more in your favor. Instead of seeing 0.4 percent, you're actually seeing a visitor-to-customer conversion rate of 5 percent. With this newfound efficiency, you could reduce your marketing budget by 80 percent and *still* see more value for your marketing money.

Effective online marketing isn't about spending money, though; it's about being smart in how you promote your company and services. It's just as much about putting in the effort to create a highly findable site and ensuring that each and every page on the site serves as an effective entry point and introduction to the business.

The best way to stretch your marketing dollars is to create innovative ways to promote your products and services, and to understand and exploit the inherent strengths of the web to best benefit your business.

Product-Based Websites

One of my favorite methods of expanding online presence is to think beyond the "one website" mentality. For a nominal incremental cost, you can have a dozen domain names and create a dozen different websites that address different facets of your business, focus on different product lines, or even feature a single product that you'd like to promote.

A company that does this to great effect is the powerhouse Proctor & Gamble. With hundreds of product lines, they've registered each product domain name and each leads to a specific website or section of the parent company's site. Examples are www.crest.com, www.clairol.com, www.folgers.com, and www.tide.com.

Proctor & Gamble don't make hundreds of unique sites, though. They minimize their development costs by using a single design for multiple websites. Figure 13.1 shows how P&G product sites can be almost identical.

Individual, focused websites are much more effective than having customers directed to the main Proctor & Gamble site. Cloning the underlying design is also considerably less expensive than developing two unique websites.

If developing more than one website seems a bit overwhelming, the least you should do is register the domain for each and every product in your lineup, then have them redirect visitors to your main site. If your product names are trademarked, you'll want to own the domain names anyway, but it's also just good branding.

Beware

Be careful that you don't have multiple websites with exactly the same content, however, because Google frowns upon that. If you have multiple sites, make sure that they aren't just clones but have different content, and you'll be fine.

BizTips

Make sure that your products include the product website address, too. Pick up a box of Tide detergent and you'll see "Visit www.tide.com" printed on the side, for example.

Figure 13.1: (Top) The Eukanuba Pet Food website. (Bottom) The Iams Pet Food website.

Another possibility is to create thematic websites associated with your product lines, even if they're just different entry points into the main site. An artist might have EarringsByLinda.biz, NecklacesByLinda.biz, and BraceletsByLinda.biz in addition to her main website at JewelryByLinda.biz. Each pair of earrings sold would include the address of the earrings site, each bracelet would include the bracelet site, and so on.

You can also use specific domain names as shortcuts to products in your catalog or areas on your site. Visiting the website www.laborposter.com, for example, actually shows a product page that's within the BusinessKnowHow.net website.

Turning Your Press Releases into Content

Press releases are tailor-made for adding to your website. They're not the same as articles, however, so smart companies create a separate media relations area on their sites. This area contains all of their press releases, along with any press coverage the company has received, review kits that detail particular strengths and capabilities of the products, white papers that position the company's service or product in the industry, and sometimes even an archive of product photographs available for download.

The Google Press Center (www.google.com/intl/en/press) is a good example of how a lot of company information can be made available to anyone who seeks it. Available information includes case studies, images, a company history, executive bios, their privacy policy, and a separate section on investor relations.

> **BizTips**
>
> Don't make your press and media center off-limits to regular visitors, as some companies do. It's content. Make it available to everyone and you'll have more ways to hook potential customers and a more findable website, too.

A well-designed media center has links to all of the media content and the main area of the site on every page. Every press release, after all, can be the very first page someone sees on your site. Figure 13.2 shows how Google incorporates links to the rest of its press center on each press release page (for example, www.google.com/intl/en/press/pressrel/print_library.html).

You can include a lot of interesting material within a press or media center, even material that might actually be of more interest to potential customers than journalists.

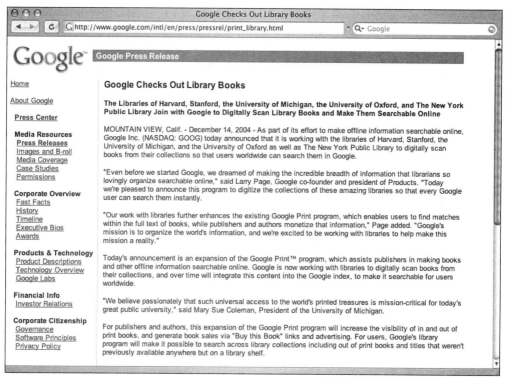

Figure 13.2: Google press releases include links to many other areas of their press center on each press release page.

Newsletters and Customer Communications

One of the areas where you can really stretch your marketing dollars is to stop sending printed materials to your customers. In the age of electronic communications, it's amazing how many companies still print up fancy multipage color newsletters that they send to their customers. That same money could be spent offering all of those existing customers a special "loyalty" discount on new products, or even gift certificates that they could share with friends and family.

Newsletters open up a new world of communication with your customers. Even the most rudimentary website can use them effectively. You don't need any web skills or graphics to produce a fun and compelling newsletter.

> **Memo**
>
> The next time you get a glossy brochure from a company, think about how they could have spent their marketing dollars instead of incentivizing you with discount coupons, free samples, or other more tangible calls to action.

Newsletters are even more useful for service providers than product-based companies, and you can include anything you think will be interesting to your customers. Further, a simple signup form on your web pages (not just your home page, remember, because plenty of your potential customers are going to go straight to a secondary page and never even see your home page) will also net lots of visitors who aren't yet customers, visitors who are nonetheless excellent prospects.

Some companies produce *HTML*-based newsletters that include graphics, fancy lay-out, and other elements that make their newsletters visually attractive, while others produce simple text-only newsletters. The advantage of an attractive design is obvious, but the unfortunate reality is that many sub-scribers don't have e-mail programs that can properly format and display the more complex newsletter. My recommendation: Either offer both format options (which means that you essentially have to produce two versions of each newsletter) or just have a text-only version.

Buzzwords _____

HTML is *hypertext markup language* and it's the lan-guage that web designers use to create web pages. It's not terribly difficult to learn and there are some very sophisticated tools that make producing simple HTML as easy as typing in Microsoft Word.

Writing Style

There are many different approaches to writing a newsletter, ranging from a dry cor-porate communication without any identifiable author to a personal letter from the company president.

As an information service provider, I have a newsletter that I send to my readers and potential customers. Rather than use a complex layout and worry about whether every-one's e-mail program will display it correctly, I just write a personal message to the list.

Here are the first two paragraphs of a typical issue:

> Hello, everyone, and welcome to another of the sporadically written Dave Taylor Author News updates. Right off the top, I'm happy to report that two of my most recent books are doing very well: *Wicked Cool Shell Scripts* continues to sell far better than we expected (I mean, it's a book about writing shell scripts for Unix! How unexciting is that? :-)) and we continue to receive good publicity for *Learning Unix for Mac OS X Panther*.

> In the hopper: I'm working on a new book that has much more of a business slant, focused on the different ways you can promote your business online using

Google and other sites. I'm excited about this one because it continues my transition into the business section of the bookstore rather than perpetually being trapped in the geeky computer department in the basement.

You can see that it's very personable. It explains in the very first sentence that it's sent to a mailing list, and has a light, humorous tone that's inclusive, with minimal jargon.

HTML-based newsletters can be expensive and tricky to design, but the process of pouring content into the newsletter can be somewhat automated if that's the route you desire.

Too Much Design, Too Little Content

Other newsletters can completely miss the point of what makes an effective and engaging communication with customers. Nikon, makers of some of the best camera equipment in the world, has superb photographers on staff, but their "Nikon News Online" newsletter is just a full-page advertisement, with no actual interesting content at all, as shown in Figure 13.3.

Memo

There's one facet to e-mail newsletters that's critically important, and that's avoiding being labeled as spam. Writing about spammy subjects like prescription drugs or get-rich-quick schemes will cause you no end of trouble with subscribers' spam filters rejecting your messages.

Before you even get to the point of sending out your first newsletter, however, it's vitally important that you ensure that you have a *double opt-in list*. This means that having someone enter his e-mail address on your website is *not sufficient* for you to add him to the list. Instead, your subscription management system should automatically e-mail him a subscription confirmation, and it's only upon his accepting that confirmation that you can safely add him to your list.

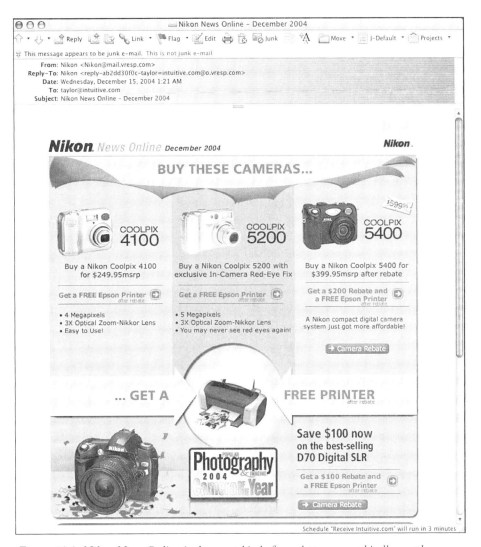

Figure 13.3: Nikon News Online is the worst kind of newsletter: a graphically complex advertisement without any actual content to engage the reader.

Sponsoring Other Newsletters and Sites

Some newsletters, particularly those that are more informational and less sales-oriented, accept advertisements or sponsorships. If a newsletter is focused at your target market, being a sponsor can be surprisingly inexpensive and an excellent way to raise your visibility with your future customers.

Find out what mailing lists and newsletters your customers follow by using the techniques outlined in Chapter 10, then start with those publications when you seek opportunities to promote your business through sponsorship.

When you find a newsletter you're interested in sponsoring, simply send an e-mail message to the newsletter editor politely asking if they accept any advertising or sponsorship. Some will inevitably reject your offer, but others might never have thought of charging money to include a few lines about a company that offers a product or service for their readership.

Hobby sites, fan sites, and even nonprofit organizations also accept sponsors or underwriters, another avenue to get your name out and promote your products within your community.

Finally, don't forget that one of the best ways to stretch your marketing dollars is by learning how to use Google AdWords. For more details, see Chapter 17.

Memo

Whether you sponsor a site or have a paid ad on a major commercial network, one of the most important things to do is ensure that you have a *landing page*, so that visitors who click on one of your ads aren't just dumped unceremoniously on your home page. The landing page should deliver the promise of the ad itself, selling your product or service directly. If you have 20 products, advertising one specific product can be much more effective because it's highly targeted. The page that visitors get when they arrive at your site should continue to focus on that specific product, sing its praises, and offer a special call to action to maximize your conversion rates.

The Least You Need to Know

◆ Multiple websites, or even multiple domain names that lead to different parts of a single website, can be much more effective than a single site.

◆ A press center on your site can offer the opportunity to add lots of overt marketing material.

◆ Newsletters, whether HTML or text-based, are highly effective methods of communicating with your customers.

◆ Always make sure your list is 100 percent double opt-in to avoid being accused of spamming.

Chapter 14

Secrets of the Online Marketing Masters

In This Chapter

- Designing search engine–friendly pages
- Understanding the importance of page titles
- Improving your keyword density
- Naming links and pages effectively
- The problem with link exchanges

When you need your car repaired, you don't pull out a spanner and overalls, and when your sink is backing up, your tool of choice is probably the telephone. In the same way, savvy businesspeople know that staying focused on their business is what produces success in the long term. When it comes time to building a website, it's time to hire someone who knows what they're doing.

The task of choosing a good website designer isn't easy because of the wide range of expertise. I'll highlight the most important criteria: experience, professionalism, and the ability to work as part of a team. Too many service professionals believe that they know what you need and that your ideas are mildly interesting when the project starts, but quickly become annoying once the actual work begins. They're not going to produce a website that you'll be happy with for the long term, and if that's the kind of person you've been working with, it's time to find someone new.

A lot of web developers also now claim that they know how to do search engine optimization (SEO) and that part of what you'll receive when they're done is a very SEO-friendly website. Having looked inside quite a few business sites, including those by companies advertising that they know how to optimize for search engine placement, I have to say that most of these people are clueless about how a sophisticated search engine like Google really works and how to develop pages that offer the best findability.

BizTips

One strategy for ensuring that your web developer is really building a site that is going to maximize your findability is to simply give them a copy of this book, or, at least, this chapter. Certainly I encourage you to use this chapter as a checklist to ensure that all of these critical elements of search engine optimization influence the development of your site.

Just a few days ago, a colleague of mine who builds beautiful websites was quite surprised when I opined that the home pages don't matter any more and that good design is now all about individual content pages. She'd never thought about this implication from the new web reality that more people see a secondary page than ever visit the home page.

Search Engine–Friendly Page Design

The best websites are those that are built around content. I keep saying this, because it's a very important concept. Any tricks or techniques that you may hear about or that your developer may espouse are likely to only work for a short period of time, if at all, and can sometimes even get you kicked out of Google and other search engines entirely. You don't want that to happen!

BizTips

It's all about content. That's the key to growing your business with Google.

Google remains true to its original philosophical foundation, a search engine that uses popularity and content analysis to figure out if a given page is a good match for a search query. Your site needs to have good, clear, coherent content, content that's focused on your business and content that's all legitimate.

Skip the Fancy Applets and Navigation Toolbars

Websites that use fancy programming techniques or *applets* for navigation are harder for a search engine to navigate than those that are simpler in design. This is why Java-based menu bars, Flash-based navigation, or even JavaScript menu pop-ups should either be avoided entirely or should be supplemented with plain text links elsewhere on the page. If a user can't easily figure out how to get around, odds are good that a search engine will also have problems. A site that can't be crawled is a site with content that'll never match queries from potential customers.

Buzzwords

An **applet** is a small, portable program that's intended to be downloaded to the visitor's computer and run. It then produces and controls some of the material on the web page. Many applets offer exciting visual effects, sounds, and animation, but it's important to balance the trade-off of eye candy versus findability.

Too Much Design Detracts from the Content

The content should always be the heart of each page, without graphics, advertisements, cross-selling, or the design itself getting in the way. Some websites have an impossible time saying "no" to element creep—the gradual inclusion of more and more content—and end up with both visitor and search engine–unfriendly pages like that shown in Figure 14.1.

Navigation on a site should also be easy, and having the site links appear *after* the content on the page is a smart way to boost findability, too, because content at the top of a page is considered more important than content at the bottom. Further, many people believe that search engines only look so far into a page to ascertain its content, so having lots and lots of sophisticated navigation code can theoretically result in the content of the page being ignored.

BizTips

Simplicity is the essence of good business website design.

Figure 14.1: By including so many ads and having graphical page elements that are indistinguishable from ads, the Weather.com site has become the worst place to find your weather forecast.

Section headers on a page are also important because search engines use the implied importance of different HTML tags as a guide to interpreting the content of the page. A web page where all the section heads are actually graphics might look more attractive, but will ultimately be less findable than one that uses the HTML h1 and h2 tags for level one and level two headers, respectively.

The Importance of Page Titles

One element of findable page design is that every page of your site should have a clear and relevant title. Websites where every single page has "Welcome to Joe's

Athletic Gear" are not well-designed. You can have your company name appear on every page, but use it like a so-called *breadcrumb trail*, where as someone goes further into the site, the title keeps lengthening as a visual clue about their location.

The Wall Street Journal website (www. wsj.com) uses the breadcrumb trail effectively. The home page is titled "WSJ.com—U.S. Home," and each subsequent page builds on that information. An article about the health risks of the drug Celebrex, for example, has the title "WSJ.com—Pfizer Says Study Shows Heart Risk from Celebrex."

Since so many sites have poor titles in the first place, the ordering of words in your title probably matters much less than simply creating good titles in the first place. If your site is built around a content management system—a weblog or similar scheme—then you can automate the creation of effective titles.

Don't be afraid to have your slogan or a few descriptive key words in the title, too. The *New York Times* does this beautifully, with the home page title "The New York Times > Breaking News, World News & Multimedia." This is also why the title on eBay's home page is "eBay—New & used electronics, cars, apparel, collectibles, sporting goods & more at low prices." It's a bit wordy, but includes lots of good key words to help their findability.

BizTips

These titles could be improved a bit to increase findability, actually, because the first few words in the title are considered the most important, and the *Wall Street Journal* is wasting those by having their domain name (not even the publication name) appear each time. A better title would be "Pfizer Says Study Shows Heart Risk from Celebrex—from the *Wall Street Journal*."

BizTips

Save the typing, never bother with the phrase "Welcome to" or "Home Page" on any of your pages. They just waste space that should be replaced with words that describe your business, products, service line, or industry keywords.

The Diminishing Relevance of Meta Tags

When the first generation of search engines began to crawl the web and analyze the content of different web pages, they let web developers include special keyword and description elements. These *meta tags* weren't visible to anyone viewing the page, but were buried in the content and were just for crawlers.

> **Buzzwords**
>
> A **meta tag** is one of a class of special HTML markup tags that weren't included in the original language definition. They all start with the word *meta*, hence the name.

In the last several years, many search engine–optimization experts have tried to use *keyword stuffing* to trick the search engines. By doing this, they've subverted the original intent of the meta tags to the point where they're almost universally ignored by crawlers. There might be some latent value to having meta tags on your pages, but it's likely that you'll reap more benefit from adding another page of content than by adding meta tags to your existing pages.

> **Buzzwords**
>
> A malicious practice, **keyword stuffing** is using tricks to increase the keyword density of certain keywords on a page without those keywords being visible to the user. This can be done by putting these keywords within comments, making up fake HTML tags that are ignored by browsers but are seen by search engines, and so on. Keyword stuffing is a bad idea, and if a crawler like Googlebot detects it on your page, it'll toss the page out of the database entirely.

The Skinny About Keyword Density

If you find yourself writing the word "it" frequently, you're going to need to learn a new style of writing to improve your findability. Google and other page analysis systems use fairly simple heuristics to figure out what words or phrases appear more than once in a passage of prose. The words that do appear more often are indicators of the meaning of the page and help that page be ranked more highly for relevant searches.

> **BizTips**
>
> Find your comfort point on the continuum of informal writing and ensuring that you have many occurrences of keywords and phrases, then stick with it throughout your different pages.

If you have a website about the glorious 1964 Ford Mustang, you'll be more findable if you keep repeating that same phrase throughout articles and commentary, rather than having slang or shortcuts like "After the Auto Show, the 'stang was an instant hit" or "It was one of the best cars on the road."

In a similar vein, you should ensure that your keywords appear within the first paragraph of your content, if not in a descriptive paragraph that floats above everything on the site.

Having said that, don't overdo it. If every fifth word is your product name, you could actually be penalized for keyword stuffing. So use the words in context, as appropriate; just be precise and detailed in your writing. I use the "read it out loud" test: if your writing is so stilted and keyword-filled that you can't actually read it out loud to someone without stumbling, it's probably time to back off a bit from having the keywords appear so often. If it doesn't make sense, maybe it's time to replace some of your indirect references with the specific name of the product or service.

Naming Links and Pages Effectively

Because many websites are developed using software tools that hide the underlying details from the developer, file names can end up being quite unfriendly. Names like "15.3.php" or "art43.htm" demonstrate this scenario. It's not that they're inherently bad, but that you're missing out on another opportunity to reinforce the meaning of each file through its name. How much more logical and understandable is a file called "wood-frames.htm" rather than "wf0001.htm"? And Google will like it, too.

The names that you give internal links are even more important than file names. Pointing to your home page from secondary pages with the text "home page" isn't a terrible crime, but if you have an article about fitting photographs into wooden frames, the links to that article should use those exact words, not "frame fit", "article 11", "latest story", or "tips" or anything else that doesn't have any descriptive value or key words.

This is also why having graphical elements as links is less desirable than having text links: graphics don't give you the ability to include the descriptive words (and words that are part of the graphic itself are invisible to search engines).

BizTips

A good strategy is to have a small set of text links on the bottom of each page that emphasizes the keyword you use to describe that particular page. My sites that point to Ask Dave Taylor, for example, do so by highlighting the phrase "help desk" to help with site findability.

Requesting Thematically Related Inbound Links

Having descriptive text links is so important that every time you see someone link to your site by showing your site address, you should immediately ask them to fix it. A link where "http://www.findability.info" is shown on the page is far less desirable than a link that points to the site, but displays "Findability and Practical SEO Tips."

You can encourage people to link to your site using the words or phrase you prefer by pointing them to a link-to-us page. Under the guise of offering easily copied HTML text, the page can improve your findability by having the same text appear again and again on other sites pointing to you. An example of a link-to-us page is shown in Figure 14.2.

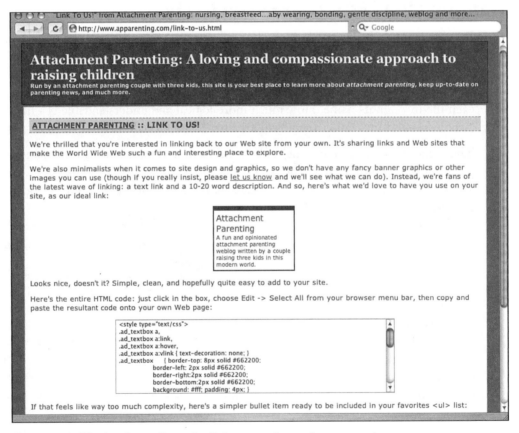

Figure 14.2: The Attachment Parenting link-to-us web page demonstrates how you can encourage other sites to use your descriptive text and your keywords when they link to you.

The Pitfalls of Trading Links

As your site continues to develop and you build a reputation in the online community, you'll inevitably find invitations for cross-linking start to appear. The offer seems reasonable: link to their site and they'll link to your site. You both win with new links, and search engines like links since they help demonstrate popularity.

There are a number of reasons why you should be leery of these link exchanges, however. Many of the sites that offer to link to you aren't at all related to your site (these are called *link farms* in SEO parlance) which means that while you do them a service by linking to them, they aren't offering you any value because they're unrelated topically or have too many other links. Additionally, many of these sites automatically remove links a few days after they invite you to cross-link, so you're left pointing to them, while they've backed out of their half of the bargain.

Never offer links off your home page with a link exchange, if you do accept an offer of this nature. As discussed elsewhere, your pages are highly valuable real estate and you don't want to waste it on invitations for visitors to go elsewhere and leave your site. If you are going to point to other sites, create a new links page and put all the links there.

On the other hand, if the site looks interesting, is professional, could be attracting your customer community, and is only pointing to other sites that you like, then swapping links is an excellent idea. Just don't offer a link on your home page that takes visitors to another site.

The Least You Need to Know

- ◆ Findability comes from good content laid out properly on web pages without tricks or sneaky SEO techniques applied.

- ◆ Reinforcing the main keywords on pages is critical and should occur in the title, headers, and even the file name itself.

- ◆ The text used to point to other pages on your site should duplicate the title of the page, not be a fragment or graphic.

- ◆ A link-to-us page can help other sites learn how you prefer to have your site listed, and a links page can give you somewhere to put cross-linked site addresses without wasting valuable real estate on your main pages.

Part 4

Promoting and Growing Your Online Business

This is the heart of the book, the million-dollar information that will help you see how to implement the ideas discussed earlier. Remember, growing your business with Google is about a lot more than just web pages, and this part explores strategies for creating a more popular website and ways that you—or someone else in your organization—can become an online expert, a transition that will pay tremendous dividends.

Three chapters in this section deserve your very closest attention, too. Chapter 18 explains all about Google's innovative—and highly cost-effective—AdWords advertising system, including very specific insider details of how to create effective ads and how to manage an ad campaign.

The chapters on AdSense and affiliate programs are even more important because they'll demonstrate ways that you can turn your website from a cost center into a potential profit center. It won't be right for everyone, but if you're tired of writing checks to cover your site, maybe it's time to start cashing checks instead.

Chapter 15

Content, Content, Content!

In This Chapter

- ◆ The importance of frequent site updates
- ◆ The need for discussion forums
- ◆ Considering games and surveys
- ◆ Finding additional content for your site
- ◆ Weblogs as content management systems

With billions of pages in its index, Google can't refine its relevance formula on a daily basis. Instead, every few months Google does what insiders call a *Google dance*, where it adjusts how relevance scores are calculated and essentially modifies the results list for every search on the site.

The inevitable result of a Google dance is that some website owners complain that they have a noticeable drop in traffic while others exult that their websites have quite a bit more traffic than they're used to. Within a day of each dance web developers are trying to ascertain what changed in the formula so they can update their sites and improve their relevance scores.

Buzzwords _____

The **Google dance** is a sporadic adjustment to the Google relevance formula that results in your pages being ranked higher or lower for specific keyword searches.

This entire approach is wrong, however, and illustrates the impossibility of trying to "figure out" and "trick" search engines. It's like a Cold War military exercise, with the search-engine developers creating new formulas that promote legitimate sites to the top and the search-engine optimizers trying to figure out the changes and devise new strategies to boost relevance scores. The losers in this exercise, of course, are both you as the website owner who has a business to run, and people who use search engines to find legitimate content on reputable websites.

The long-term goal of all the tweaks and modifications to the Google relevance score formula—and, by extension, to the Yahoo! search and MSN search relevance engines—is to be able to identify real content and present it as the best possible match for any given search. This means that even if websites aren't ranked highly today, as time passes and analysis improves, sites with lots of good, relevant content will continue to move up and gain traffic and visitors.

This isn't to say that you shouldn't apply the techniques highlighted in this book to better your chances of being identified as high-quality content, but to emphasize that it's the _content_, your articles, information sheets, product literature, white papers, and even commentary on industry events that is so important.

Update Your Site Frequently

When you introduce a new product in the market, announce a new service for clients, or even just add new material to your website, it's terribly demoralizing to realize that it might take weeks or months for that content to be found by the search engines and added to their databases.

BizTips _____

Remember: The more frequently you update your site, the more often Google and other search sites will reindex your content, making everything more findable.

Earlier we talked about Googlebot, the software crawler that explores your site, finding and analyzing all the pages thereon. What wasn't mentioned is that Googlebot doesn't visit on a daily basis. It might not visit for weeks.

During this interim period, any changes that you make to your website, any updates, press releases, new products, or updates to existing products, are unknown to Google and therefore can't match a search query. Sometimes it can feel like hosting an open house, just to stand at the door for hours waiting for someone to pop in and look around.

The exact details of how frequently Googlebot decides to visit a given website are shrouded in privacy, but there are two reasonable conclusions that can be made by observation:

◆ While PageRank (as discussed in Chapter 5) might not be important for improving your relevance score on a given search query, it is an indicator of how important Google finds your site, and therefore an important factor in how frequently Googlebot comes to visit.

◆ Also important to Googlebot's visits is how frequently your site changes. Websites that have been sitting untouched for years also find that their content is ranked as less relevant, everything else being equal, than the same content on a site that has been updated more recently.

You can boost your PageRank by having more sites point to you, as discussed in Chapter 5, but that can be difficult to accomplish and the PageRank values aren't recomputed for months at a time. An easier way to encourage Googlebot to visit more often is to *change your site frequently*.

BizTips

Sites that change frequently have Googlebot visit more frequently, too, which means new content is included in the Google database quickly.

My understanding of the basic strategy Googlebot uses for calculating how frequently to visit sites is based on reading hundreds of different discussions on the topic. When Google first finds a page, it starts with a 90-day visit cycle. Every three months, Googlebot visits the site to see if it has changed. If it has, then Googlebot moves it into a 45-day visit cycle. The next time it visits, Googlebot will move it into a 22-day cycle if it's again changed, and so on up to some busy websites that are visited on a daily basis. If a page isn't updated between visits, the site probably moves back down to a less frequent visit schedule.

This isn't completely accurate because it doesn't factor in that high-PageRank sites start out with more frequent visits than low-PageRank sites, but it's a good starting point. The importance of having a constantly growing, evolving, updated website is now clear. Not only do active websites benefit from more frequent visits by Google and other search engine crawlers, but their content is also ranked as more relevant because they're active sites.

Which begs the question: Where do you get all this content from?

Adding Discussion Forums

One smart way to add content to your site is to create a user's group or industry discussion forum on your site. Then your customers and potential customers are actually doing the hard work of writing new material each day while you're reaping the benefit of having a website with frequent updates.

Beware

Make sure you have the community to support a discussion forum before you add one. A forum without discussion isn't appealing and can convey quite the wrong message to visitors.

Unless you have a strong readership and busy online community that doesn't already have a discussion venue, however, adding a discussion forum could be a mistake. To have a good discussion forum, you need at least 100 regular visitors, of which at least 50 should make frequent contributions to the site.

The problem with a discussion forum that doesn't have enough people involved is that it just languishes and looks dead. Worse, new people will be discouraged from joining the community if they don't perceive it as already busy and interesting. This process is exactly analogous to how busy restaurants stay busy while quiet, empty restaurants repel, rather than attract, potential customers.

If you have a half-dozen people who track what you're saying and occasionally add their two cents, you get some nice comments on a weblog and look popular, as I'll discuss later in this chapter. If you go to a discussion forum where there are two discussion threads and a typical message has three viewings and no responses, it might reflect the same number of contributions from the same number of visitors, but it looks far, far worse and is much less likely to cause someone to bookmark the site or recommend it to friends.

To be fair, not everyone believes that a discussion forum needs to be busy, but a lack of contributors will stymie your goal of the discussion forum producing frequently updated content.

Should you add a discussion board to your site? If you don't already have a busy user or client community, I suggest not.

If you do want to proceed, the fastest solution is to have the actual discussion forum running on its own server. It can still be part of your domain, it would just be called "forums.yourbiz.com" or similar instead of being part of the "www" server. (Having the same top-level domain name is important because the discussion forum should be an integral part of your company website, not a completely separate entity.)

Two well-regarded discussion-hosting companies are Invision Power Services (www.invisionzone.com) and InfoPop (www.infopop.com).

Surveys and Games

Another approach that some business websites use to generate traffic and content is to have daily, weekly, or monthly surveys. The survey box appears on every page on the site and the survey results page, constantly updating as people vote. This can be a fun and interesting way to generate some customer feedback, but just as giving away unrelated services generates traffic but doesn't draw potential customers to your site, surveys should be thematically relevant and of interest to your clients or potential customers.

An artist who specializes in murals might have a survey about what famous murals his visitors have seen, a dog groomer might have a survey about favorite dog breeds, and the Porsche mechanic might have a survey about what Porsche visitors own. In all cases, surveys should be written to be as inclusive as possible, so if the visitor doesn't have a Porsche, the optional survey answer might be "None. Yet!" rather than leaving the visitor feeling unwelcome.

Games can add content to a site, too, but it's going to be a one-time addition (since a game is unlikely to produce a steady stream of new content as a discussion board could), and it's also potentially risky because you could end up paying the cost of hosting a popular game without actually attracting any new customers to your site.

> **BizTips**
>
> If you opt to host a game on your site, be alert to higher bandwidth costs. If the game becomes popular, you could have hundreds or even thousands of people visiting on a daily basis. Your web-hosting company probably meters how much data you send out to your site visitors and this can easily push you into the next pricing tier.

This isn't to say that with some creative thinking you couldn't contract with a game development company and have a game that is tied into your industry. Examples could be an online version of the children's game "Operation" for a pediatric surgeon as a way of making their site more friendly, a quiz where visitors are asked to match beer brands and company slogans to promote a bar, or a shoe-sizes-of-famous-people quiz for a shoe store.

To encourage visitors to play the game, offer them an online discount or a printable coupon that they can bring into your store.

Finding Content for Your Site

Many business websites now include the latest industry news on their websites as a way of having constantly updated content and making the site look more topical. Large news organizations like the *New York Times* offer the ability to include their news headlines on your site for free, and many more news organizations offer RSS feeds that can be transformed into news feeds on your site, too.

> **Memo**
>
> Industry news is a welcome addition to most sites, but if it's too prominent, your visitors might well click on the headlines and leave your site without seeing your product line or services.

Figure 15.1 shows how easy it is to add a custom *New York Times* news feed to your web pages. To sign up for this program, go to www.nytimes.com/gst/nytheadlines.html.

While news headlines constantly change, you aren't actually adding new content to your site with each news story, so this is inferior to adding articles each week, writing a weblog, or even adding a discussion forum.

Weblogs as Content Management Systems

To be honest, it's not easy to add lots of content to your site with frequency. After all, you're busy running your business, whether it's fixing leaky pipes, sewing quilts, boxing up products you've sold on eBay, or calibrating oven temperatures for your next batch of gourmet snacks.

Relying on customers and your community seems like a good idea, but there are only so many customers and there are lots of websites in any industry you can imagine, from surfboard manufacturing to rock-climbing gear. There are also many industry publications and community interest groups competing for those same folk, so most businesses need a different strategy for creating content.

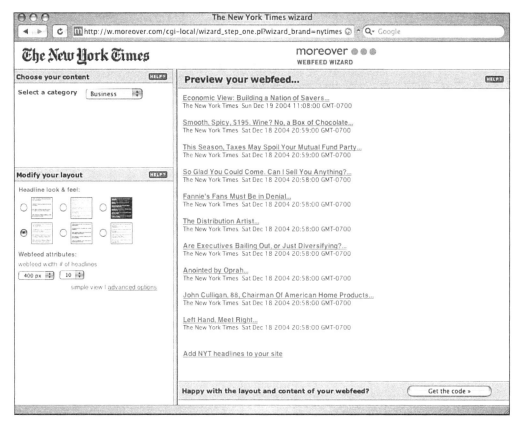

Figure 15.1: The New York Times *business news headlines can be easily added to your website.*

I suggest that this strategy is creating and maintaining a weblog, an online diary of sorts that's focused specifically on your products, services, and topics of direct interest to your customers. If you have someone on-staff who is outgoing, engaging, and enjoys interaction with your customers, he or she could be the perfect author for this new area on your site. If there are a few opinion leaders in your customer community, they might be quite interested in contributing to your weblog for a small fee or even for occasional free merchandise.

Of course, you might be the best choice of all. You're enthused about your company products and services and you are Internet-savvy!

Just as there are both hosted discussion forum solutions where the actual forum resides on a different computer and solutions that are installed on your server as part of your website, so there are two choices with weblogs, too. The two most popular

---

Memo

When the muse hits, I add 3- to 4-paragraph articles to my weblog, creating a brand new page and updating a variety of other pages with the new content, all in 10 to 15 minutes.

---

options for hosted weblogs are Blogger (www. blogger.com, a Google company) and Typepad (www.typepad.com). Weblogs that are installed on your server and then reside on the same computer as your website are more complex, but more flexible. Three of the leaders in this category are Movable Type (www.movabletype.org), WordPress (www. wordpress.org), and Blogsite (www.blogsite.com).

Incorporating a Weblog into Your Site

Without going into the technical details of how a weblog works, the best and least intimidating way to think about business weblogs is that they're a venue for you to send communiqués to your customer and potential customer community. These messages (*articles* in weblog parlance) can be a few sentences long, highlighting a new product, or they can be dozens of paragraphs, long essays on the state of the industry or the implications of the latest market news.

Weblogs can be incorporated into your own website as an adjunct, as print publication *Fast Company* has done with its FC Now weblog (at http://blog.fastcompany. com) or they can actually *be the website*, as with technology provider Myst Technology (www.myst-technology.com) where they use a weblog to maintain every page of their site. Figure 15.2 shows the FC Now weblog; Myst Technology is shown in Figure 15.3.

Whichever approach you take, weblogs make it remarkably easy to add new content and modify existing content, all without the intervention of a web developer, webmaster, or anyone from the IT department. That alone is sufficient to excite many businesspeople, because there's nothing more frustrating than having to wait weeks for new pages to be included on your site.

BizTips

A weblog manager can enable multiple people in your company or customer community to post to your weblog, without any of them being able to touch any other content on the site.

If you think through these implications, it also means that someone in marketing could be given the ability to post press releases, someone in engineering could post manufacturing updates, and someone in customer service could answer troubleshooting questions, without giving them access to the rest of the site.

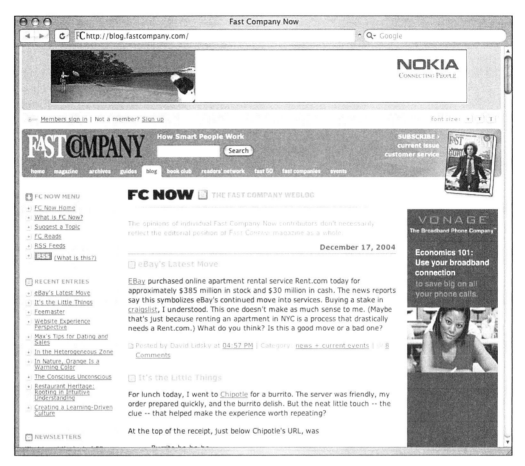

Figure 15.2: Fast Company *magazine's FC Now weblog is an integral part of their website and helps them frequently add new content.*

The Value of RSS, Really Simple Syndication

Newcomers to the world of weblogs are confused by the syndication concept, where you essentially publish a newswire feed of just your content and articles. RSS, XML, and RDF buttons on these blog sites lead to incomprehensible pages of text with no layout. To understand why this syndication capability is a boon to a business website, consider the dilemma of a customer wanting to keep track of your company through your website.

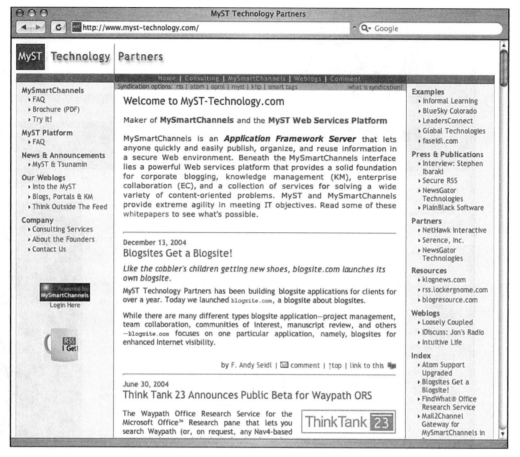

Figure 15.3: Myst Technology uses a weblog system as the underlying structure of their entire website.

Memo

A new competitor to RSS that also offers syndication capabilities is something called *Atom*. The technical differences are irrelevant; just think of it as another type of feed, joining the possibilities of RSS, RDF, and XML.

Even the most dedicated web surfer won't consistently visit a site every week to find out about what's new. They might visit for a few weeks, then once a month when they remember, then, eventually, you drop off their proverbial radar screen. A syndication system allows these potential customers to subscribe to a text-only version of your website content and keep up-to-date on your company without ever having to visit the site again.

The text-only information is formatted in a special markup language called RSS, RDF, or XML. They're all essentially the same thing; and although all require that you use a special reader application or subscribe to a web-based service that understands RSS feeds, they're a breeze to use.

You can create and maintain an RSS feed that mirrors the content of your site or includes excerpts or teaser articles, but it's much smarter to have a site management tool that maintains the RSS feed data without any human intervention. That's another reason for including a weblog somewhere on your site, because it produces RSS data that helps customers and other interested parties stay up-to-date on your product and service releases.

Figure 15.4 shows NewsGator Online, a free web-based service that lets you keep track of your favorite sites with RSS feeds, along with many major news and wire services.

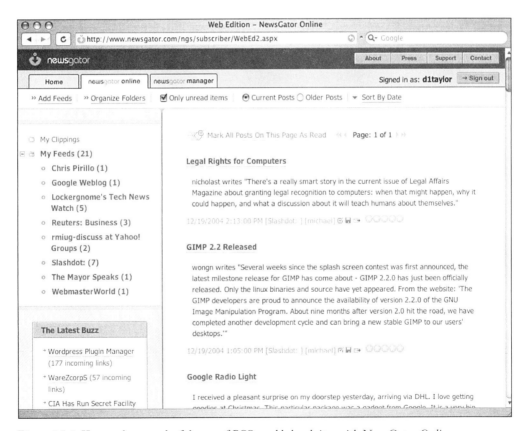

Figure 15.4: You can keep track of dozens of RSS-enabled websites with NewsGator Online.

Writing for a Weblog

Many companies set up a weblog but never use it (over 15,000 new weblogs come online every day). The main reason this occurs is because of what I call "published writer's block." If you think about writing articles for your website as a column in the *Wall Street Journal*, then you'd want to refer to your marketing person, a professional writer, possibly a lawyer to vet the article for any possible legal problems, and generally end up publishing about one article every two to three months.

> **BizTips**
>
> Imagine that every time you step out of your office, two or three of your most loyal customers are standing there, asking, "What's new?" It wouldn't be hard to update them on your industry, your business, or your products, would it?

Instead, imagine that you're actually sending out a personal e-mail message to your potential customers, and that they've told you that they're fine with you sending as much as you'd like, even more than one message in a day. Each message could be as short as "We just signed a distribution contract with REI! Give it a week, then go into your local REI outlet and ask about our new IceDigger axes," or the message could be three, four, or even ten paragraphs or more.

You need to remain on topic and ensure that your messages are relevant to your business, industry, or customers. You also don't want to speak poorly of your competitors. Otherwise, everything's fair game, from sharing customer testimonials to news about new contracts, what's going on in the research lab, new holiday hours in the mall, or even an invitation for subscribers to see a new mural you just finished.

Having read hundreds of different weblogs, my primary advice is to keep the writing friendly and enthused. Every salesperson already knows that enthusiasm for your product produces a similar level of enthusiasm in the majority of customers.

The Least You Need to Know

- The more frequently you add content and update your site, the more quickly changes are incorporated into the Google database.

- Discussion forums can be an excellent way of letting your customers generate new content for your site, but only if they remain busy.

- Weblogs offer an excellent approach to content management and automatically generate an RSS feed that allows your customers to stay current on the news from your business.

Becoming a More Popular Site

In This Chapter

- ◆ When to submit your site to search engines
- ◆ Search engines for weblogs: blog indices
- ◆ How to request inbound links
- ◆ Creating your own mini-stores

All of the website design and promotional techniques discussed to this point have been fairly insular, focused on how to tune your site for best results. The Zen of Growing Your Business, if you will.

It's time to expand our horizons and look outward, to learn how to find topical search engines that are worth requesting inclusion, how to identify which sites should be pointing to your business site, and why it's valuable to have a presence on eBay, Froogle, Yahoo! Shops, and similar sites.

Submitting Your Site to Search Engines

While the popularity of search engines waxes and wanes, Google is likely to be the top dog for quite a while. There are other search engines on the web, not just the big players, but industry- and topic-specific directories that are important, too. Finding them isn't always easy, but it's important to have your site listed in as many different places as possible because you never really know how your next customer is going to find your site.

BizTips

Remember, PageRank is a measure of how many links you have pointing to your page, and how "important" each of those linking pages are on the web overall.

Search engines that crawl the web, like Google, offer a web address submission feature, but you don't need to bother submitting your site, as long as you have at least one inbound link. Chapter 15 explained how PageRank affects how frequently the Googlebot crawler visits a page, so to get your site included in Google's database, your best bet is to have a link pointing to your site from a page that has a high PageRank.

Since Yahoo! Search and MSN Search are crawling the same web as Google, it stands to reason that if Google can find you quickly, then these other sites are going to find you and start indexing your pages quickly, too.

There are hundreds of different indexes and search engines, however, and while some rarely add new sites, many others are automated and happily add your site if you submit it.

Yahoo! Directory

The original Yahoo! website was a directory of other sites in a nicely organized and easily searched form. Rather than automatically finding new sites, the directory was built upon site descriptions dutifully submitted by website owners. That directory is still part of the Yahoo! site, and it's worth spending a few minutes to request that your site be added.

BizTips

Note that it can take months to be added to the Yahoo! directory.

Start by going to Yahoo! and clicking the Directory tab along the top, then search for your industry using high-level keywords. A broad search will include "related directory categories" in the results. If your search is too specific, you'll only see individual site matches and need to try again.

Once you're on the best category page, you'll see a link on the top right called "Suggest a Site." Click that link and you'll find that Yahoo! has two ways you can submit a commercial site. If you don't want to pay anything, you can submit for free, but it takes an unknown amount of time to add your file. Or you can opt for their special "7-Day Guarantee" which costs an exorbitant $299. Read the small print, though: even if you pay for the seven-day option, you'll find that it only guarantees that they'll evaluate your site within seven days, not that they'll include it. If they don't include the site, you're still out the $299.

BizTips

The 7-Day Guarantee is wildly out of line with the value of being in the Yahoo! Directory. Submit through the free system and then go back a month or two later to see if it's been included. You can resubmit your site every 30 to 60 days without penalty.

The Open Directory Project

The Open Directory Project, known informally as DMOZ, is an excellent alternative website directory. Found at www.dmoz.org, it's incorporated into a number of different search engines, including Google, AOL search, and Netscape search. DMOZ is a volunteer project with unpaid editors, however, so getting your site added to a given category depends on the luck of the draw. I've submitted sites and six months later not had them added, but I've also submitted sites in different categories and found them in the directory a few weeks later.

The submission process for DMOZ is typical for a directory site. Your first step is to search for companies like your own, and then choose the category that best matches your own business from the list of possible matches. This can be quite time consuming, particularly if you're a service provider.

Each category on DMOZ is listed along with the number of entries in that category shown in parentheses. For example, the DMOZ category Computers:Education: Internet has 108 entries, while Computers:Internet:On The Web:Personal Home-pages has 11,422 entries. If you have to choose between two or more appropriate categories, select the category with the least entries, so that your listing has a better chance of standing out from the crowd.

When you've found the best category, click the "suggest URL" link at the top of the page, and you'll see a long, wordy input form as shown in Figure 16.1. (I've scrolled the screen down a bit so you can see some of the input fields.)

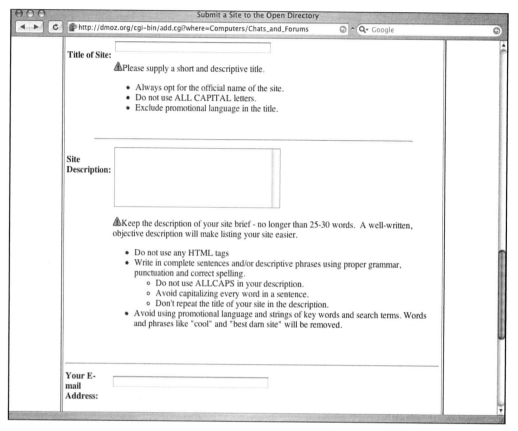

Figure 16.1: The process of submitting your site to the Open Directory Project can be time-consuming, but is well worth the effort.

Crafting a good description is important, and since you're likely to want a succinct description for other places, too, something you should save. One good place you can include your well-written site description is on your "link to us" page, as discussed in Chapter 15. Remember to sprinkle the description with your keywords, though ensure that it's still readable so that it won't be rejected by the DMOZ editor.

About.com

Another online directory of websites that's managed by volunteers is About.com. A commercial enterprise, the site can be more difficult to read, but again, the basic idea is to search the site for either your category of business or a few well-known competitors.

Most likely, you won't get to the right category directly, but on any page that's close to your desired category, you'll see a set of breadcrumb navigation elements on the top. On the page I landed on, I saw "You are here: About > Computers & Technology > PC Hardware / Reviews".

Surf around the site until you find a page with a small picture of a Guide at the top. Click the Guide's name and you'll be able to send them an e-mail message requesting that your site be included in their category. Make sure you include your website address, title, and a brief description that they can just cut and paste if they agree to add your site.

> **Memo**
>
> About.com was purchased by the *New York Times* early in 2005. Look for changes and more news-related content to appear as they integrate the two businesses.

Topical Web Directories and Search Engines

In addition to web-wide search engines, there are also topical search engines and web directories focused on offering a good starting point for people who don't want to match everything in the world. Finding these can be a bit more difficult, however. A good first stop is to use Google.

Finding these topical directories is a two-step process. First, search for your competitors' websites. If you have an online shoe store, search for "shoe store". A sculptor could search for "sculpture sculptor artist studio", and a bicycle designer could use "designer custom bicycle bike".

Now, for each of the top 5 or 10 entries, search Google to identify what sites point to that site. This is accomplished by prefacing your search with the special Google tag *link:*.

The sculptor's search results, shown in Figure 16.2, show sculptor.org, a directory of sculptors, as the top match. That's definitely a place to request a listing.

Most of the other search results are specific sculptors, but pay close attention to the specifics of the matching pages. One of the top matches is a sculptor's website, but it's actually the "links to other sculptors" page on that site. That's worth a quick visit to request they add your site.

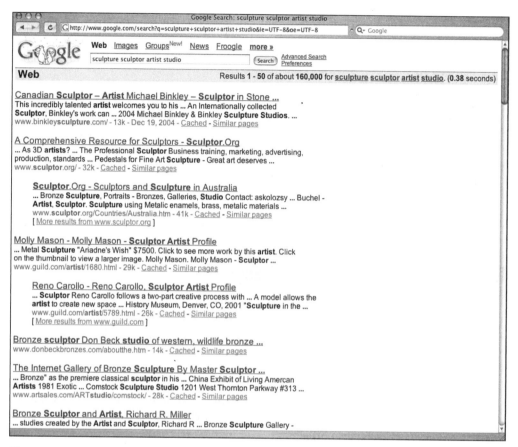

Figure 16.2: A sculptor can use Google to identify topical directories and other sculptors for linking.

Other sites are the art world's version of topical search engines: artist collectives. The matches include web pages for sculptors on guild.com, artsales.com, yourartlinks. com, collectiblestoday.com, artrealm.co.uk, and gallerysites.com. All of those should be investigated.

Continuing our process, the matches include a number of competing sculptors. For each matching site, you'll want to find out what sites point to their site. To find out who points to sculptor Bruce Gray, for example, search for "link:www.brucegray. com". This produces a list of sites that point to Bruce's website. Skim through the list to see if there are any directories shown. If so, add your site to each directory on the list.

If there isn't a link for adding new entries, but there's an e-mail address shown, send them a message requesting that they add your site, and list your site title (usually your business name), website address, and a 20- to 25-word description.

This process of going to the sites that point to your competitors will be re-examined shortly, when we consider how to request inbound links to your site with link exchanges.

Submitting Your Weblog to Blog Indices

If you are going to use a weblog as either an adjunct to your website or as the foundation of the site, there is another set of weblog- and RSS-related sites that you'll want to ensure know about your site.

Memo

As weblogs are exploding onto the scene—over 14,000 new ones every day—it should be no surprise that there are hundreds of blog index sites and directories. Start with the ones listed here and then explore a bit to find additional options. One excellent strategy for this is to look at what indices your favorite weblogs list at the bottom of their pages: you should show up everywhere they show up.

Since many weblogs are noncommercial, some of the weblog directories aren't appropriate for your business site. An excellent place to start is with the five weblog directories listed in the following table.

Weblog Directories

Site Name	Web Address
Syndic8	www.syndic8.com
NewsIsFree	www.newsisfree.com
Technorati	www.technorati.com
Daypop	www.daypop.com
Feedster	www.feedster.com

There is also an extensive list of weblog directories that Robin Good has assembled on his website, with much useful and informative commentary. I don't agree with all of his site assessments, but his list remains a good place to find the most important weblog directories.

BizTips

Robin's site has two different weblog directory lists, one is free, and for the other you have to pay a modest fee to download. The free list can be found at www. masternewmedia.org/rss/top55.

Requesting Inbound Links

As you browse the web, you'll find other sites that you like and that you'd like to request they link to you. This is known in the industry as cross-linking and it can be a powerful way to improve your findability with potential customers and also help your PageRank with Google.

A word of warning, though. Cross-linking is most effective when the two sites are similar in topic. Some sites are just blatant lists of links and you want to avoid those so-called link farms like the plague because they're not going to drive any meaningful traffic to your site and because many search engines detect and automatically ignore links on link farms.

Another strategy for creating cross-links is to contact the owners of every site that links to any of your competitors. You can identify this list by using the "link:" special search on Google, as shown earlier in this chapter.

When you identify a site with which you'd like to swap links, your best bet is to communicate via e-mail with the site owner. You can almost always ascertain their e-mail addresses from their websites, or use a contact form to query them directly.

Don't offer links from your home page, however, since that real estate is just too valuable for link exchanges. Instead, add a page to your site that's just for links to other sites, perhaps called "Elsewhere on the Web," "More Industry Web Sites," or something similar.

Here's the type of e-mail I send to a website owner when I'm requesting a link exchange:

> Leo,
>
> While surfing the web I came across your site, Ask-Leo.com, and was impressed with the depth of your knowledge, the value of your answers, and the volume of questions you've fielded.
>
> I have a similar Q&A site focused on Mac, Linux, and business topics, but we're definitely working in the same space.
>
> I'd like to link to your site and would request that you add a link to my site so we can enjoy the benefits of a link exchange.
>
> If you're interested, I'd suggest the following link:
>
> > Ask Dave Taylor <http://www.askdavetaylor.com/>
> >
> > From technical questions to publishing, parenting to business topics, Dave's ready to answer anything, free!
>
> I'll add a link to your site on my sitemap page, found at http://www.askdavetaylor.com/sitemap.html. I'm hoping we can work together!
>
> Best regards,
>
> Dave Taylor

There are software programs that can automate the tedious process of finding related sites and sending out link exchange requests, but you should shy away from them. First off, these programs aren't narrow enough in identifying compatible sites, and secondly, sending a form letter is sure to minimize your success in gaining additional inbound links.

Don't expect every message you send to result in a link. If you have 50 percent of the recipients respond favorably, you're doing well. Since it doesn't take long to send out a request to a dozen site owners, however, it's still time well spent.

Creating Mini-Stores

If you have products to sell, whether informational or physical goods, you can gain a lot of value from building rudimentary online stores in two of the biggest shopping centers on the Net, and in ensuring that your products are included in Google's shopping engine, Froogle.

In addition to the three profiled here, eBay, Yahoo!, and Froogle, there are a number of other venues worth exploring, including the popular Amazon Marketplace program.

Memo

Amazon actually has two very different seller programs, Advantage and Marketplace, with quite different terms and commission structures. Adding unique products that aren't already part of their database (as an artist would need to do) is an expensive undertaking, while offering discount pricing on books, music, video, consumer electronics, and other brand name merchandise already sold on Amazon can be quickly set up. Learn more about these programs at www.amazon.com/exec/obidos/subst/misc/sell-your-stuff.html.

Opening an eBay Store

You may think that eBay is completely focused on auctions and variable price sales, where customers set the value of a given product by bidding a certain amount, but eBay also has an entire shopping area of fixed-price products called *eBay Stores*.

There are a number of fees associated with selling through an eBay store, and to be eligible for an eBay store you need to be a registered eBay seller and have a feedback score of at least 20. A basic store costs $15.95 per month and allows you to have your product listing pages plus an additional five pages. More advanced stores can cost up to $499.95 per month, and include live 24-hour telephone support from eBay.

BizTips

The eBay store qualifications suggest that you should be buying and selling on eBay to qualify for a store, and therefore that the cost of the auctions should be tax-deductible as a business expense. Double-check with your accountant before you go crazy, though, just to be safe!

Just as eBay auctions have lots of little charges that add up to the seller's end-of-auction fee, so eBay Stores also have fees associated with each product you list. Each 30 days that a product is listed in your store costs $0.02 plus a percentage of the selling price that's calculated using a sliding scale of 8 percent of the first $25 in value and 5 percent of the rest of the price, up to $1,000. Above $1,000, there's an additional 5 percent fee for the amount above $1,000.

This means that if you list twenty $100 sculptures for six months and sell half of them on the very last day, you'll incur a total cost that's the monthly store plus the listing fees, plus the final transaction fees. A grand total of $50.87 in fees against $1,000 in sales. If you use eBay's popular PayPal program to process the transactions, PayPal will take an additional fee on the sale, too.

The fastest and easiest way to get started with an eBay Store is to download eBay's Turbo Lister program and import your inventory information. Turbo Lister is free to use (though you'll still have to pay the listing and merchant fees) and is found at http://pages.ebay.com/turbo_lister.

> **Memo**
>
> Wondering where that $50.87 figure came from? I calculated the end of auction fee as 8 percent of $25 plus 5 percent of $975, which is $2 plus $48.75. Then add a $0.12 listing fee since the auction is for one type of item listed for six months, and that's $50.87.

Joining the Yahoo! Shopping Program

While Yahoo! might be playing catch-up with its search engine, one area where Yahoo! has a leadership position is Yahoo! Shopping. It's quite popular; one in eight stores on the web are hosted by Yahoo! Small Business. Start at: http://smallbusiness.yahoo.com/merchant/.

There are three levels of Yahoo! Shop available for merchants, ranging from a starter setup at $39.95 per month and a flat 1.5 percent transaction fee to a professional store at $299.95 per month and a flat 0.75 percent transaction fee. Importantly, all Yahoo! Shops include customized domain names, so your website could be your Yahoo! store, for example, or you could have a store address similar to "store.yourdomain.com". Yahoo also has a free software application to enable quick store management, Yahoo! SiteBuilder, and a separate Catalog Manager for inventory management.

Unlike eBay, Yahoo! Shops requires that you have a merchant bank account for your business, an account that allows you to transact business online. This shouldn't be too difficult to set up, whether you're brand new or an established business. Just call your local bank and ask about the terms and conditions.

> **BizTips**
>
> Make sure that your merchant account enables you to conduct online transactions. Many banks have a higher transaction fee for online versus in-store merchant accounts.

Yahoo! Shops also offers a nicely integrated suite of tools that will help your online shop look professional, including a secure shopping cart and transaction management system, email verification of transactions, UPS shipment tracking, and settings so that Yahoo! notifies you automatically if any of your inventory levels drop below a preset threshold.

Figure 16.3 shows an example of an online store that's built entirely around the Yahoo! Shop merchant solution.

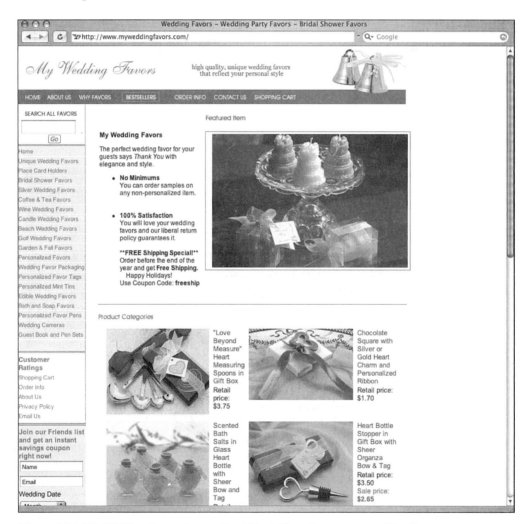

Figure 16.3: My Wedding Favors is actually a Yahoo! Shop. See www.myweddingfavors.com.

The more expensive Yahoo! Shop packages include a number of useful merchandising options, including gift certificates, cross-selling of products, a coupon manager, and support for building an affiliate program so you can empower others to help sell your products.

With its connection to Shopping.com, BizRate, Overture, Google AdSense, the Commission Junction affiliate program, and more, if you're selling products online, then Yahoo! Shops is well worth investigating as either an adjunct store or as the foundation of the commerce side of your site.

Joining the Froogle Merchant Program

Froogle is a pleasant alternative to the previous two, a free shopping search engine from Google. Getting your products in the Froogle database can be highly technical but it's worth it because being a part of Google can reap significant benefits. You sign up for Froogle at www.google.com/froogle/merchants/apply. You'll need to indicate how many products you have in your store, what type of merchandise you carry, whether you ship products overseas, and the specifics of your store name, website address, e-mail contact address, and so on.

It typically takes anywhere from two days to a week to receive approval from the Froogle team, at which point you'll start building your product data feed. While Google itself crawls your site, including your product pages, the Froogle system needs to know exactly what products you have available, in a very specific format. For each product you'll need to have the product web address, the name, the description, the web address of a picture of the product, the category that best matches the product, and the price.

The following listing provides an example section of a Froogle feed from FlowersFast, a site discussed earlier in Chapter 12.

> **offer_id:** A15-CS
>
> **name:** FTD Chicken Soup Bouquet
>
> **price:** 36.90
>
> **shipping:** 7.95
>
> **product_url:** http://flowersfast.com/fcsa.htm?source=froogle
>
> **image_url:** http://flowersfast.com/fcsl.jpg
>
> **category:** Shopping > Flowers > Get Well Selections
>
> **description:** Tender Loving Care—fresh from the heart.
>
> **brand:** FTD

offer_id: A16-BH

name: FTD Big Hug Bouquet

price: 36.90

shipping: 7.95

product_url: http://flowersfast.com/fbha.htm?source=froogle

image_url: http://flowersfast.com/fbhl.jpg

category: Shopping > Flowers > Father's Day Items

description: They'll drink in your gleeful message, as a plush bear hugs a mug full of fresh flowers.

brand: FTD

This isn't something you want to build yourself! It's not even something that you want your web developer or IT person to build by hand. Have a programmer create a simple application that goes through your product database and outputs the data in the form that Froogle needs.

Once you've built your data file, Froogle requires that it be sent to them via a crude file transfer mechanism called FTP. There are many FTP applications available for Windows and Macintosh, and the actual uploading process is straightforward, if unpolished.

That's all there is to it. The Froogle folk will check the feed to ensure it's in the correct format; then you can upload new data feeds as you add new products or change pricing, as frequently as once each day.

The Least You Need to Know

- While crawlers like Google will find your site automatically, you should submit your site information to Yahoo!, the Open Directory Project (DMOZ), and About.com.

- If you have a weblog, you can submit information about it to a variety of weblog search engines, too.

- Businesses with physical products often find great value in creating additional storefronts at eBay and Yahoo!.

- Google's Froogle shopping search system allows you to include your products for free and is a great adjunct to having your own store.

Chapter 17

Becoming an Online Expert

In This Chapter

- ◆ Learning to give information away
- ◆ How to be popular on mailing lists
- ◆ Learning from discussion boards
- ◆ The scoop on weblogs and weblog comments
- ◆ Figuring out what's happening in Usenet groups

Instant messaging, IM for short, is a simple technology that lets you directly communicate with someone else on the Internet. Chatting happens by sending lines of text back and forth, so it hasn't taken long for shortcuts and cryptic acronyms to invade the world of IM. The most important of these for our purposes is TANSTAAFL, which stands for "There Ain't No Such Thing As A Free Lunch."

In many ways, this chapter is all about that truth, that there is no such thing as a free lunch when you're growing your business online. Retail shop owners know this intuitively, that you can build the most beautiful store in town, but if no one knows about it, you'll go out of business before you start earning a profit.

Offering your knowledge to the online world is good because you're giving back to your community and helping people learn more about your industry and profession. But philanthropy doesn't grow a business and doesn't pay the mortgage, so there's got to be another reason to devote some of your precious time sharing your expertise with the community: becoming seen as an expert establishes your business online and can drive significant traffic to your website.

There are lots of ways you can share your expertise with the online community, the worst of which can produce the opposite effect to what you desire, making you a pariah in the community. Obviously, it's critical to know the best strategy and stay far away from the worst.

> **BizTips**
>
> Recalibrate your thinking to get the most value out of this chapter. Stop thinking in terms of trade secrets and confidentiality and start thinking about sharing information and educating your customer base.

Information Wants to Be Free

When a potential customer comes into your store and asks about your merchandise, you happily spend time explaining the strengths of your product and why it's an ideal purchase. You might even have brochures, fact sheets, specifications, or other literature that you give prior to them departing the store.

If that same customer approaches you through your website and asks about your products and about the market space itself, do you willingly share information in the same way?

Earlier we talked about taking all the questions that customers ask and turning them into a Frequently Asked Questions (FAQ) area on your site or even creating a Q&A format weblog to disseminate this information. Those are both excellent steps on the path to becoming an online expert, but they're still passive in the sense that your potential customers still have to come to you before they achieve enlightenment. The prototypical "guru on the mountaintop" just doesn't sell as much enlightenment as the "guru on the street."

The knowledge that you have about your industry and profession needs to be out on that street, too. You need to be spreading enlightenment wherever there are people seeking it.

Service providers often leverage their knowledge into information products that they can sell or seminars that can generate revenue for their company. Those are smart strategies, but they'll find that there are more buyers and more attendees if they give away some of their knowledge rather than put a price tag on everything.

Who Are These Experts?

One way to gauge who are industry experts is to skim through industry publications. Who gets quoted? Why? What about that person makes them more expert than you? Further, those industry experts are sharing their insight and wisdom with the populace, and it's not a coincidence that they're also the most successful people in the industry.

In your business community, there are seminars sponsored by different clubs and organizations every week. The people that speak at these events are sharing their knowledge with the audience. Do attendees think, "Gosh, I now know everything that she knows, there's no reason to ever call her," or do they think, "Wow, this woman sure knows what she's talking about! I need her card so we can call her"?

 BizTips

Business cards and brochures are inexpensive and invaluable. Always have lots on hand.

There's a critically important idea here. Not only does information want to be free, but the people who benefit from free information are the first to pay for even more wisdom from an expert. Giving away information, sharing your expertise, is actually a very savvy marketing strategy that can quickly build your customer list while also raising your visibility in the community.

To translate this into the online world, you need to devote the time to participate in relevant discussion forums, mailing lists, and similar online venues so that you can both learn from your customers and establish your expertise in your customer community.

A couple that runs a café and bookstore, for example, could participate in discussion groups about the esoteric world of coffee and book groups. A store that sells cellular telephone equipment might allocate an hour each day to have a salesman answer questions on a popular cell phone mailing list. A published writer could join an authors group and quickly become the resident expert about contract negotiations and offer insight into what happens to a book project after an author finds a publisher.

There are thousands of ways that you can become involved with the online community, but they all have one thing in common: You're sharing your knowledge and time with your customer community and building a reputation as an expert.

The Secret Benefits of Being an Online Expert

This expertise-building often spills over into publications (since reporters also read discussion groups), industry events (conference organizers often approach experts with invitations to speak), and business dealings with suppliers, buyers, and even companies with an interest in acquiring your firm (savvy business people are plugged into their community, online and off).

The title of this section is provocative and should have caused you to stop and think for a minute. Does information really want to be free? How can you be in business if you're giving your expertise away?

At this point I hope that you're thinking about this differently.

A consultant meets with a client and explains how his services can help them achieve their business goals, without charging for the initial consultation. Retailers happily answer questions about their products to potential customers. Your time spent online is similarly valuable. Or even more so, because each time you answer one person's question, hundreds or thousands of potential customers are reading your response and learning about your business.

Mailing Lists

The discussion of mailing lists in Chapter 9 revolved around how to find lists that were thematically relevant to your industry or product line. It didn't talk about whether you should participate in the discussion and if so, how best to present yourself to the online community.

The answer is straightforward: If you're seeking to grow your business online, you *must* participate in customer mailing lists and share your knowledge—or even ask questions—with the rest of the group. However, note that slick salespeople who constantly promote and hype their own products are soon shunned or kicked out of online communities.

E-mail as Advertisements

Every single message you send to a mail-ing list is a virtual calling card, a chance for you to advertise your business and gain new customers. But wait! If this is as far as you get in this chapter, you'll find that the earlier prediction about possibly becoming a pariah will come true, because in the online world *your advertising is peripheral to the knowledge and information you're sharing.*

BizTips _____

Advertising being peripheral to information is beautifully illus-trated on the Google search results pages. There are ads shown, but there's no question that the focus of the page is on the search results themselves.

You're a professional wedding photographer and part of a busy mailing list for both amateur and professional photographers. A question arises from an otherwise un-known participant, "My brother's getting married and wants me to shoot the wed-ding. Should I do it, or should he hire a professional?"

There are two ways you can answer this question. You can take the easy way out and respond with something like:

> Weddings come once in a lifetime. Hire a professional. I'm available: visit www.mywebsite.com to learn more.

I hope you can see where sending out that message would be a tragic, potentially unrecoverable mistake. Marketing yourself online is all about *sharing your knowledge,* remember; not about spreading your pitch.

Beware _____

Most online communities are quite forgiving about mistakes, because every-one was new to the group at some time, and everyone forgets about the group rules occasionally. Just as in real life groups, however, there are some gaffes, some mistakes, some things you can say that are unforgivable and that will taint you forever. One mis-take of this gravity is to post a crass marketing or advertising message. Don't do it. It's better to not respond at all if you can't find a way to answer in an informative manner.

Here's an alternative answer that offers good insight to the audience and simultaneously establishes your credentials as an experienced professional. Always remember that the entire list is reading your response, too, not just the questioner:

> That's a tough call. Most pro photographers avoid shooting their own family events because if something goes wrong, you don't just have an unhappy client, you have a furious brother, sister, or cousin.
>
> If you're looking to build your portfolio, volunteer to shoot weddings where you don't know more than one or two attendees, but my advice from 18 years of shooting weddings is to avoid the potential wedge that could be driven in your relationship with your brother and hire someone else to shoot the wedding.
>
> Then you can attend and *enjoy* the wedding!

This simple message offers good advice, establishes the credibility of the author, and therefore justifies why the advice is worth following.

The Importance of Signatures

The secret to these mailing list postings isn't in the message itself, however; it's in the so-called signature block that's included immediately after the message.

Buzzwords

A signature block is a sequence of three to five lines of text that is automatically appended to each and every message you send out, whether to individuals or mailing lists.

Marketing yourself through mailing lists is all about having content wrapped in marketing materials. The marketing materials aren't typically in the message itself, though, but in this signature block.

A good signature block contains your name, contact e-mail address, website address, phone number, and a one- or two-line advertisement for your business. Signatures are something that everyone on a mailing list reads, particularly after reading a cogent and thoughtful message.

Here are some exemplary e-mail signatures:

```
Steve Loyola <sloyola@bestwebbuys.com>
Best Web Buys <http://www.bestwebbuys.com/>
Forbes "Best of the Web" pick for Comparison Shopping
Money magazine's choice for "Textbook Bargains"
```

```
John Locke
Manager, Freelock Computing
The Open Source for Business Solutions
http://www.freelock.com
john@freelock.com 206-579-4836


Dan Murray
Internet Marketing Strategist
RavenwoodMarketing.com
Performance-based search marketing
dan@rmiug.org
ph 303-447-3475



Salvatore F. Iozzia
accelerator/owner
Chain Reaction Web — <http://www.chainreactionweb.com>
Toll Free (800) 294-8182—support@chainreactionweb.com


* Kit (Riley) Cassingham, The B&B Lady * Sage Blossom Consulting *
            Member ISHC
http://www.TheBAndBLady.com     http://www.ECOnomicallySound.com
http://forum.TheBAndBLady.com   http://forum.ECOnomicallySound.com
            * (970) 626-2277 *
```

Notice that the specific information, length, and layout varies between these signatures, but that they all serve as effective mini-billboards. In all cases, if you'd just read an article written by one of them, their signature would convey more information and give you an avenue to learn more about their business.

If you really want people to be interested in your signature, you need to write thoughtful and informative messages. Don't *you* want to learn more about someone after you've heard them say something really smart or insightful? The more they pay attention to your signature, the more likely they are to visit your website, and that's what it's all about!

Another benefit of participating on mailing lists is that most lists now have online discussion archives, hundreds or thousands of web pages that are also indexed by Google and other search engines. Your message to a list not only can enlighten the members of the list, therefore, but hundreds or perhaps thousands of other people over time. And every one gets a clickable link to your website.

> **BizTips** _____
>
> When you include your website address in your signature, make sure that you preface it with the "http://" notation and that you either have the address at the end of the line or have a space after the address. This will help e-mail programs recognize it as a website address and automatically make it clickable.
>
> Having said that, when you include your website address on marketing collateral, business cards, fliers, and so on, I recommend that you _omit_ the "http://" notation because readers will already understand the context.

Mailing List Do's and Don'ts

Only answer questions where you have a lot to say or have great insight that hasn't already been offered by someone else on the list. Coming across as an expert isn't the same as monopolizing the conversation. Don't answer every question and don't feel obligated to participate in every discussion.

I've been on lists where someone only submits one or two messages a month, but because they have a reputation for expertise, each post is eagerly read and often saved or shared with others who aren't on the list.

Similar to your first few minutes at a party, a smart strategy for becoming a member of a mailing list is to wait a week or two before your first posting. Some lists are very formal and professional, while other lists commonly have contributors using lots of slang and industry jargon. Matching the predominant style of interaction will help you come across well and avoid any embarrassing gaffes.

Don't talk about politics, don't talk about religion, and don't talk about anything that's not directly related to your business, product line, or service. A software programmer might have strongly held political beliefs, but if they're seeking to improve their reputation in the industry and gain more programming jobs, their politics should be channeled to a different venue or remain offline completely.

Finding Good Mailing Lists

The two most common places to search for mailing lists are Yahoo! Groups (www.yahoo.com) and Topica (http://lists.topica.com).

Memo

Spelling counts. Grammar counts. Most importantly, coherence and politeness count. If someone disagrees with a message you've written, even if his or her response is hostile and questions your bloodline or worldview, it's always in your best interest to respond politely and without rancor. If you need to go for a walk first, do so.

Never try to use sarcasm, and even humor can often backfire in the online world. The Golden Rule works wonderfully online: communicate with others the way that you'd like them to communicate with you.

A personal trainer, for example, could search for "fitness" or "exercise" or "trainer" and see what lists come up. Unfortunately, neither of these search engines can do an AND search, so looking for "personal trainer" would really be a search for "personal OR trainer" which, as you might suspect, would generate many useless results.

Another strategy for finding lists is to use Google, and search for the phrase "mailing list" along with two or three keywords. You might find yourself playing detective as you find individual messages and track backwards to a page that discusses the specific list.

BizTips

A good mailing list can quite literally change your professional life. I am a member of two or three lists that have helped me find new clients, identify new business opportunities, and make dozens of new friends and colleagues.

Finally, once you're on one mailing list, you can ask the participants of the list individually if they can recommend two or three other good lists that you should join.

Hanging Around Discussion Boards

While mailing lists are an excellent venue for establishing your reputation for expertise and friendliness, many online communities are moving to web-based discussion forums. Where your customers go, you should go, so identify the most popular discussion boards (which you can often do by just asking your current customers) and sign up.

Check the website of popular industry publications, as many of them now have discussion forums. A publication-sponsored board can be a great place to gain visibility in your industry and possibly garner some attention from the publication itself.

Additionally, a few Google searches will reveal a number of different discussion boards. For example, a landscape architect could search for

"landscape architect" (bbs | "discussion forum")

and quickly find links to a number of different discussion boards in his field.

BizTips

Sophisticated Google search techniques are discussed in Chapter 4. The above search can be read as search for the phrase "landscape architect" along with either the word "bbs" or the phrase "discussion forum."

Discussion boards are similar to the cocktail lounge at a trade conference, where serious discussions are interspersed with irreverent comments and even some misinformation from competitors. As with mailing lists, the smartest strategy with a discussion board is to spend a few hours or longer reading through the current discussions, paying particular attention to writing style, level of accuracy, formality, and how much contributors talk about their own work and projects.

You'll find that on some discussion boards everyone just talks about themselves, while on other boards many authors don't even have a one-line signature, relying instead on interested participants reading their online bios.

Discussion boards allow you to include a signature with each posting you make, but most people try to minimize their signature to a single line in this context. Instead, if the discussion board has user profiles, go and fill yours out to highlight your business and be sure to include a website address.

Memo

Some mailing lists and discussion boards have moderators, people that serve as an editorial control board to ensure that the discussions stay on-topic and polite. If your submissions are polite and professional, then you'll probably never even know they're around.

If you're not sure about whether a particular message you'd like to send is appropriate, an excellent strategy is to e-mail the proposed message to one of the moderators of the group, asking for their approval. If they like the message, you've raised your visibility with an opinion leader in the group, and if they don't like the message, they'll almost always tell you why, avoiding a potentially embarrassing mistake on your part.

Weblogs and Weblog Comments

In addition to mailing lists and discussion forums, weblogs are becoming another venue where you can find opportunities to answer questions and share your expertise. It's a slightly different environment, because weblog comment etiquette suggests that you never want to say that the original author is wrong (even if they are). After all, it's their weblog and you're just adding your two cents.

To find weblogs that are worth reading, you can use any of the search engines discussed earlier, including Technorati, Feedster, Syndic8, and Daypop. Figure 17.1 shows the result of a printer going to Feedster and searching for "commercial printer".

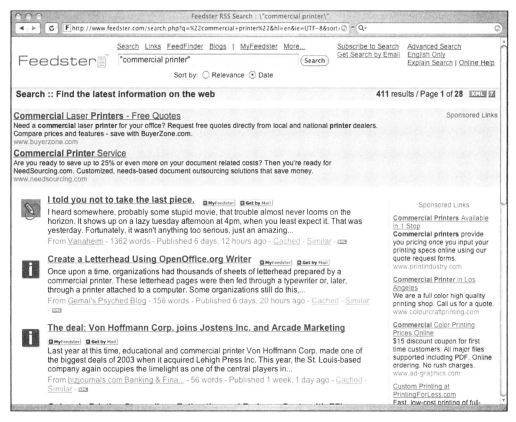

Figure 17.1: Feedster can find Weblog entries related to a specific company, product, or industry.

The majority of weblog owners take their sites quite seriously, and will quickly delete any comments left that are rude, insulting, crassly commercial, or even just politely representing an opposing viewpoint. Some weblog authors will post their own comments in response to your addition, while others never add comments of their own, preferring their readers to continue the discussion.

In all of these cases, rather than a cocktail lounge, it's best to think of visiting a weblog as being invited into someone's home for a small gathering. You're only allowed to stay while you remain a positive influence on the gathering.

> **BizTips**
>
> A best practice: weblogs where the author responds to comments creates a much more cohesive community than those where the weblog author posts articles and then apparently ignores any subsequent discussion.

Usenet Groups

Years ago Usenet discussion groups were the main place where people built communities online, ranging from the purely social to the professional. Lacking meaningful moderation and the ability for articles to be cancelled after they've been posted, Usenet has become almost completely overrun by irrelevant postings and spam.

Depending on your profession or industry, however, you might just get lucky and find that there's a Usenet group that has a majority of interesting and useful articles. Start by searching at Google Groups (http://groups.google.com) for articles that discuss a topic of interest.

As an example, a search for "yoga instructor" reveals that there are 1,560 matching articles, of which the first is listed as being in a group called "misc.kids.pregnancy" and the second in "misc.health.alternative". Rather than select the individual article, clicking on the name of the group produces a summary of the most recent discussions and can instantly reveal whether the group is worth joining or not.

> **Memo**
>
> Many Usenet groups also have Frequently Asked Questions (FAQ) postings that appear every few weeks. Keep an eye out for them and do read through them if you have the opportunity.

Guidelines for participating in Usenet discussions are quite similar to the guidelines for mailing lists. Read a few dozen messages to gauge voice and professionalism, be friendly and polite, and make sure that you add useful information to the discussion.

Don't forget to include your signature file, but with one important difference: Never include your e-mail address in your posting. Spammers often spider the Usenet archives to extract e-mail addresses, and by posting in a specific group, you also identify an exploitable interest.

That's why you'll often see e-mail addresses that look like "taylor@ NOSPAMintuitiveNOSPAM.com" where it's expected that humans will easily extract the real address for e-mail, while software programs will stumble and end up storing the wrong, bad address. The yoga article mentioned earlier in the Usenet group "misc.kids.pregnancy" has the author's e-mail address listed as "pliss@fakeaddress.com" for just this reason.

How important is Usenet nowadays? Not very. I've ordered the topics in this chapter by what I believe are their value to a businessperson. A good mailing list can be a fabulous resource, a discussion forum can be an enjoyable diversion, and weblogs can give you the chance to answer a rant or explain a perceived customer problem.

The Least You Need to Know

- Participating in an online community is about sharing your knowledge and helping others learn your craft. Advertising, while not forbidden, should always be secondary.

- A critical step toward becoming an online expert is to participate in a few industry- or product-specific mailing lists.

- Discussion boards can be found through various sites and searches and can also be an important place to share your knowledge and gain new connections in your community.

- An occasional search for weblog discussions about your product or industry can yield a superb venue for sharing your knowledge and helping customers understand your industry or business.

Chapter 18

Advertising Your Business with Google AdWords

In This Chapter

◆ Taking a closer look at AdWords

◆ Identifying great keywords

◆ Monitoring your campaign

◆ Writing ad copy that sells

The popularity of Google as a search engine has changed the entire advertising model on the web. Banners, pop-ups, and interstitials (ads shown between pages) are passé, bother viewers, produce poor results, and often cost much more than they're worth.

Google AdWords offers a different view of advertising where short text-only ads are displayed adjacent to search results. These ads represent a new advertising paradigm because they're contextually relevant rather than *interrupt-driven advertising*.

What's revolutionary about AdWords isn't the ad format, but the method that Google uses to determine which ads should be shown. AdWords advertisers list desirable keywords or search queries, then Google automatically includes the best matches as it generates search result pages. There's no fixed cost for these advertisements either.

> **Buzzwords** _____
>
> **Interrupt-driven advertising** is advertising that interrupts what you're doing and forces you to view the advertisement. Television commercials are interrupt-driven advertising, while sponsor billboards on the side of a soccer field are not.

All ad space is sold through a bidding process where the most sought-after keywords for advertisers produce the highest bids.

One more wrinkle: AdWords charges *per click*, not per display, so if five thousand people see your advertisement and none of them click on it, you'll owe Google nothing. If your advertisement underperforms, however, generating too few click-throughs for the impressions it receives, Google will automatically pull it out of the rotation and require that you modify the ad text or change your keywords.

It's all rather complex, but once you understand the basics, you'll realize that for as little as five or ten dollars per month, you could have your products and services included in AdWords ads and be creating new customers every day.

Understanding How AdWords Works

Imagine a new cell phone owner who seeks a hands-free headset for her Nokia phone. She searches for "buy nokia cell phone headset" and Google produces a set of matching web pages and a list of AdWords advertisements for various related companies.

Each of these advertisers has bid on one or more keywords or key phrases that match the Nokia query. Each time someone searches for, say, "cell phone" or "headset" and clicks on the advertisement the advertiser will pay Google a small fee. The advertisers at the top of the AdWords listing are generally those that have the higher per-click bids, and those at the bottom have the lower bids.

In extremely competitive categories, the highest bids might be a few dollars or more per click received, but many categories offer you the chance to have your ad included for as little as $0.05 to $0.10 per click.

You can cap your daily AdWords expenditure to spread your advertising budget across a period of time, rather than having it all consumed in the first day or two of your campaign. You can also specify a start and stop date for campaigns, so it's possible to have a campaign that only runs for a few days, or to have a series of teaser ads leading up to a holiday, industry, or national event.

AdWords advertisers have many different elements to consider when creating a new campaign, including the best keywords, start and stop dates, optimal bid price (which is impacted by desired placement in the search results), and the wording of the advertisement.

Finding the Best Keywords

The first, and most important, step in creating a new AdWords campaign is to identify the best keywords for your ad, keywords that will identify customers interested in buying your product or service. Your instincts might be quite poor in this regard, so it's imperative that you use research tools to ascertain what keywords will work best.

For example, a camera lens store might be tempted to bid on the keyword "lens" or "lenses", but then they'll be pointlessly advertising on searches for "replacement contact lenses", "design of home telescope lens", and "closest lens crafters Kansas City, MO".

You might think that having your ad display on overly broad keyword matches doesn't matter because you don't pay by the ad impression, only by the click. If your advertisement's ratio of impressions to clicks gets too high, however, Google will freeze your ad due to "underperformance." Even before that happens, your placement will begin to suffer because Google factors ad performance into ad placement.

Google offers a useful keyword suggestion tool as part of AdWords, but savvy AdWords experts also use a service called WordTracker (www. wordtracker.com) to research keywords and identify those that are best suited for a given ad campaign.

> **Memo**
>
> AdWords placement based on click-through performance is critical to keep in mind as you proceed with your advertising campaign. It's always preferable to be displayed less often but have a good click-through rate than to have lots of impressions but a lower rate.

Picking Good Keywords

Because AdWords is a completely different advertising medium, it's important to acknowledge that your gut instinct about good keywords might be wrong. To achieve the best possible results for your advertising expenditure, keyword research is critical. You don't always want to pick the most popular keywords in your industry. You want to pick keywords that are highly specific to ensure that you engage buyers while simultaneously being as general as possible to capture more potential customers.

Keyword advertising exists on a continuum from extremely general searches (think "shop online") to extremely specific ("buy large blue sweater free shipping"). This continuum also represents the product-buying cycle that starts with researching alternatives, then in-depth research on a specific product, then research on a vendor, and then, finally, the purchase transaction itself.

General search terms are going to produce the most ad displays, but the goal isn't to have lots of people see your advertisement; it's to have the *right people*, the people who are ready to buy your product, see your ad. This is an entirely different philosophy and one of the most difficult hurdles traditional advertisers face when moving to AdWords.

> **Memo**
>
> General keywords should bring customers to high-level pages on the site, and specific keywords should bring customers to detailed product information pages.

This also means that you should almost never have an AdWords ad lead to your business website home page. If you're paying to advertise at that high a level, you're probably wasting your ad budget on attracting visitors instead of buyers.

Working with WordTracker

There's a free WordTracker interface that was shown in Chapter 10, but it's worth paying for access to the full keyword research service for an advertising campaign. The results are more detailed and there are better tools available with a paid subscription.

After you've created a WordTracker account, log in and choose a "compressed keyword search" to begin your keyword research.

BizTips

When researching keywords remember that the data represents the previous 60 days of searches. This makes planning ahead for seasonal promotions quite difficult because the December/January searches, for example, aren't going to be indicative of what terms would be good keywords for a Valentine's Day promotion.

There are no easy answers to this dilemma other than to rely on your imagination and industry experience and, as you work more with WordTracker, perform important keyword searches immediately after holidays and save the results. A search late in February of 2005 would offer useful suggestions for an AdWords campaign starting in January of any year.

Start your searches with general terms. An online camera lens store could start with the general "camera lens", which analyzes the 352 million search queries in the WordTracker database to find the 500 most frequently occurring related search terms. This is shown in Figure 18.1.

The data produced by WordTracker gives you an immediate sense of the frequency of searches for each of the terms specified. The phrase "camera lens" has a count of 248, which means that there were 248 search queries in the last 60 days on the sites WordTracker analyzes. Since the WordTracker data isn't from all online search engines—Google isn't included, for example—there's a multiplier that maps the count value to a predicted number of searches across the entire Internet on a *daily basis* that's shown as "Predict." "Camera lens" has a count of 248, which leads WordTracker to suggest that there are 225 searches using this exact keyword phrase across the entire Internet each day.

Knowledge of your industry segment now comes into play when narrowing down keyword results. Sigma, Canon, and Nikon are all brands likely to be carried at a camera lens store, but searches for "Sigma camera lens" happen 35 times daily, "Canon camera lens" occur 32 times each day, and "Nikon camera lenses" is only sought 26 times each day.

There's also critical data about singular versus plural keyword searches here, too: "camera lens" is predicted to have 225 searches each day, while "camera lenses" is estimated to be searched for only 163 times each day.

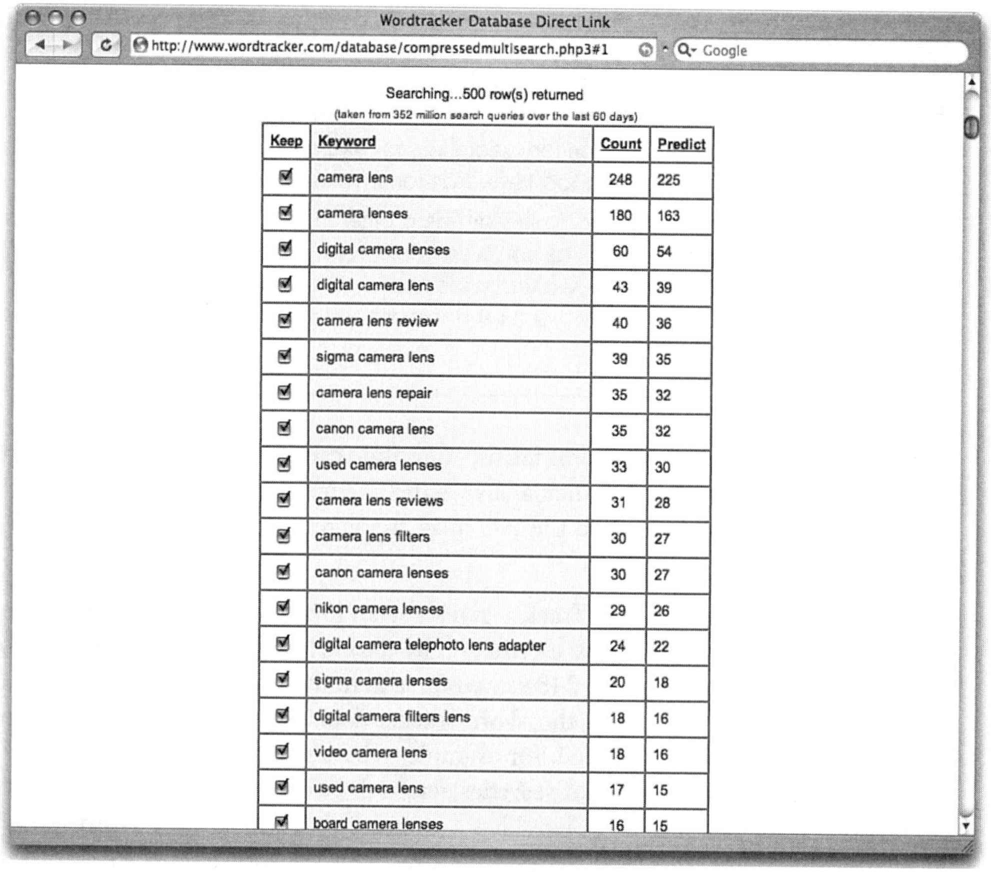

Searching...500 row(s) returned

(taken from 352 million search queries over the last 60 days)

Keep	Keyword	Count	Predict
☑	camera lens	248	225
☑	camera lenses	180	163
☑	digital camera lenses	60	54
☑	digital camera lens	43	39
☑	camera lens review	40	36
☑	sigma camera lens	39	35
☑	camera lens repair	35	32
☑	canon camera lens	35	32
☑	used camera lenses	33	30
☑	camera lens reviews	31	28
☑	camera lens filters	30	27
☑	canon camera lenses	30	27
☑	nikon camera lenses	29	26
☑	digital camera telephoto lens adapter	24	22
☑	sigma camera lenses	20	18
☑	digital camera filters lens	18	16
☑	video camera lens	18	16
☑	used camera lens	17	15
☑	board camera lenses	16	15

Figure 18.1: WordTracker offers detailed data and keyword suggestions.

Google AdWords allows you to associate an advertisement with an almost infinite number of different keyword terms and combinations, so a good AdWords strategy is to bid on "camera lens", "camera lenses", "digital camera lens", and "digital camera lenses", and then see which actually has the highest click-through rate.

BizTips

AdWords will automatically adjust your advertising campaign so that the most effective ads are displayed most often, and actually disable any campaign ads that have poor results.

Resist the urge to think of your advertising as a popularity contest. You do *not* want to simply pick the most frequently searched topics, because your goal isn't to have lots of ads displayed, it's to attract the right buyers, bring them to your site, and close the sale. There are many savvy AdWords buyers who have ads only shown a few times each week, but each time the searcher is pulled to the perfectly targeted ad, comes to the site, and purchases the product.

In addition to identifying what keywords you should bid on, WordTracker also helps you begin building a *negative keyword* list. Negative keywords let you avoid having your ad displayed on searches that aren't your target customer, or are your target customer, but just not at the desired point in their buying cycle. For example, if you're bidding on camera lenses, you might have "repair" as a negative keyword because you don't want to match "camera lens repair" as that's not your target customer.

Buzzwords

A **negative keyword** is a word or phrase for which, if it's included in the search query, your advertisement shouldn't be shown. You can either use these as block words in AdWords so that your ad will never show up with these searches, or bid a minimum amount on these keywords just to see what happens. A knife seller would identify "make" as a negative keyword to avoid matching searches for "how to make a knife".

Keyword Research with Google AdWords

Google offers a keyword research tool for AdWords customers, too, but unlike WordTracker, it offers no data about how frequently a given search might occur. The real strength of the Google keyword tool is that it has a far more sophisticated variation engine than WordTracker.

Figure 18.2 shows the Google keyword tool's three categories of suggested keywords associated with "camera lens", broken into More Specific Keywords, Similar Keywords, and Additional Keywords to Consider.

If you bid on the keyword phrase as entered into the keyword tool, your ads will not only be shown on searches that are shown as More Specific, but also on those that are listed as Expanded Broad Matches, too. It's critical to the success of your campaign that you closely examine the Expanded Broad Matches list and add to your negative keywords list any searches that aren't relevant to your specific product line or businesses.

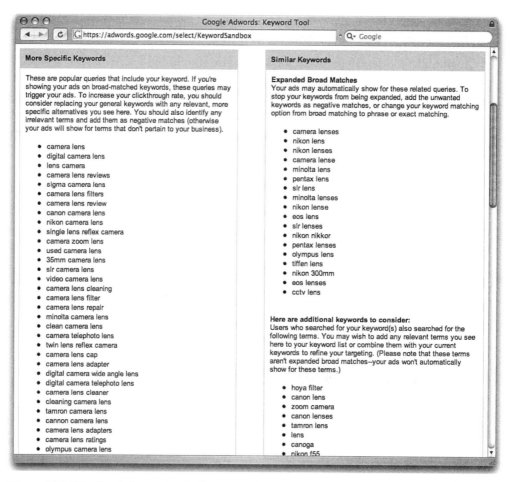

Figure 18.2: The Google keyword tool offers excellent alternative keywords, but no predicted or actual search frequency data.

In this instance, since our store only sells camera lenses, a search for "cctv lens" (video lenses, not camera lenses) will be a waste of money and should be blocked with a negative keyword.

Creating an Ad Campaign

An advertiser creates campaigns that include one or more AdGroups, each of which contains one or more individual ads tied to specific keywords. You can specify a maximum cost per day for each campaign so you can ensure that your advertising budget extends through the duration of the campaign, not just the first few days. Each specific keyword in each AdGroup can have a separate maximum cost-per-click bid price, too.

Before we start, a word of warning: Google suggests that this is a simple four-step process, but you'll see that there are actually more steps involved. Not a lot more, but certainly more than four discrete tasks.

Step 1: Language and Location Targeting

To create an AdWords campaign, click on "create new campaign" and then choose between a global or nationwide campaign, a regions and cities campaign, or a customized campaign. If your business is limited to a geographic area, choose one of the latter to ensure that your ads are only shown to candidate customers. A customized campaign only displays ads for searchers within a specified distance from a location, while regions and cities only shows your ads to people in the specified location. If you can ship throughout the nation or globally, then global or nationwide is your best choice.

Step 2: Create AdGroups

The second step in creating a campaign is to create an AdGroup, as shown in Figure 18.3. Notice that this figure also shows the five fields of an AdWords advertisement: headline, description line 1, description line 2, display URL, and destination URL.

The headline is the title of the ad, and it's the most important two or three words in the entire advertisement. If it doesn't draw the attention of the web searcher, then the rest of the descriptive text will be useless.

The description, which should not be longer than 70 characters, should be engaging and entice users to click on the advertisement. It can be quite a challenge, but using the Sponsored Links tool to read through competing descriptions can serve as excellent inspiration.

BizTips

Before you create your own headline, use the Google Sponsored Links tool to view all the advertisements currently shown for your search terms. Go to www.google.com/sponsoredlinks to get started. Remember, your headline is competing with all the advertisements shown.

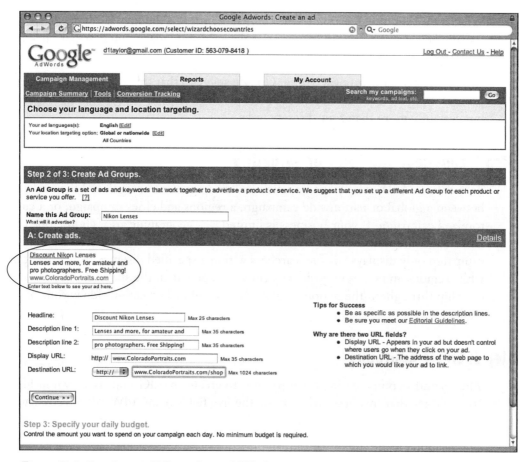

Figure 18.3: Creating an AdGroup for an AdWords campaign.

There are two website addresses associated with an advertisement, which can be confusing. Most advertisers have the display URL, the website address that's shown in the advertisement, be the domain name of the site. The destination URL is the address of the specific page visitors will be sent to when they click on your advertisement. It should also be the page on your site that's most likely to convert these people into buyers.

After you've done what you feel is a reasonably good job with your advertising information, it's time to move to the third step in creating an advertising campaign.

Step 3a: Choose Keywords and Maximum Cost-Per-Click

Here's where AdWords can be a bit confusing. The third step is to specify your daily budget, but before you can do so, it's time to specify the keyword list that you want to use with your new advertisement. This is where all the earlier research with WordTracker and Google Keyword Tool will pay off, as you'll have real data upon which to base your keyword list, not just guesses.

AdWords lets you bid on three different classes of keyword phrases: broad matches, phrases, or exact matches. There's a subtle notational difference between the three, as shown in the following table.

Google AdWords Keyword Specification

Keyword Phrase	Type of Match	Example Matching Search
camera lens	broad	fix broken lens and camera
"camera lens"	phrase	buy new camera lens
[camera lens]	exact	camera lens

Enter a few keywords or key phrases, remembering the three notational options listed in the previous table. I'll use "Nikon lens", "Nikon lense" and "Nikon lenses" in all three forms, broad, phrase, and exact. The second key phrase is a misspelling. Don't forget to add them to your research list! Common misspellings and typos are important sources of lower-priced keywords. And while I'm talking about misspellings and typos, it's worth popping back to WordTracker, too, because the WordTracker system also has a slick misspellings tool.

Once you've entered a list of keywords and key phrases, Google will display them all, along with a suggested maximum cost-per-click bid. Typically, this estimate will get you into the top two or three advertisements shown for each keyword, as shown in Figure 18.4.

Figure 18.4 shows that this is a competitive keyword space and that it's fairly expensive to be in the top few positions. This is also the first place in the AdWords system where you'll encounter information about how frequently each of your keywords occurs on a daily basis. You can see in Figure 18.4 that the broad key phrase "Nikon lens" should, on average, generate 140 clicks per day on your ad (which means that it'll be shown considerably more times than 140), each of which will, on average, cost $0.71 for the click. That'll cost you an estimated $98.34 each day, with an average position of 1.2 for that broad search.

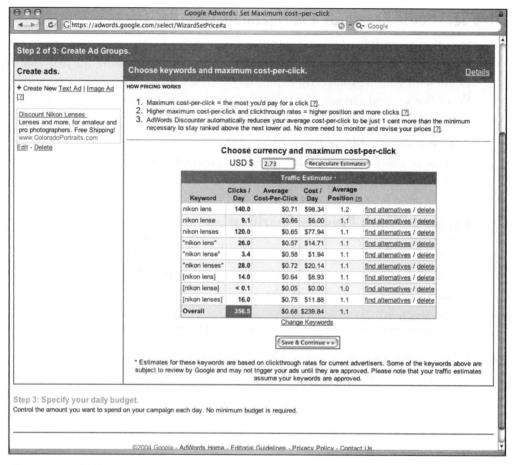

Figure 18.4: AdWords estimates traffic and average position for a set of keywords given a maximum cost-per-click bid of $2.73.

The overall predicted statistics for this ad group is 356 clicks at an average of $0.68 per click for a daily total of $239.84. You could run with this value and use the Daily Budget to limit your expenditure, but it's a much smarter move to enter a lower maximum cost per click and see what happens.

Changing the maximum cost per click from $2.73 to $0.68 dramatically lowers the cost of the ad without significantly impacting the net results. Fewer clicks per day (291) and an average cost per click of $0.38 produces a daily expense of $107.97 with an average position of 1.7.

Memo

Your maximum cost per click shouldn't be computed based on your desired position, however, but based on your actual return on investment for the product or service that you're selling. If you run an advertisement and ascertain that only one out of each 200 potential customers buys your product, and that you earn a profit of $75 on each sale, then your advertising must cost less than $0.38 per click or you're losing money.

Far too many businesses that get involved with AdWords ignore the return on investment (ROI) of their ad campaigns and do what AdWords professionals call *ego bidding*. That's a bad business strategy and is certainly not going to produce good results in the long term.

Once you've estimated your ROI and decided on a reasonable maximum cost-per-click bid, you can save the ad group and either create another ad group or continue to step three.

Buzzwords

Ego bidding is bidding whatever price is necessary to have your advertisement appear in the #1 position.

Step 3b: Specify Your Daily Budget

Google suggests a daily advertising budget for your new ad group that will ensure that your advertisement appears each time someone searches on any of your keywords or key phrases. The AdWords suggestion for the Nikon Lens campaign is $170.00 per day. Fortunately, you can adjust this figure if it starts out too high (as it probably will). Remember that your monthly ad fee will be 30 times your daily budget. A $100-per-day budget will produce an end-of-month advertising bill of $3,000.

When you activate your first ad campaign, AdWords will show it as "active," but it'll actually be held for a few days waiting for someone in the AdWords team to review the ad, check the destination website, and make sure everything is okay. Once it's approved, then you'll finally begin to appear in search results.

Editing and Modifying Your Campaign Settings

Once you've created your first ad campaign and started to have advertisements displayed, you'll be able to change your maximum price-per-click for specific keywords, your maximum budget per day, and other critical settings. Unfortunately, these options are presented in a bewildering fashion with buttons, text links, and features that are only accessible after jumping to intermediate pages.

The Campaign Summary offers a lot of useful information on active and completed promotions. Notice especially the Campaign Daily Budget and negative keywords sections, as seen in Figure 18.5.

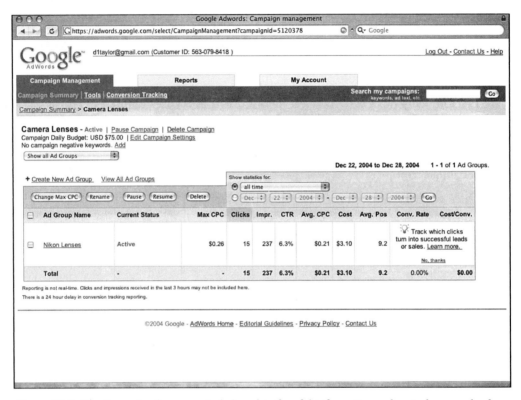

Figure 18.5: The Campaign Summary includes a lot of useful information and control over each ad group.

This campaign has just started, so the clicks and impressions are still low, but already the summary shows that the "Nikon Lenses" ad group has generated a 6.3 percent click-through rate with an average cost-per-click of $0.21.

Note here that there's a critical bit of small print on the Campaign Summary page: "Reporting is not real-time. Clicks and impressions received in the last 3 hours may not be included here." The lack of true real-time reporting has tripped up more than one advertiser who sits poised over their AdWords report, waiting to see the effect of a new ad campaign, additional placement, higher bid, or a similar change.

There are a number of important settings accessible from the Edit Campaign Settings link, and you should always go to the Campaign Settings area at the beginning of any campaign. This is where you can change the daily advertising budget for the campaign, specify a stop date for the campaign, and indicate whether or not to have Google automatically optimize the ads, all shown in Figure 18.6.

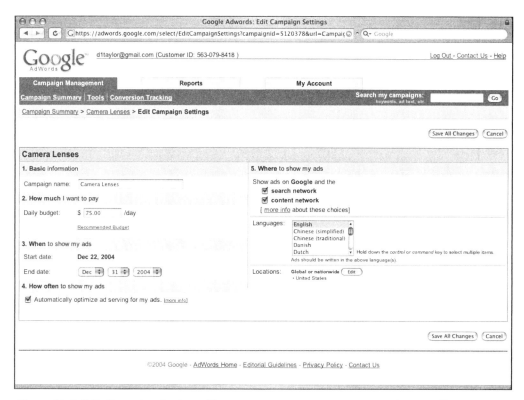

Figure 18.6: Edit Campaign Settings offers access to many important settings that can affect the success of a campaign.

Always allow this optimization as it's one of the great features of AdWords. Without any intervention, Google tracks click-through rates on your different ads and automatically begins to show those ads with a higher CTR more frequently than those with a lower CTR. This means that you will see better and better results for your advertising over the course of a campaign, and by the end of the campaign your top performing advertisement will be shown far more often than any other.

Another critical choice on the Edit Campaign Settings page is whether you want to have your advertisements shown just in Google search results (the "search network"), just on third-party AdSense web pages that match your topic (the "content network"), or both. By default, Google chooses both networks, but many in the AdWords community have found that the search network offers better results than the content network. You should pay attention to your results and shut off the less valuable network if it isn't profitable.

Setting Per Keyword Maximum Cost-Per-Click

There's one more setting that's important to tune before beginning your advertising campaign, and that's changing your maximum CPC (Cost-Per-Click) for individual keywords. This is accomplished by clicking into a specific ad group, which produces a page similar to Figure 18.7.

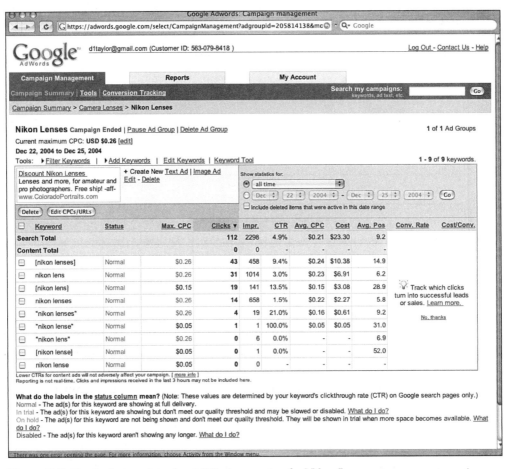

Figure 18.7: Results from a three-day AdWords campaign for Nikon Lenses, at an average maximum CPC of $0.26.

Notice the button Edit CPCs/URLs in Figure 18.7. Select all of the active keywords in the campaign, and then click the button to move to Change CPCs and URLs, as shown in Figure 18.8.

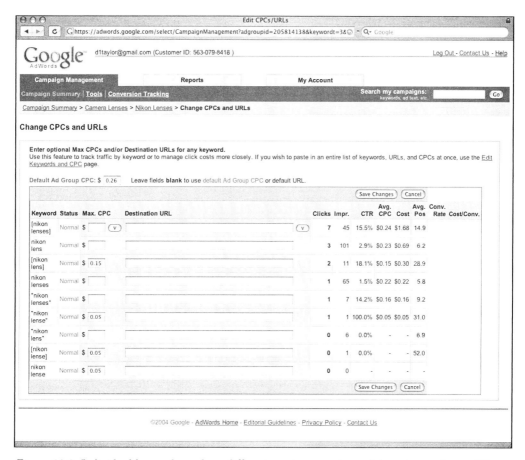

Figure 18.8: Individual keywords can have different maximum cost-per-click settings and even different destination URLs, all within the same ad group.

The exact match key phrase *[Nikon lens]* has a bid of $0.15, quite a bit lower than the $0.26 default ad group CPC, and keywords that include the misspelled word *lense* have the lowest allowed max CPC bid of $0.05 to experiment with whether they generate any useful leads.

Don't leave this page once you've changed your settings. Instead, click the Edit keywords and CPC text link near the top of the page and you'll move to an area that lets you see all your keywords and maximum CPC presented as text. The key phrase

Nikon lense with a max CPC bid of $0.05, for example, is shown as *Nikon lense ** 0.05.* Don't worry about understanding this notation, just notice the critically important Estimate Traffic button on this page.

By using the Google estimate traffic capability, you can fine-tune the max CPC of each keyword to get the optimal placement and display frequency for your advertising. Figure 18.9 shows the traffic estimates for my current maximum cost-per-click bid values. The two searches where I have the worst placement at the current settings are *[Nikon lens]* and *"Nikon lenses"*, where my estimated average position will be 8.3 and 4.6, respectively.

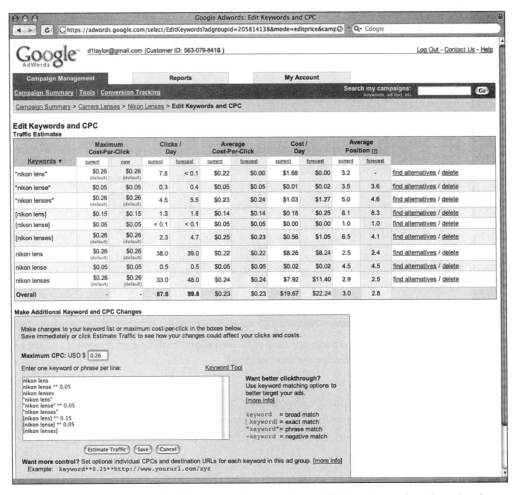

Figure 18.9: Edit Keywords and CPC gives you fine control over CPC per keyword, with predicted traffic and position values for the new amounts.

Without modifying the overall Maximum CPC, I'll bump up my max CPC for *[Nikon lens]* to see if I can get into the top five. To do this, I change the $0.15 max CPC by changing the line "[Nikon lens] ** 0.15" to "[Nikon lens] ** 0.30" in the lower box, then clicking on Estimate Traffic again. The result is shown in the "forecast" column: Jumping up to $0.30 max CPC puts me at average position 3.1.

That's a bit too much, however, so I'll drop it down to $0.25 and see what happens to my predicted position by again modifying the line from "** 0.30" to "** 0.25". The result is a predicted average position of 4.0. That's a good result, so I'll save the changes and launch my campaign!

Monitoring Your AdWords Campaign

Once your campaign has been running for a few days, you'll be able to access detailed campaign reports that list keywords, the maximum cost-per-click for each keyword (you can adjust your maximum CPC for individual keywords), how many times your ad was shown for each keyword, how many times it was clicked, and the resultant click-through rate. There are additional AdWords statistics, too; average cost per click, overall cost, and the average position of your advertisement in the search results.

This is all illustrated in Figure 18.7, shown earlier. In that figure you can see that the total cost of this three-day campaign was $23.30 and that produced 112 click-throughs from 2,298 impressions, a good click-through rate of 4.9 percent. The average position of the advertisement was 9.2, which means that on average it was in position 9 or 10, that is, the ninth or tenth ad on the search results page.

The more useful information is found in the per-keyword information. Here I can ascertain that the key phrases *[nikon lens]* and *[nikon lenses]* had the best CTR, 9.4 percent and 13.5 percent, respectively. These two exact matches also accounted for over half of the click-throughs and both also had very low positions, an average of 14.9 for *[nikon lenses]* and 28.9 for *[nikon lens]*.

The statistics let you ascertain your visitor acquisition cost against each keyword pattern, too. It cost $10.38 to pull 43 customers with the *[nikon lenses]* keyword ($0.24 per click), while the ad *[nikon lens]* did considerably better, costing only $0.15 per click to pull in 19 visitors, a total expenditure of only $3.08.

BizTips

Remember that it's critical you always keep your ROI costs in mind when looking at the statistics. If you make $10 profit off the sale of your product, are paying $1.15 per click, and are only seeing 10 percent of these new visitors making a purchase, you're losing money on your AdWords campaign.

Finally, in three days no one searched for *nikon lense*, and only one person searched for *[nikon lense]* or *"nikon lense"*. It might be safe to jettison these misspellings as being too rare to be worth the effort.

The AdWords experts pay very close attention to their reports pages, constantly adjusting both their maximum CPC and the wording of their ads to minimize the expense and maximize the results.

Writing Good Ad Copy

Producing high-yield advertisements is about more than just picking the right keywords. It's also about writing good ad copy, a task that's considerably more difficult when there are only 70 characters available. The goal is to create AdWords advertisements that compel people to click and come to your site.

The first important rule is that the headline should match the user's search, if possible. Bidding on overly vague key phrases can cause a mismatch, so one strategy for ensuring that the headline is relevant to the searcher is to err on the side of using very specific keywords. You can also create different ad headlines for different keyword sets.

BizTips

The mantra of all good advertisers is *test, test, test!* Run 2 advertisements with different wording, or, heck, 50 different versions of an advertisement and see which produces the best results. Then create 20 new variants based on that ad, again and again, until you've identified the best possible ad wording to bring in your customers.

This also holds true with what words or phrases you bid on. Keep trying different variations and track all your click-through data (a tool like www.ClickThruStats.com can be a neat solution) so that you can simultaneously identify which keywords or key phrases produce the very best results for your advertising dollar.

Your ad needs to stand out from other ads that will be displayed along with the search results (or on a content network page). Make sure you do some Google searches to see how the other ads are worded and try to make yours even more appealing.

Special offers always attract attention, so be sure to include "free shipping," "10 percent discount for new customers," or similar offers, if applicable. Grammar also counts, so make sure that your ad makes sense and is readable. That'll also instill confidence on the part of the searcher, increasing the likelihood that they'll click on your advertisement.

Try three or four different versions of the ad and let Google's automatic weighting based on click-through rate let your campaign migrate to the most effective advertisement, then delete (or further modify) the less effective ads.

Feature important concepts for your customers or industry in your advertisement, too, as space permits: speed of shipping, ISO-9000 compliance, breadth of selection, discounts, warehouse pricing, bulk sales, guarantees, industry endorsements, certifications attained, and so on.

Test your advertising with different levels of specificity, too. One ad might say "Nike shoes" while another says "Nike Air Jordan" and a third says "Nike Air Jordan 1-20 $69".

The Least You Need to Know

- ◆ Google AdWords is a contextually driven advertising system that greatly improves the click-through rates of advertisements.

- ◆ Advertisers compete for ad placement by bidding on how much they'll pay on a per-click basis.

- ◆ Both Google and WordTracker offer excellent keyword research tools and should be utilized before starting any campaign.

- ◆ Ads can be targeted by various types of searches, by whether they should appear on the search or content network, or various other options.

- ◆ Good ads have at least one element that appeals to the customer, whether the words "discount," "free shipping," "ISO-9000 certified," or similar concepts.

- ◆ Start with simple ads and more common keywords, then iterate based on results to refine your advertising campaign.

Making Money with Google AdSense

In This Chapter

♦ Taking a closer look at AdSense

♦ Where to incorporate AdSense on your site

♦ How to block ads from competitors

♦ Some additional thoughts about AdSense

Most of my recommendations for growing your business have involved spending money or time with the intent of driving new customers to your site and closing the sale. This is a traditional method of generating revenue and expanding a business, of course, but there's another way to attain your target revenue.

Instead of paying to advertise on other sites or paying for people to help optimize your website for maximal findability, Google will pay you to include advertisements from other companies on your web pages.

Can you generate thousands of dollars a week from your website? Probably not. But if you'd like to have your website break even rather than be an expenditure each month, or you'd like to add a new area to your site that helps you monetize the incoming traffic, then Google AdSense could be an excellent fit.

BizTips _____

Advertising on your site has pros and cons. Read through this entire chapter and think about the implications of moving from a writer to a publisher carefully before you decide to jump into AdSense.

Even if you don't think you want to add advertising to your website—and there are a number of reasons not to, as we'll discuss shortly—this chapter is still worth reading because you can always create a second site that's filled with reference materials and pays for itself through advertising.

The best feature of AdSense isn't that it lets you easily include advertising on your site, however, but that the entire system is managed by Google and once you've included a few simple lines of HTML code (or, better, gotten your IT person to add it) all the advertising shows up without further intervention and you're paid each month as long as you earn at least $100 in that pay period.

Understanding How AdSense Works

AdSense is the flip side of AdWords. It's the mechanism whereby the ads purchased through AdWords are displayed on web pages. You'll recall that when you bid a certain amount on specific keywords through the AdWords program, your ads are then displayed on various websites, ranked based on how your bid compares to the other bids for the same keyword or keywords. When running an AdWords campaign, you can also opt whether to have your ads displayed on the search network or the content network.

BizTips _____

AdSense actually displays a block of ads on a given page. The block can contain anywhere from one to five individual advertisements, depending on their sizes and configurations.

The content network is the network of millions of web pages across thousands of different websites that display Google AdSense ads.

What really differentiates AdSense from more traditional online advertising alternatives is that you don't have to specify the topic of your web pages and you still get finely targeted, contextually relevant advertising. This magic is done by the Google relevance formula, the same engine used to compute the best matches for a given search.

A page that discusses travel and finding hotels in foreign cities will automatically have travel ads included by the AdSense system. Ditto a site about skateboarding, knee surgery, growing roses, selecting an interest-free credit card, or setting up an outdoor thermometer.

You get paid each time someone *clicks* the ad, not each time you display an advertisement on your page. Remember, AdWords prices are based on the number of clicks, not the number of people who saw the ad.

Some keywords are extremely popular and can be bid astonishingly high, over $100 per click. This means that the payoff for the AdSense partner who displayed the clicked ad also reaps a high payoff. Other keywords are noncompetitive and the AdSense payoff is only a small percentage of the $0.05 minimum AdWords bid.

BizTips

The AdWords keyword research tool can help you identify some of the most expensive keywords, but don't get sidetracked. The theme of this book is building good, relevant, industry-specific content. It's wisest to stay focused on your core business and see AdSense as an adjunct income stream.

Once you're approved to join the AdSense program, log in and you'll be able to configure the advertising that's going to be displayed on your pages and examine a variety of performance and revenue reports.

The biggest decision you'll have to make regarding AdSense is the size of the ad: a bigger ad block is going to include more individual AdSense ads and draw more attention, but it's also going to be more invasive. You need to pick advertising versus content, blatant versus subtle, or perhaps even crass versus ineffective. It's not always an easy decision.

Configuring an AdSense Ad Block

Ad blocks can be configured as banners and buttons, towers, or inline rectangles, either as text ads or graphical ads. Different sizes and orientations allow for more individual ads to be included. The following table summarizes the different sizes and how many different advertisements can be included in each.

Different AdSense Layout Options

Name	Dimensions	Ads Displayed
Leaderboard, text	728×90	4
Leaderboard, graphic	728×90	1
Banner text	468×60	2
Banner image	468×60	1
Button, text	125×125	1
Half-banner	234×60	1
Skyscraper, text	120×600	4
Skyscraper, graphic	120×600	1
Wide skyscraper	160×600	5
Vertical banner	12×240	2
Medium rectangle text	300×250	4
Medium rectangle, graphic	300×250	1
Large Rectangle	336×280	4
Square	250×250	3
Small rectangle	180×150	1

The layout of the web pages will probably dictate the ad block size. Figure 19.1 shows a web page with a large rectangle AdSense ad block included in the middle of the page.

The ads in Figure 19.1 blend in with the content of the page because of the specific configuration of that ad block. AdSense lets you fine-tune colors to match (or contrast) with the existing color scheme of the website. You can change the title color, the text color, the link color, the background color of the ad block, and the border color. Setting the border and background color to be identical effectively removes the border from the image.

The AdSense ad block shown in Figure 19.2 is configured to stand out more by contrasting with the color scheme used on the page, rather than blending in.

Figure 19.1: In this figure, there are four individual ads shown in a large rectangle format.

One advantage of a weblog or similar content management system is that the special code needed for Google AdSense can be automatically included on each new page. You can then create compelling and engaging content to attract your customers, and reap the benefits of however much additional revenue you see from the AdSense program.

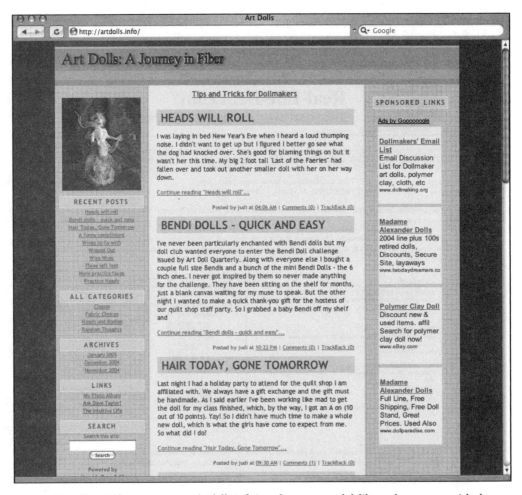

Figure 19.2: The AdSense region on Artdolls.info is a skyscraper and deliberately contrasts with the colors on the page.

Maximizing Click-Through Rates

There are many theories about what type of ad design encourages the best click-through rates. If your visitors have their attention drawn to the ads, click on them, and, hopefully, buy the products advertised, you'll earn more for having those ads on your site. Make it too obvious, though, and your click-through rate will increase, but your traffic will decrease as the advertising repels more people.

One very important AdSense capability is *channels*. A channel is a group or collection of web pages that all have an AdSense ad block displayed. You can either specify channels by a top-level domain (if you have more than one website, for example), or you can create your own custom channels and give each advertising block a different channel so that AdSense can track your results.

BizTips

You can include AdSense ad blocks on as few as one or two web pages, or you can include ads on every page. You also aren't limited to one ad block, you can include up to three ad blocks on a single web page, even if the blocks are configured to be completely different sizes or colors.

How Much Money Can You Make?

Figure 19.3 shows my own Google AdSense report for the first three weeks of December, 2004. Since I have a number of different websites that include AdSense, this report offers a consolidated overview, but I can use previously defined channels to split out the revenue report on a per-domain or per-project basis. I can also download a version of this data ready to be imported into any of a dozen different spreadsheet programs for further trend analysis.

Each line of output includes the number of times an AdSense ad was displayed (page impressions), the number of times someone clicked on one of the ads (clicks), the resultant click-through rate (also known in the industry as CTR), the effective *CPM*, and the overall earnings for that period or that channel within the given period.

Buzzwords

CPM is cost per thousand. The "M" comes from the Latin *mil*, thousand, just as a *millimeter* is a thousandth of a meter, not a millionth. Here's how Google explains it: "CPM is a useful way to compare revenue across different channels and advertising programs. It is calculated by dividing total earnings by the number of impressions in thousands. For example, if a publisher earned $180 from 45,000 impressions, the CPM would equal $180 divided by 45, or $4.00."

The first line of results, for Wednesday, December 1, shows that there were 7,174 page impressions and 157 clicks, producing a click-through rate (CTR) of 2.2 percent. Note that page impressions is not the same measure as overall website traffic, which Google can't calculate. Ads aren't shown on all pages of the websites, and some pages include more than one AdSense ad block. There's only a loose correlation between impressions and overall site traffic.

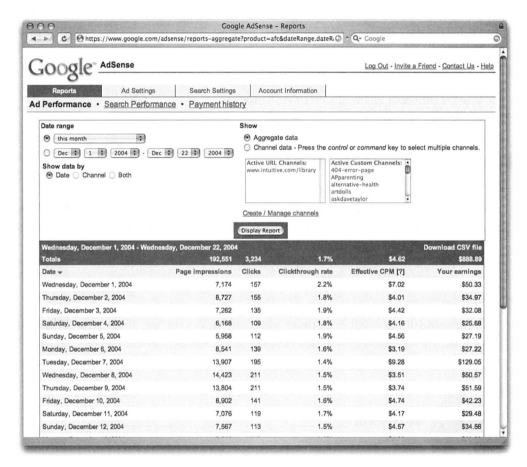

Figure 19.3: Google AdSense offers the chance to earn real revenue from your web pages without the hassle of having to maintain ad campaigns.

Google doesn't share the value of each individual ad click, but you can extrapolate rough numbers from the effective CPM shown. December 1 saw an ECPM of $7.02, which turned 157 clicks into AdSense earnings of $50.33. Divide the earnings by the total number of clicks and it reveals that each click on this particular day was worth $0.32.

The CPM rate varies based both on the popularity of the keyword and the time of day, time of month, and season. For example, in July keywords associated with Valentine's Day are not at all competitive, but come early February, it's guaranteed that they'll become extremely competitive again. Notice that while the effective CPM on December 1 was $7.02, the overall effective CPM across the 22 days shown in the report is a much lower $4.62, against 192,551 net page impressions.

This same 22-day period produced 3,234 clicks against a total earnings of $888.89. That works out to $0.27 per click, showing that the ads displayed on the first of December were more valuable than the overall ads displayed throughout the month. This makes intuitive sense because as it got closer to Christmas, more advertisers had used up their advertising budgets when they could ship their products before Christmas Day. In fact, keyword prices on December 26 are likely to be quite low.

> **BizTips**
>
> The value of a given advert click varies by the time of day, day of the week, and day of the year. A company paying to advertise its Halloween costumes might have an ad running year-round, but its bids will be much higher (because the competition will be greater) in the last few weeks of October each year.

Stay Focused on Your Business

Some of the entrepreneurs who participate in the AdSense program get very excited about these numbers and decide that building high-traffic websites focused on valuable keywords is a savvy path to a revenue stream without the hassles of dealing with actual products or services. For a small percentage of these entrepreneurs, this AdSense-centric site development strategy works, and they prosper for a while.

In the long term, however, sites that are built to maximize AdSense revenue aren't going to be successful because each time Google tweaks or tunes its relevance formula, these sites typically drop in relevance and there's then a commensurate decline in traffic. I have heard colleagues share their stories of a Google dance producing 60 percent, 75 percent, or even 90 percent drops in traffic and revenue.

You'll also notice that this book isn't titled *The Complete Idiot's Guide to Getting Rich Quickly!* because you already have a business, whether it's selling a product line or offering a professional service. AdSense can be a nice adjunct where it fits into your business website, but growing your business is not the same as creating a completely new business based on an ephemeral and perpetually fluctuating revenue model.

If you're dying to explore AdSense opportunities, however, I do have an area at www.findability.info that talks about some additional best practices. But remember, success comes from staying *focused*, not getting sidetracked with noncore business ideas.

Figuring Out Where to Include AdSense Ads

Having shared all those disclaimers and warnings, let's consider where you should add AdSense ad blocks to your business site.

 BizTips

Some online shopping consultants say that you shouldn't have *any links at all* on a sales page other than links that let the customer add the product to their shopping cart or complete their transaction.

First off, and most importantly, each and every AdSense advertisement is an invitation for your visitor to leave your website rather than explore and possibly purchase some of your products. For this reason alone, you should never have AdSense ads on any pages where you also have any sort of purchase or buy buttons.

Every page of your site might be the first page a visitor sees, so there are undoubtedly secondary pages where AdSense can be profitably included without an adverse impact on your conversion rate. On my busy AskDaveTaylor.com website, I don't allow ads on the first page, but include a large rectangle ad block within the articles on all subsequent pages.

Once you've decided what pages can have AdSense, you again face the decision of how subtle or overt your ads should appear. Make the ads too subtle and they won't be noticed, won't be clicked, and will serve no purpose other than as a visual filler on the page. Make them too overt, however, and you risk having everyone who visits your page leave immediately, with a highly unfavorable impression of the site and, by extension, your business.

Seek a balance, making sure that your internal links are higher on the page and presented in a manner that ensures that visitors realize what else is on the site. Then take unused or dead space for an AdSense ad block or two. The skyscraper layout is easily incorporated into many sites because of the popularity of vertical navigational columns. Instead of having the lower portion of the column empty, slip in an AdSense skyscraper and monetize the space.

AdSense for Search

If you don't have a search engine on your website already, you can utilize AdSense for Search and have a search system that includes AdSense ads that pay you if they're clicked. This is a hotly debated feature in the business community, however, because it's often inadvisable to offer chances for your visitor to leave the site when they're busy searching for something that you hopefully discuss on a page or two.

Further, the majority of website owners I've surveyed share that while they might make a respectable revenue stream from the AdSense program, almost none of it is because of AdSense for Search. Your site, your visitors, and your experiences may certainly vary, of course, but while it's important to include a search engine on your site, utilizing one that includes ads might not be in your best interest.

Also, if you don't have at least 30 to 40 pages on your site, don't add a search engine. Keep building content until the chances of someone finding what they seek on your site are higher than having no matching search results. If you prefer not to utilize Google for your internal search system, there are a number of other options that your webmaster or IT person can incorporate into the site with relatively little work.

BizTips

You should pay close attention to searches for two reasons: so you can save the queries your users are entering as a way to glean insight about their interests or problems; and so you can ensure that more and more searches meet with success as your site grows and evolves.

Avoiding Ads from Direct Competitors

If you're adding content that's relevant and useful to your potential customers, it's also going to be useful and interesting to the potential customers of your competitors, too. This is a significant problem because even if you'd make a small fee each time someone clicks on your competitors' ads, the potential customer has left your site for the competition. That's not a good thing!

Fortunately there's a way to indicate which URLs cannot have their ads displayed on your AdSense-enabled pages. This URL filtering is simple to configure. Log in to your AdSense account, then under Ad Settings choose URL filter and type in the website addresses of your main competitors, as shown in Figure 19.4.

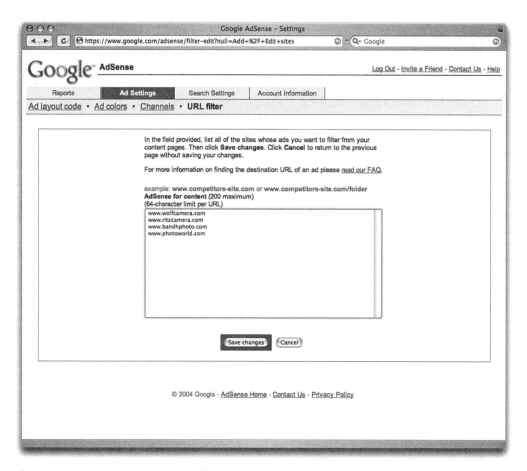

Figure 19.4: AdSense checks ads against your URL filter, which lets you prevent competitors' ads from showing up on your pages.

When you're building up a list of URLs that you'd like to filter out, it's important not to click on the ads that AdSense is displaying on your pages. Instead, move your cursor over the ad, then look on the very bottom of your web browser to see the target web address for that ad.

> **Memo**
>
> Each time an ad is clicked, you earn money. It doesn't matter if the person spends time at the resultant website, and it's not dependent on anyone buying anything. It can be hard to resist occasionally clicking on your own AdSense ads to make a buck or two. Don't do it: it's fraud and it'll get you kicked out of the AdSense program.
>
> Even with those warnings, AdSense participants click their own ads and even hire others to click, convinced it's a sneaky way to earn some quick cash from Google. What they don't know is that Google has highly sophisticated anti-fraud tools that can detect when this type of activity is occurring. When a pattern of fraudulent clicks is detected, Google kicks the AdSense participant out.

BizTips

An easier and more accurate alternative method of identifying the target web addresses of competitive ads is to use the AdSense Preview Tool, which you can download for free. Start at the AdSense home page (www.google.com/adsense) and then click the Help link in the top-right corner. One of the resultant choices is the AdSense Preview Tool. Unfortunately for Mac users, the AdSense Preview Tool is a Windows-only application.

Some Additional Thoughts About AdSense

AdSense offers an easily maintained way of monetizing some of your web pages. Since it's just as easy to create two or three websites as a single site, you can also now see why the Porsche mechanic creating two websites is such a smart idea. One of the sites would be the actual repair service while the other hosts Porsche reference materials. This offers more revenue-earning possibilities to the mechanic in addition to being great content to improve his site findability and demonstrate his expertise with Porsche cars.

Not everyone will want to devote the time required to produce AdSense-friendly content. Others will find that the risk of competitors appearing on their web pages far outweighs any possible benefit from allowing ads. That's okay. Some businesses seek to minimize expenses, and can use AdSense revenue as a method of paying for product or service-specific AdWords campaigns, while others eschew all revenue possibilities other than direct sales of their own products or services.

The AdSense terms of service prohibit you from including other advertising that's similar in appearance to AdSense on your website. This means that the mock Google ad pointing to your cousin's tire store can get you in trouble, though a more generic graphical advertisement or text link is just fine.

Just as smart AdWords participants test different ads to identify which generate the best click-through, there's no reason why your webmaster or IT person can't change the color scheme of a Google AdSense ad block every few days to ascertain what combination offers the best click-through rate and revenue opportunity.

As with much of website design itself, the design and placement of AdSense ad blocks is as much an art as a science. Choose a few pages and experiment with different layouts and color schemes to see what kind of results you see, before you push the layout changes onto the rest of your site.

The Least You Need to Know

- AdSense is a program through which Google will pay you to allow advertising on your web pages.

- Balance is critical, however, between the zeal to produce AdSense-friendly pages and maximize your potential advertising revenue and the needs of your business and business-oriented website.

- AdSense reports offer excellent statistics and can quickly help identify which pages and which ads are performing the best.

- Some business website owners decide after an evaluation period that advertising isn't for them and only include AdSense ads on noncritical pages on the site.

Chapter 20

The Advantages of Affiliate Programs

In This Chapter

- ◆ Understanding affiliate programs
- ◆ What makes a good affiliate terms of service agreements
- ◆ Knowing what to ask in an affiliate application
- ◆ Adding affiliate products or services to your own site

Would you pay a commission to someone who helps sell your product or service? Do you offer customers a merchandise credit or discount on their next bill if they refer new customers? If so, then you already have an affiliate program, and extending it into the online world is a logical next step. If you don't have an affiliate program, then now is an excellent time to consider whether it would be profitable to create an extended sales force.

This chapter will offer you a quick tour of the world of online affiliate marketing, with an emphasis on why you might want to create an affiliate program of your own and how you can do that while minimizing the possibility of fraud.

Affiliate Programs in a Nutshell

A good affiliate program requires minimal intervention, particularly the affiliate programs through Commission Junction, LinkShare, MyAffiliateProgram, and Performics. Even the most rudimentary affiliate program can help you rack up more sales as it empowers your colleagues and customers to sell on your behalf.

Just like anything else involved with making money on the Internet, however, there are unscrupulous entrepreneurs who will happily sign up for a new affiliate program knowing nothing about the product, then spam millions of e-mail addresses trying to make two or three sales. One step toward creating an affiliate program is to learn how to distinguish the good affiliates from the bad, before there's trouble.

This points out the trade-off associated with running an affiliate program. On the positive side, it's a straightforward way to create an extended sales force with a minimal initial cash outlay, just commission payments. On the negative side, though, your logo, company name, and even products move further from your direct control and there are risks associated with that.

You can also make some additional revenue from your own site by joining other merchant affiliate programs. When you recommend a particular book, magazine, or service provider, you can then earn some additional website revenue each time someone acts upon your recommendation and purchases the product.

The most popular of these programs is the Amazon.com affiliate program. If you have a list of recommended books that you include on your site for people interested in learning more about your industry, or have a weblog where you point interested readers to cogent magazine articles about your industry, it's worth joining the Amazon.com program.

BizTips

A press release or advertisement about an application should include a link that takes interested parties directly to the product page, not the home page.

How Affiliate Programs Work

Product-based business websites are organized so that each product has its own web page. If you sell computer software, you'd have one page for your word processing program, one for your spreadsheet program, one for your customer retention management program, and so on. Each of those product pages has a unique web address, or URL, that allows you to point customers directly to that page rather than force them to navigate through the site to find what they seek.

The most rudimentary affiliate programs work by including a unique affiliate identification value to that web page address. If the word processing program information is at "word-processing.html", then affiliate program member Roy, id #23, might instead point customers to "word-processing-23.html". The pages are identical, but now you have a simple way of looking at your website traffic reports and identifying which affiliates are generating the most traffic to your site.

You don't want to pay for traffic, but for sales. AdWords charges you each time someone clicks an advertisement and lands on your site, but you don't want to structure an affiliate program that way. The likelihood of fraud and the chances that your costs could skyrocket without you ever seeing any of those visitors convert to paying customers are too great. Instead, an affiliate program needs to track the customer through the purchase process, not just onto the site.

The simple way to implement an affiliate program if you don't have too many affiliates is to create unique product *SKUs* for each product and affiliate. It then becomes easy to match the purchases with the affiliate links that produced the sale.

If you have 4 products and 10 affiliates, this approach means that you now need to manage 40 SKUs, not 4. If you have thousands of products and hundreds of affiliates, this clearly won't work and it's time to move to a more sophisticated solution.

> **Buzzwords**
>
> An **SKU** is a *stock keeping unit* and it's a unique identifier that allows both merchandise and inventory control.

Sophisticated Affiliate Management Systems

Many online shopping-cart systems can store and track additional information that is hidden from the customer. PayPal, for example, allows product pages to include a hidden affiliate ID. That data is sent from page to page as the customer completes her transaction, and finally is saved in the transaction data record. In this situation, affiliates would link to product pages using a different notation. Instead of "word-processor-23.html", the link might be "word-processor.html?aff=23".

If you have a lot of products or want to plan for a lot of affiliates, then your best strategy might be to build your store at a site that supports affiliate programs or just go straight to an affiliate management vendor.

If you've built your store with Yahoo! Shops and opted for the Merchant Professional level (which costs $299 per month, as detailed in Chapter 16), you can use the built-in Yahoo! affiliate program, or you can hook your store directly into Commission Junction. If you're seeking lots of affiliates, then joining Commission Junction as a merchant is a smart strategy.

BizTips

You can learn more about Commission Junction by going to their website at www.cj.com.

Regardless of where your store is built, the best third-party affiliate management program is Commission Junction, which has a team of engineers ready to help you integrate your affiliate program into your store and thousands of affiliates eager to hear about your new company, product line, and commission structure.

When you have affiliates helping sell your products or services, your affiliate management program will help you keep track of the return on investment (ROI) of the program. A good system will show reports that list the top affiliates, the traffic each has brought to the site, the gross sales from each affiliate, the commission rate for each affiliate, and the commission paid.

Figure 20.1 shows a report from Commission Junction for an account manager who has a number of different affiliates. Note especially the columns Commission Paid, Sale Amount, Sales, and Clicks. Affiliate "publisher1", for example, has generated $2,113.78 in sales, earning a commission of $274.79 which was produced from 133 clicks (people visiting the affiliate's site and clicking on the special affiliate link to learn more about the product) that led to 9 sales.

A common strategy for affiliate managers is to offer bonuses to the top one percent of affiliates and drop the bottom one percent of affiliates out of the program on a monthly or quarterly basis.

The Affiliate Terms of Service Agreement

There are risks associated with offering an affiliate program, the greatest of which is that you don't have complete control over the methods your affiliates use to promote your products. One way to minimize this risk is to have a strongly worded terms of service (TOS) agreement.

The terms of service for your affiliate program are critically important to forestall any difficulties with potential fraud, brand protection, or spamming. While it may be tempting to sign up everyone who wants to help sell your product, it's much better to manually approve affiliates, an online analog to interviewing new employees.

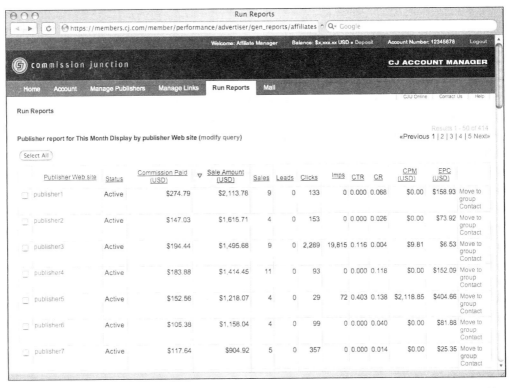

Figure 20.1: A Commission Junction merchant affiliate report, showing how many products were sold by each affiliate, the gross revenue, affiliate commission, and much more.

To avoid any potential problems, outline exactly what you consider acceptable and unacceptable promotion in your affiliate agreement. This is captured in the TOS agreement, though it's really a contract between you and your affiliate. A Google search for "affiliate program terms of service" will give you 12 million matches, more than enough to find inspiration for your own agreement and help you avoid missing important clauses or restrictions.

Nonetheless, let's examine the key elements of a good affiliate TOS agreement, because it's an excellent way to learn more about the possible pitfalls of having your own affiliate program and how to circumvent these dangers.

Acceptable Sites

Businesses seek to be promoted by like-minded organizations, and online businesses are no different. When you sign up affiliates and have them promoting your products on their websites, through their newsletters, and in other venues, you want to ensure that their approach is compatible with your own and that they won't alienate potential customers because of other content on their site.

This idea is captured in your TOS agreement by enumerating what you consider acceptable and unacceptable sites for promoting your products and business. The Apple iTunes store affiliate program has a typical list of unsuitable sites that include, but are not limited to, those that:

- Infringe trademark rights of yours or any third party or otherwise violate the rights of any third party

- Contain sexually explicit materials

- Contain hate/violent/offensive content

- Promote discrimination based on race, sex, religion, nationality, disability, sexual orientation, or age

- Promote illegal activities or otherwise violate any applicable laws, including those targeting "spyware," "adware," or spam

- Violate any intellectual property rights, including, without limitation, scraping text or images from the Apple websites

- Do not clearly state an online privacy policy to their visitors

- Otherwise are considered offensive or inappropriate at Apple's sole discretion

Your acceptable sites list might be shorter, but there's a lot of value to ensuring that your TOS agreement is consistent with the TOS of some of the biggest affiliate programs on the net. After all, they've already gone through all the bad experiences that you hopefully won't encounter, but against which you still need to protect your business.

Ownership of Intellectual Property

One of the most important clauses in a TOS agreement is that the affiliate parties must agree not to represent themselves as a part of your company, employed by your company, or affiliated in any way other than as a website affiliate. They shouldn't issue a press release saying that they've partnered with your firm as a way of raising their standing in the community, for example.

You also need to ensure that you retain control over anything that's your intellectual property, whether it be product pictures, customer testimonials, press releases, or your corporate logo.

The Geneology.com affiliate program states it as follows:

> You may not represent Genealogy.com or use its trademarks, logos or other branding in any manner other than providing approved links or Approved Content. Approved Content is content regarding data points (number of databases, number of names, etc.) on Genealogy.com. This approved content must be kept up-to-date.

Acceptable Promotional Techniques

The greatest risk in an affiliate program is that you sign up an affiliate who then presents your company or products in an unfavorable light. The danger isn't that they'll post a negative review with affiliate links (that wouldn't make much sense, after all). It's that they'll promote your product in ways that alienate the very online communities within which you're trying to ingratiate your business.

Specifically, I'm talking about spamming: the transmission of unsolicited commercial e-mail, the bane of the Internet, and the very last thing that you want your company associated with. It's critical that you explicitly prohibit any promotion of affiliate links through unsolicited e-mail. Affiliate TOS agreements quite commonly state that an affiliate found spamming will not only be kicked out of the program, but also forfeit any earned commission to date.

ThinkGeek sells a variety of clothes and other products and their affiliate TOS agreement captures this anti-spam requirement well:

> Under no circumstances shall you send commercial electronic mail messages as defined in the new Federal spam law, the CAN-SPAM Act of 2003 [the "Act"], with respect to ThinkGeek's Program. For clarification, this does not prohibit you from sending transactional or relationship messages as defined in the Act. ThinkGeek reserves the right to collect, withhold, or cancel any and all compensation related to the content you send via commercial electronic mail messages.

BizTips _____

Sneaky and banned search engine optimization tricks are discussed in more detail in Chapter 21.

In addition to spamming, affiliates that use sneaky and banned optimization tricks to artificially boost their search engine relevance scores can be a problem, too, because you never want to be associated with someone who isn't a good online citizen. Again, a clause in your TOS agreement can detail what you consider acceptable website promotional methods and prohibit those that can get their company—and by extension, your company—into trouble.

Another way to control the use of your material and ensure that it'll be utilized in a manner that's consistent with your business goals is to require that affiliates already have a website and that you have the opportunity to review the site when they apply for the program.

Commission Structure and Payment

Clearly state the goals and rewards of joining your affiliate program. If you only sell one product that costs $150, state explicitly in your TOS agreement that the affiliate payout is $15, $20, $30, or whatever figure you choose. Your goal in picking a payout amount is to make it low enough that it doesn't consume your profit from the sale and high enough that it motivates affiliates to hawk your wares.

Most sites offer a percentage of sales as a commission structure, so a site with lots of low-priced items might offer 15 percent of the transaction, while a site with high-ticket items might limit the cost of sale by having a 5 percent commission with a bonus if the customer purchases more than a set amount. Dell Computer's Canadian division has an affiliate program, for example, that pays 1 percent of all home and office purchases, while the eBay affiliate program pays a flat $30 for each user who joins eBay and bids on an auction.

BizTips _____

Affiliate commissions can vary quite a bit. One $90 product I know of offers a $30 per unit affiliate commission, and a $995 educational training package has a $250 per-sale fee.

The affiliate signup page should also clearly state when that payout will be distributed to participants. Some companies pay out immediately upon completion of the transaction, others pay monthly, and some pay quarterly. To minimize your work, set a minimum threshold on payout. If your affiliate payouts are $0.17/product, state that affiliate payment is only generated on a balance of $25 or more.

What to Require on an Affiliate Application

The applications for big affiliate programs are useful examples for your own affiliate application, and it's one area where caution and reticence is far better than adding even one questionable affiliate.

Since you're going to be issuing payments to your affiliates, you'll need to collect their tax ID or Social Security numbers so you can file 1099-MISC reports at the end of each year. In the interest of preserving your affiliates' privacy, store their account information in a secure place that is *not* your server or any computer that's accessible from the Internet.

Some companies ask their affiliates to identify how they'd like to receive payment and offer gift certificates as an option (which is brilliant), along with direct deposit or payment by check. Others issue checks for every affiliate, and some programs even charge a check issuance fee if the balance is under a certain threshold.

Applications should also require that affiliates indicate the name of their websites, the website addresses, descriptions of the sites, and how the applicant plans on marketing your products or services.

Finally, require that applicants agree to all of your TOS agreements by having a checkbox that links to the TOS itself. Amazon's affiliate program states "Check here to indicate that you have read and agree to the terms of the Operating Agreement."

BizTips

Always ensure that you have the appropriate wording in your affiliate agreement or TOS contract that allows you to approve or deny anyone for any reason, without explanation.

When to Add Affiliate Products or Services to Your Site

Chapter 19 introduced the somewhat radical idea of generating revenue from your business website by joining the Google AdSense program. Including advertising on your site is a big step, however, and many business sites eschew that possibility in the interest of staying pure to their business vision.

Affiliate programs offer another way to generate revenue for your website, a way that lets you retain much more control and that can be much more consistent with your business.

Flip back to Figure 19.1 (in Chapter 19) and notice that, in addition to the Google AdSense advertising on the Real-Life-Debt.com website, there's also a book recommendation with a picture of the book, price, and Buy button. That book is offered through the Amazon.com affiliate program and any visitor who decides to buy the book by clicking on the button generates a small commission for the website owner.

There's a whole world of affiliate programs. Far from being constrained to just those products sold by Amazon.com, a quick visit to the leaders in managing affiliate programs, Commission Junction and My Affiliate Program (www.myAP.com), reveal that the range of products and services you can offer on your site is staggering.

A Sampling of Affiliates

All of the following businesses offer affiliate programs through Commission Junction (www.cj.com):

Citibank	Marriott Hotels
Fossil Watches	eBay
Backcountry.com	Quicken Loans
Barnes & Noble	Home Shopping Network
Staples.com	Home Depot
Best Buy	Expedia
The *New York Times*	

There are few online businesses that can't find compatible products and services that they could offer through an affiliate program. Even if it only generates $100 per year, that's still an additional revenue stream that helps turn your website from a cost center to a potential profit center.

A gas station might offer map sales through Barnes & Noble, discounts on car rentals through Expedia, and information on local backpacking expeditions along with some featured gear through Backcountry.com.

A real estate broker could include affiliate links to popular restaurants and shops in town, maps of the area, and even discounts on moving, painting, and remodeling services.

A veterinarian could have links to books and magazines aimed at pet owners, links to online pet product stores, and even open up an adjunct affiliate-based store of their own that lists the top 20 products for dog and cat owners.

Unlike the Google AdSense program, there are no limitations on how many different affiliate programs you can join and how many (or few) products you offer on a given web page. Further, AdSense prohibits other similar advertising on a page, as discussed in Chapter 19, but including affiliate links on your pages in no way violates the AdSense TOS agreement.

Figure 20.2 shows a typical affiliate report from online superstore Amazon.com. Notice that this shows the same basic data as the Commission Junction account manager view shown in Figure 20.1: gross sales, affiliate commission, clicks from the affiliate site to Amazon.com, and number of items ordered.

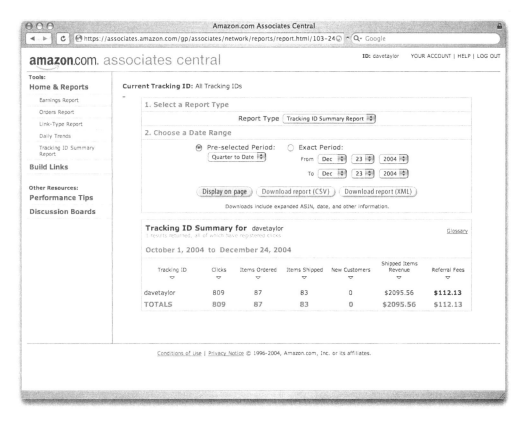

Figure 20.2: An Amazon.com affiliate report, showing that this affiliate was responsible for 809 visits to Amazon.com that led to 87 products being sold, earning the affiliate $112.13 in commission.

Signing Up

To join Commission Junction you'll need to have an active website and either some web savvy or the ability to have your webmaster or IT person help with construction of the special links that you need to ensure proper credit for sales. How to create an affiliate link is beyond the scope of this book, but all affiliate management systems include link-building wizards or similar aids, so it's not impossibly hard, just a bit tricky the first time.

I don't encourage businesses to go wild with affiliate links for the same reason that I'm leery about having too many advertisements on business website pages. If you have a weblog where you talk about industry trends, however, it's quite reasonable to post occasional book reviews or answer the inevitable visitor's "how do I start" questions with a list of recommended reading. Using affiliate links for these books can generate a small amount of income and help offset the time required to write that article.

What's particularly nice about sophisticated affiliate programs is that many of them keep track of how a customer found the site and pay out commissions on products purchased days, or sometimes even weeks, later. This means that your book review could lead someone to Amazon.com who decides not to purchase the book after all, but instead opts for a new DVD player or camera bag. In both cases you would still earn an affiliate commission.

Affiliate programs call this longer-term credit for affiliate-initiated sales *cookie tracking* because of the underlying web browser technology. The specifics of how cookies work are beyond the scope of this book—and you'd probably be bored reading about it anyway—but the concept is that the visitor's web browser gains persistent memory across computer restarts.

The Least You Need to Know

- If the idea of an extended commission-only sales force is appealing, then you should create an affiliate program.

- Successful affiliate programs are characterized by the merchant carefully screening affiliate applicants and retaining control over how his business and products are presented by the affiliate.

- In no instance should you allow affiliates to send unsolicited e-mail to promote your products or services.

- Many business websites also join affiliate programs themselves to make a few dollars off promoting compatible and complimentary products from other vendors.

Chapter 21

Avoiding Dumb Online Promotional Mistakes

In This Chapter

- How to recognize bad SEO consultants
- The optimization techniques you should avoid
- The optimization tools you should avoid
- The smart alternative to tricking the system

The difference between being the first and twelve thousand five hundred third match for key search queries in your business segment can be significant for your business and revenue stream. It's no surprise that an entire industry has cropped up to try and trick the system, to improve your search ranking, and help you garner more traffic through any means possible.

There's danger lurking around every corner of this treacherous jungle, however, because for every search engine–friendly modification you can make to the design and implementation of your business website, there's a trick that can backfire, lowering your ranking or even getting you banned from the search engines completely.

The worst part is that the so-called search engine optimizer (SEO) consultants face considerably less risk than you do. If your site gets banned from Google, for example, they aren't adversely affected (indeed, their contract probably states that they're not responsible or liable for any adverse consequences of their SEO techniques utilized on your site) but your business is suddenly pushed out of the mall, off the grid, and invisible to all those potential customers.

Most web designers are uninformed about search engine optimization techniques, good or bad, but some have just enough knowledge to be dangerous. That's just as much a danger as hiring SEO consultants. The end results are still the same, and your site is still either artificially ranked lower in search results or banned completely, while they're off to help their next client.

The most dangerous promotional strategy, however, is one that works. Some of the top-ranking websites use many of the techniques discussed in this chapter, techniques and tricks that are explicitly prohibited by Google, MSN, AOL, Yahoo!, and the other major search engines. Why is that dangerous? Because it can lull you into a false sense of confidence, a belief that if an SEO consultant can do it for one of his other clients, that he can do it for you, too. But ranking on Google and other search sites can be quite ephemeral, and if known bad techniques are being used, it's just a matter of time before the crawler penalizes your site.

How to Recognize Pay-for-Placement Scams

You're reading through your morning e-mail messages, answering customer questions, and chatting with friends when you come across an e-mail message entitled "Search Engine Secrets Discovered" that's selling a CD-ROM for a few hundred dollars that will teach you:

- Three different methods we use to pick the best traffic-producing keywords for any website ... and how you can have a list of hundreds of popular keywords in only a few minutes.

- How quick and easy it is to create "doorway" and "hallway" pages for the search engines so that you could possibly have thousands of different pages on your domain, all pulling in visitors for your site 24 hours a day, 7 days a week.

- The secret weapon that gives you an "unfair advantage" over your competition ... and virtually assures you will reach the top positions (don't let your competitors hear about this one first or you will be in trouble).

◆ How to submit your pages to the search engines and assure that every single one of them gets listed. (If you listen to one of those amateurs tell you how to list your site, you may just get banned for life.)

◆ How to use pay-per-click search engines to receive over 10,000 visitors for only $100.

◆ The infamous Yahoo! backdoor … You can get listed and we will show you the quickest and easiest method for doing so!

◆ And much, much more …

This is a scam. This person might well have produced a CD-ROM that has information on these topics, but every single one of the suggestions is a recipe for disaster. That disaster won't befall the CD-ROM producer—since they're only guaranteeing that the CD-ROM will play on your computer (if anything at all), not that the techniques will accomplish what you seek—but your business.

What's particularly insidious about this type of e-mail is that it appears to address these very concerns, talking about how if you submit sites *without* the knowledge of their secret techniques that you could "get banned for life." The legitimate ways that you can improve your site, like creating content around popular keywords, keywords that you've found using WordTracker or similar tools, have been covered in Chapter 18. The illegitimate, dangerous techniques you should just avoid.

The demonstrated lack of professional ethics and disrespect for your time shown by someone sending you unsolicited spam messages isn't a good way to start a relationship either, is it?

In case that's not enough, here's another one:

Be the very first listing in the top search engines immediately.

Our company will now place any business with a qualified website permanently at the top of the major search engines (for example, Yahoo!, MSN, Alta Vista, and so on). This *SERP* promotion includes unlimited traffic and is not going to last long. If you are interested in being guaranteed first position in the top search engines at a promotional fee, please reply to us promptly to find out if you qualify. PLEASE INCLUDE THE URL(S) YOU ARE INTERESTED IN PROMOTING. This is not pay-per-click. Examples will be provided.

Sincerely,

The Search Engine Placement Specialists

No search engine placement company can legitimately make this offer, particularly to place you "permanently at the top." Here's what Google says about this kind of offer: "Beware of SEO's that claim to guarantee rankings, or that claim a 'special relationship' with Google, or that claim to have a 'priority submit' to Google. There is no priority submit for Google."

Managing a Link Farm

Not all SEO consultants are going to spam you, however. Some might be pleasant enough fellows that you meet at a local business mixer or an entrepreneurial conference, people who assure you that they don't do anything wrong but still have amazing results. One way that they sometimes can achieve these results, albeit temporarily, are through having dozens or hundreds of sites that primarily link between each other, but also have some links to third-party sites such as your own. On the surface that doesn't sound too bad because Google bases its PageRank on how many inbound links there are for your site.

When the sole purpose of a site is to provide links to other sites, however, it's considered a *link farm* and Google automatically ignores it and any links it may contain. You can't be penalized for having a link farm point to you, but if you then swap links and point to one of the link farm sites, you *can* be penalized. Worse, as discussed in Chapter 5, each link off your page bleeds a bit of PageRank, so instead of reserving your PageRank for important links, you're giving PageRank to the link farm along with paying them for your improved placement.

Link farms are a bad idea. Links from any page or site that's primarily a list of website addresses have no real value and should be avoided.

Ranking for Obscure Keywords

Another common thing that you'll hear from SEO consultants that are looking to part you from your money is that they can guarantee good placement on selected keywords. The way they accomplish that is by *selecting sufficiently obscure keywords so that no one else is in that space.*

Being in the top 10 for the search "pizza" would be an impressive accomplishment since there are 21 million matches. Being in the top 10 for "pizza "wheat crust" Tucson" is not impressive (in fact, there are only 33 matches to this search query). That's exactly what these so-called experts are really offering. They don't say top placement in the keywords *you want to match* because that's not what they can deliver. It stands to reason. If it were just a matter of some tricks to be in the top 10 for any key word, wouldn't *their website be matched* on the appropriate searches in the first place?

Ten Dumb Tricks to Avoid on Your Website

Rather than work with a placement consultant, you might have a webmaster, IT person, or nephew that's read about all the ways you can fiddle with your site and get top search engine placement. Any tips beyond "build a really good, content-rich website" are going to be tricks that can eventually get you banned from the search engines completely.

Ensuring that you have good title tags, using descriptive file names, and repeating your key words a half-dozen times on the page are all recommended strategies. Anything more, and you're playing with fire.

Even the placement experts recognize the dangers in the different optimization techniques. One spam e-mail I received warned me about picking the wrong optimization techniques by pointing out:

> A lot of traffic sellers utilize a technique known as pixel linking. You put about a million one-pixel links onto a web page. The person selling the traffic then has a website that gives away something for free, so that page (where your one-pixel link is) gets a lot of hits. Here's where you lose out. The pixel link acts just like a banner. No one even has to click on it. When the page it's on is viewed, your link registers a hit.

What's interesting about this claim is that there *are* people who believe that having a lot of links on a single page is sufficient to fool a search engine into thinking that your site is phenomenally popular. There's really no end to the ingenuity of these so-called experts. Avoid them all and, as a general rule, you should *never* respond to any unsolicited e-mail offering to sell or give you something anyway.

Hidden or Cloaked Text

Another popular trick is to have information on your web page that's hidden from view but is still part of the active content on the page. Search engine crawlers try to mimic a regular web surfer reading a web page, but they're not actually humans, so people try to trick them. The hidden text trick is to have text on an identically colored background (for example, white text on a white background), have slightly different colored text, or have text with a size specified as "0 percent" or "0 pixels" or "0 point." Regular users who visit your page see nothing other than perhaps some odd spacing, while the crawler sees and incorporates all the words listed.

If our Porsche mechanic had poor judgment, he might add the phrase "best Porsche mechanic, Porsche, Porsche cars, fix Porsche" as white text against the white background of the page, thinking that the additional repetitions of the word Porsche will improve keyword density (which I'll discuss in a minute) and therefore make his web page more relevant to Porsche-related searches.

Search engine companies understand this trick, though, and have very sophisticated software that can detect these techniques and penalize your web page for using them.

Keyword Stuffing

Repetition of your keywords is very important to your pages being ranked properly in search results. A web page for a comix store should have the word "comix" appear in the page title, in a level one header, and at least twice in the first paragraph.

There's a world of difference between having your keyword or key phrase appear a half-dozen times in 20 paragraphs and having it appear 20 times in one paragraph, however.

> To keyword show you keyword what I mean keyword, it's keyword impossible to believe that keyword normal writing has this keyword density of keywords appearing normally.

There are more subtle forms of keyword stuffing, too, including making sure that the keyword or keywords appear within every markup tag, as the names of image files, as the names of other pages linked to this page, and a half-dozen times on the bottom of the page, too.

Analyzing keyword density and calculating if it's occurring naturally or is forced is an easy task for a program and this strategy does not work for any of the major search engines.

Doorway Pages

A more subtle strategy that's used by a lot of placement consultants is to create a set of *doorway*, *gateway*, *bridge*, or *hallway pages*. They're all the same thing, pages that are built specifically to be highly relevant for a specific keyword or key phrase, pages that don't have anyone pointing to them, but point to your home page. The intent is to have spill-over relevance because hundreds of doorway pages optimized for different keywords in your industry segment all point to your own site.

A website that sells sporting goods could, for example, create a page that's focused completely on tents. The tents page would be designed to rank highly only in the search engines for the term "tents". Once the user found this doorway page, she would then be quickly channeled to the main website.

A variation of doorway pages are so-called *splash pages* where there's a company logo, an animated introduction, or a small graphical billboard, with various other text and keywords lurking behind.

Not only is this bad website design, it's also again something that the search engines will detect and in extreme cases can lead to having your site banned.

Different Pages for Different Visitors

You might not realize it, but every time you visit a website you are sending information about your computer and Internet connection to that server. Don't worry, though, it's not your credit card information or Social Security number. Instead, it's information about the actual web browser in use, something that encourages unscrupulous placement people to try and trick the system.

When you use Microsoft Internet Explorer for Windows, it sends a browser ID similar to "Mozilla/4.0 (compatible; MSIE 6.0)". Web crawlers from different search sites send out browser ID strings that identify them as crawlers. The following table lists some of these strings.

Some Common Search Engine Crawler IDs

Partial Browser ID string	Search Engine
Ask Jeeves/Teoma	Ask Jeeves
Googlebot/2.1	Google
Mediapartners-Google/2.1	Google
msnbot/0.3	MSN Search
Yahoo! Slurp	Yahoo! Search
YahooFeedSeeker/1.0	Yahoo! Search

Because search engine crawlers identify themselves to a web server when requesting pages, there are some people who think that producing a highly optimized custom keyword version of a standard web page for the crawler is legitimate. If you or I visit the site we see the standard content, but when the search engine visits, it sees a completely different page.

This is another bad idea and is clearly cheating. Worse, most of the people that utilize this trick forget that there's nothing to stop Googlebot, MSNBot, Yahoo! Slurp, or any of the other search engines from occasionally sending false credentials to compare the page received. If the two pages are different, this can result in a very significant penalty for the site or an outright ban on all the pages on the site.

Refresh Pages

Through the addition of some simple scripting, web pages can be created that automatically redirect visitors to a different page, or even a different site, all within seconds of arrival. This technique is quite commonly used with doorway pages so that users who search for a specific phrase are taken to the highly optimized page, and then promptly redirected to the main page of the website, a page that isn't particularly relevant to the original search.

Some sites use this refresh technique for legitimate reasons. Point your browser to the *New York Times* home page and every 5 to 10 minutes it'll automatically reload itself so that you'll always have the latest news on your screen.

Pages that use an automatic refresh (sometimes also called a *meta refresh* because of how it's implemented in HTML) to lead someone to another page or another site can be quickly detected by the search engine crawlers and will cause you to be penalized.

SEO "Content" Pages

If you work with some of the less scrupulous search engine optimizers, don't be surprised if they ask whether they can send you some additional pages that they'd like to add to your site. The pages will reside on your web server and be shown as part of your domain name. They just want the smallest of links off your home page to these new content pages.

This is another really bad idea. Every page on your site, every page with your domain name, should properly reflect the values of your online business. Those pages are more evil than that, however, because they're either link farm pages or gateway pages. The optimizers reap the benefit of having these keyword-optimized pages on your website while you gain nothing, risk your corporate integrity, and possibly get in trouble with the search engines.

Too Darn Many Links

One of the many reasons that link farms don't work is that search engines become suspicious of any web page that has more than 75 to 100 links on it, whether they're internal links to other pages on the site or external links to other websites. While having your website listed on a remote site that has lots of links won't penalize you, per se, it's also completely valueless in terms of you gaining PageRank.

This isn't to say that sitemaps and other pages that logically can have a lot of content are bad. It's just that if all the links point offsite, it's going to set off a warning bell inside the Googlebot and can produce adverse results.

Memo
Because Google pays such close attention to the number of different websites that point to your site, many people are afraid that if a bad site, a site that uses sneaky tricks for better placement, or even a hate site points to you, you could be penalized.
Rest assured, this cannot happen.
One of Google's stated views is that because you can't be in control of what sites point to you, your site will never be penalized for links from bad sites. Obviously, you don't want links from sites that aren't going to be attracting your potential customers, but if one does appear due to whatever peculiar circumstance, rest assured it won't cause trouble.

Duplicate Content

If one website full of content pages is a good thing, then surely duplicating that content with just the slightest tweaks should be even better, right? That's why some consultants recommend that you register similar domain names to your own and republish all your content in an identical form on these other servers. If each page is a hook in the vast information ocean, then this is just throwing out more hooks.

Again, search engines can detect and catch this, recognizing when two or more pages are either exactly identical or almost exactly identical. If this is found, then all of the pages on the different sites will be penalized, and if there are many pages with the exact same content on a single site (for example, an information page on a specific product linked to by other pages on the site using 15 different common keyword phrases), they can be penalized, too.

ALT Text and META Keywords

Good web pages have proper and complete HTML code. In fact, Google and other search engines routinely recommend that website owners spend time ensuring that the pages on their site are proper, correct, and can be validated by various tools. One important element of proper web pages is that every time there's an image included, an ALT tag should be used to offer a meaningful narrative description of the image for people who cannot, or opt not to, view the graphic.

You can imagine how some people take that as a license to do surreptitious keyword stuffing in these ALT tags. An innocuous inclusion of a product photograph isn't described in the ALT tag as "travel mug, 18oz" but rather as "travel products, travel store, vacation, holiday, packing, vacation planning, travel gear".

As discussed in Chapter 14, search engines allow sites to include certain description and keyword lists called META description and META keywords, but rather than a simple list of a dozen keywords, the same people who like to exploit ALT tags also like to stuff as many keywords as possible in the META keywords and META description tags, often including the same keyword 10, 15, or even 20 times.

If you guessed that the search engine crawlers can detect this sort of obvious keyword stuffing in the ALT and META tags, you're absolutely right. Do yourself a favor, therefore, and limit yourself to no more than five or six words in your alt tags, no more than 15 keywords, and no more than a 20-word description.

TITLE Tags

The title of your web page is one of the most important single elements for establishing the topic of the page. That is why it is vitally important that you always ensure that you have at least your two or three most critical keywords in the title.

The HTML standard specifies that you can only have one title, specified in one title tag. I'm sure you're not surprised to learn that some so-called experts suggest including more than one title tag, and having them all stuffed to the gills with keywords. It's a bad idea and easily detectable.

What Tools to Avoid

In addition to all the different tricks and techniques outlined in this chapter, there are also various software applications available that purport to help you track and improve your placement on search engines. Some of them probably do help, but almost all of them violate either good SEO recommendations or business ethics.

Position Analysis Tools

Popular programs like WebPosition Gold monitor your site's position on the major search engines for a set of keywords you identify. They do this by running searches on Google on a daily basis for each of the specified keywords and counting how many results pages are requested before your site appears.

Doesn't sound too bad, except Google explicitly says:

> Don't use unauthorized computer programs to submit pages, check rankings, etc. Such programs consume computing resources and violate our terms of service. Google does not recommend the use of products such as WebPosition Gold that send automatic or programmatic queries to Google.

When Google says "does not recommend," it's accurate and wise to interpret the phrase as really meaning "if we find you doing this, we'll penalize your website."

Backlink Farming Tools

Some applications let you type in a keyword, automatically identify the top matches, then search backward (using the "link:" search) for the top sites that point to each of those matching pages. The program then analyzes these *backlink* sites for contact addresses and either automatically sends requests for your site to be linked or offers you the chance to send a custom written form letter requesting the same.

Buzzwords

Backlinks are pages that point to a given web page.

Requesting links from your competitors' backlink sites is a good idea, because you probably won't ask your competitors to link to you. The sites that link to your competitors might be quite interested to learn about yet another source for the product or merchandise, however, and might be happy to add your site.

What makes using these tools a poor strategy for achieving this goal is that it's a programmatic query to Google, which violates their terms of service. Worse, with hundreds of sites to e-mail, people don't bother to customize the messages and therefore the messages are easily recognizable as spam and discarded. This also lessens the likelihood that a later personal e-mail request for a link would meet a favorable reception.

The Smart Alternative

There are a remarkable number of ways that you can try to trick the system, game the crawlers, and try to edge out your competitors to achieve the best possible positioning on the search results.

Memo

Always use a clear and descriptive title on each page, create separate pages for each product or discussion topic, use a simple text-friendly design, use meaningful file names and a good domain name, and pay attention to the words that sites use to link to your site.

The best strategy for maximizing your findability and growing your business online are those that have been discussed in this book. From creating findable web pages with search engine–recommended elements to adding content to produce a destination site rather than a billboard, growing your business online isn't about tricks and secrets. It's about hard work, about creating a good site that promotes needed products at a competitive price.

Don't be conned by these so-called search engine optimization and placement experts. Real expertstell you to build a bigger site with more legitimate content pages and gain visibility through becoming an online expert. Circumventing the system has measurable costs and risks, and you always have a lot more to lose than any of these consultants. Just say no!

My personal guideline before making architectural changes to any of my sites is to ask myself whether I'm doing it for my visitors—my potential customers—or not. Is this going to make it harder for my visitors to understand and enjoy the site? If the answer is yes, I think long and hard before I proceed with any changes, however much my colleagues may recommend them.

The Least You Need to Know

- There are lots of people who claim to know secrets and insider tricks to top search engine placement. They're all inviting you to take grave risks with your business website and should all be avoided.

- Even without placement experts, many web developers try to play tricks with websites to improve placement, tricks that can be detected by Google and other search engines, tricks that can get your site banned completely.

- Search engine optimization (SEO) tools can be dangerous, too, and should be used with great caution.

- Following the rules in this book and putting in the time, effort, and patience to grow and evolve your business online produce the best websites.

Part  5

What's Next on Your To-Do List?

One of the things I dislike about consultants is that when they're done telling you what's wrong with your company, they always seem to forget the part where they help you identify specific, tangible, measurable things you can do to fix the problems.

This part continues the theme of building content-centric business websites and offers some ingenious and time-saving strategies for identifying and adding content to your site with minimal or no cost.

Finally, the future of online business websites is discussed, especially what happens when Google is knocked off its throne as king of the search engines. It's not going to be the end of the web world as we know it, but there are some very interesting implications that unquestionably will impact your online strategy.

Chapter 22

Growing and Expanding Your Content

In This Chapter

- ◆ Copyright law and fighting content thieves
- ◆ Acquiring content for your site
- ◆ Syndicating your own content
- ◆ Publishing your own e-mail newsletter
- ◆ Establishing content-based stores

Content should be the cornerstone of your website, but you don't have to create it all yourself. There's more than one way to identify and acquire quality articles, columns, Q&A, and other material. This chapter explores different ways to find content for your site, and also considers different ways that you can leverage your own unique content on other websites in a mutually beneficial manner.

Whatever methods you use, the goal is that most of your articles and material should become *evergreen content*, content that will be just as interesting to your visitors a year from now. Too many websites create highly topical material that can be interesting to read this week, but ends up adding little value to the website over the course of time.

The Importance of Copyright Law

The World Wide Web makes it easy to ignore copyright laws and steal information from other sites without permission. This theft ranges from copying a paragraph or two of text up to wholesale clones of large business websites, hundreds of pages that are identical to the original except they have new logos and new affiliate links or product purchase links.

> **Buzzwords**
>
> Just as evergreen trees never lose their leaves, **evergreen content** is material that will be as relevant in a year as it is today. A website with evergreen content becomes a resource for industry and customers alike.

These tactics are wrong and reflect poorly on a business besides. As a businessperson, you don't want to pay for a package design, a logo, or a professional photographer just to find that others have subverted your efforts and included your unique material on their own site. Worse, sometimes these other sites are direct competitors.

There are no effective ways to avoid this other than to rely on the protection of copyright and trademark laws and to have some vigilance yourself.

Memo

Copyright law protects your content, even if you don't include a copyright notice, but you should always have one on each page of your website regardless. A properly formed copyright notice has the copyright symbol © followed by a year, followed by the name of the person or business that claims copyright. For example, "© 2005 by Dave Taylor".

A second level of copyright protection is to register your copyright with the U.S. Copyright Office or equivalent entity. The Copyright Office charges less than $50 to register material, and if you submit your entire site as a single entity, that fee will give you further legal protection.

You can find more information on this subject on the book's website at www.findability.info.

To see if your material is being ripped off, every so often use Google to search for sentences that you know occur on your own site to see if they also appear on other sites. Figure 22.1 shows the kind of result you want to get, where only your own web page is matched.

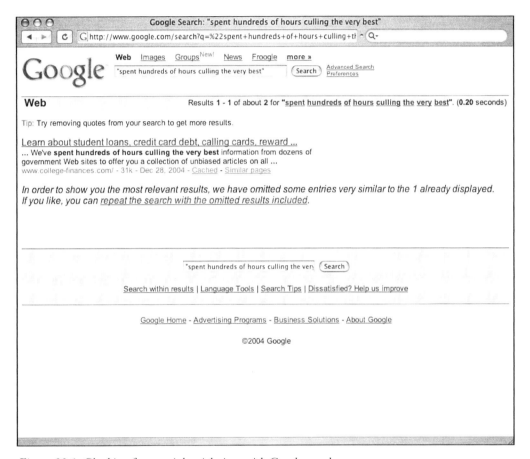

Figure 22.1: Checking for copyright violations with Google search.

If your material does appear on another site, a short cease-and-desist letter to the website owner almost always causes the offending site to be removed promptly from the web.

What do you say in a cease-and-desist letter? Here's an example e-mail:

It has come to my attention that your site, Mike's Million Dollar Branding Secrets, is an identical copy of my own copyrighted Branding Secrets website.

On your home page alone I count nine paragraphs that have obviously been copied and pasted from my own site, in violation of U.S. and international copyright law.

If your material remains accessible on the web 72 hours from now, I will begin the process of filing the necessary paperwork to proceed with a copyright violation suit. I would prefer not to do that, but will pursue this to the fullest extent of the law.

Please respond in a timely manner so we may proceed without any unnecessary difficulties.

You can start with a simple e-mail message; then, if that fails, a certified letter. Then it's time to call an attorney and explain the situation. If the competitor is overseas, however, you might not be able to find satisfaction depending on their local copyright laws and the amount you're willing to spend pursuing the case.

BizTips

Ironically, one of the tools that image thieves prefer is Google. Google's Image Search capability makes it simple to find photographs or graphical images in almost any category imaginable. Go to http://images.google.com.

To avoid having images or photographs stolen, you can include a small copyright notice on the image itself, but those can be easily deleted by an enterprising criminal. If you can't bear the idea of your images appearing anywhere else on the web, then you might reconsider which you include on your site, or create a different design that incorporates smaller images.

Licensing Content

The ease of stealing information, and the ease of finding those same scofflaws using Google search, make it imperative that your business be built upon a firm, legitimate, and fully legal foundation. This doesn't mean that you have to create all the content on your website yourself, however!

Republishing Magazine Articles

There are many ways that enterprising business website owners add new content to their sites, including receiving permission to reprint articles from other websites, hiring writers to produce new articles, and even adding freely available content from writing syndicates.

When I began pulling together a website about parenting, I knew that I wouldn't have the time to write original articles with any frequency, so I contacted some of the parenting magazines and asked about reprint permission. (Actually, with three small children at home, I'm lucky to get anything accomplished on a given day!)

A few of them said that it wasn't allowed, but one publication, *The Compleat Mother*, said that we could republish any of their articles as long as we had a source link on the bottom of the article pointing back to their website. A very fair deal: They win because of the additional exposure—and backlinks—gained by my inclusion of their articles, and I gain by having access to hundreds of articles that are already in a web-friendly format.

"Wait a sec," you might well be thinking, "earlier you warned that search engines don't like duplicate content. How is republishing an article that's already on the web not duplicating content?" That's an excellent question. By the nature of the web, some material is inevitably going to appear in more than one spot, so the best belief of the search engine community is that it's wholesale page-after-page duplication of content where the site name is different, but everything else is identical, that gets you into trouble.

If you compare a page on my APparenting.com parenting site with the original article presentation on *The Compleat Mother* site, you'll see that while the words of the article are obviously the same, the overall web pages are quite different.

This is ultimately something I'd counsel should be governed by professional and ethical behavior. If it's reasonable to have the content appear in more than one place, there's no reason that you should be penalized in any form.

Finding Authors to Republish

If the magazines in your industry aren't amenable, then perhaps the trade associations or individual writers might be interested in appearing on your website instead. Visit association websites and talk to the marketing or public relations director (not the webmaster) to find out whether there's a possible synergistic opportunity. Most trade associations and professional associations are happy for any visibility they can gain online.

BizTips

One savvy way you could incorporate individual opinion articles into your business site is to create a "Voice of the Customer" or "Voice of the People" area, prominently sponsored by your company. This also helps avoid the appearance of their articles being endorsed by your company, however tacitly.

To identify individual authors, search some of the weblog directories—Syndic8, Feedster, Technorati—to find articles written about your industry or segment. If these would be a good addition to your business website, contact the authors asking for reprint permission. It's a rare author who won't be pleased and complimented by the query.

Excerpting Articles on Your Site

Extended excerpts—where you only include the first few paragraphs of an article and then point back to their website for the remainder of the piece—can also help you produce content that helps web searchers find your business site.

You do need to carefully assess the value of including the first few paragraphs of an article against the danger of having a "continue reading this article" link that takes customers away from your site. Ironically, the better the article, the more likely you'd lose that potential customer and instead end up serving as a traffic conduit for the author.

Working with a Writer's Syndicate

There are websites that offer freely republishable articles as part of a writer's collective or syndication program. One such site is EzineArticles.com, shown in Figure 22.2.

Hundreds of writers submit their articles to the EzineArticles.com database in a wide range of different topics, from stock market investment tips to home improvement, car shopping to gardening, cooking to photography. You can—for free—copy articles that you would like to incorporate into your own website, up to 25 articles per year.

Articles include short author biographies that always include a link to the authors' websites, and that must be included as-is when you reprint the article. That's the primary motivation of the writer in the first place; it's an ingenious form of advertising and producing more backlinks. For you, the website owner, EzineArticles.com is a simple way to have new content for free.

Other sites that offer articles for your website include ideamarketers.com and yellowbrix.com.

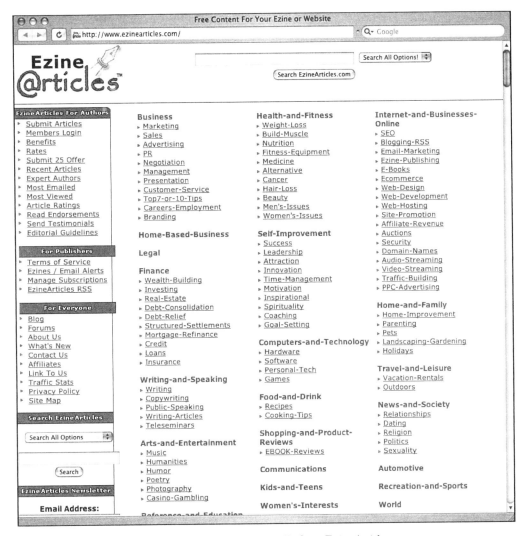

Figure 22.2: You can republish up to 25 articles annually from EzineArticles.com.

Hiring a Writer

Yet another possibility is to hire a writer to produce unique and original content for your site. Start by contacting the writing department at a local college: Many journalism and English majors would be delighted to earn even $50 for a two- to three-page article.

BizTips _____

You can buy exclusive rights (which means that the article becomes your property), first publication rights (which means that they can republish it elsewhere after it's been on your site for a certain amount of time), or just publication rights (the article might already be elsewhere on the web).

BizTips _____

An essay competition where the winning essays are featured on your site could produce dozens or even hundreds of new articles for the cost of a few gift certificates or products to give away.

There are also sites like eLance.com and Craigslist.com who offer an easy method of finding and hiring freelance writers who might be located across the ocean or halfway around the world. Some of my colleagues have a steady stream of quality material coming from overseas for $10 to $20 per article.

You can also solicit your customer base to find a few enthused contributors, likely to be opinion leaders in the community.

If you do hire a writer, make sure that you spend a few minutes checking Google to see if the content they've sent you really is new and exclusive. Some less scrupulous freelancers might copy and paste material from an obscure source and try to pass it off as their own. If that does happen, you'd be liable for the copyright violation if the material ends up on your site.

Finally, don't forget your own employees when you consider sources for new and original content. An enthused salesperson or development engineer might be thrilled at the chance to share their thoughts and opinions with the online world. The greatest challenge will be to keep them focused and ensure that they primarily write about your industry or products.

A supermarket, for example, could have a very interesting "Behind the Cash Register" weblog that relates the weekly experiences and ruminations of one of their clerks. A plumber who wrote an occasional journal humorously entitled "Don't Try This At Home" could garner an extensive following.

Syndicating Your Own Content

You should also consider syndicating or otherwise making available your own content for publication on other websites. One method would be to sign up as an author at iSyndicate.com and similar companies. If you include a small "This article can be added to your website for free: learn more" link at the end of your articles, you'll get queries from other websites, too.

On Ask Dave Taylor, every article includes the following advertisement: "Want to feature Ask Dave Taylor Q&A articles like this on your site, for free? You can! Find out how." The last few words link to the syndication information page shown in Figure 22.3.

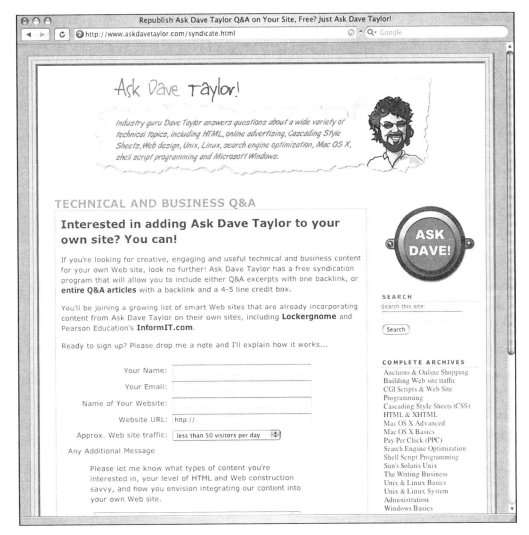

Figure 22.3: Other websites can freely include content from Ask Dave Taylor if they link back properly and ask permission first.

Regardless of how you choose to syndicate your content, it's imperative that every page republished include a small resources, contact, or bio box that lists your name, your company, a two- to three-line description of your product or services, and, most important of all, a link back to your own website.

Here's an example of an unusually long resources box from an article at EzineArticles.com about car insurance for seniors:

> Jacqueline Marcell is the author of "Elder Rage, or Take My Father … Please! How to Survive Caring For Aging Parents", a Book-of-the-Month Club selection. Endorsed by: Hugh Downs, Regis Philbin, and the National Adult Day Services Association—who honored her with their Media Award. She received "Advocate of the Year" from the National Association of Women Business Owners at their Remarkable Women Awards. Also a breast cancer survivor, Jacqueline advocates for caregivers to monitor their own health. She also hosts a radio program heard worldwide on: http://www.wsradio.com/copingwithcaregiving.

You can easily envision how a four- or five-paragraph article about your own industry or service can serve to anchor a small billboard that is then included on any number of other websites or even included in company newsletters.

This type of republishing is a great deal for both parties: The original author gains an additional publishing venue and an inbound link from an additional site, and the subscribing site gains an additional channel of information that they can include on their own site, expanding their content offerings, too.

Publishing Your Own E-mail Newsletter

Another excellent method of staying in touch with your community, turning potential customers into actual customers, and being perceived as a market leader is to produce your own weekly or monthly newsletter.

Newsletters don't need to be expensive or sophisticated productions with graphic designers and a team of marketing experts, as discussed in Chapter 13. A plain text-only e-mail message from the company CEO is much more personable than any fancy design.

BizTips

Any e-mail sent from your company risks being perceived as spam, which would be counterproductive. Minimize the risk by requiring that subscribers "double opt in" before you add them to the distribution list. This means that they should sign up on a web page, then receive a confirmation e-mail message. It's only upon their responding positively to the confirmation that they're actually added to the mailing list.

I have a newsletter associated with my AskDaveTaylor.com website that is produced completely without intervention. The newsletter has a brief introduction, usually a paragraph or two of gossip or industry news, followed by a brief excerpt of each article added to the site in the previous two weeks. Each excerpt includes a link that takes the reader to the full online article with a click. The newsletter allows me to leverage the articles I've added to the website and a second opportunity to engage my customers and bring them to the site.

Other newsletters are more formal, with full articles and other must-read information. While those often include content written by someone in the company who serves as the "public face," most web content syndication sites—including EzineArticles.com—also allow their articles to be freely republished in company newsletters.

Some companies, like Other World Computing, have built enormous subscription lists by prefacing their featured product listings with a three- to four-paragraph introductory message from the company president. Rather than just send out a list of computer bargains, they've created a popular newsletter by spending an additional thirty minutes adding an introduction to each issue.

An archive of back issues can also be included on your website, allowing yet another repurposing of your original content. Each back issue should be modified to prominently feature sign-up information and new products and services elsewhere on your site.

Most important for any newsletter is that it be interesting and useful. Just as the magazines you most enjoy reading are those that offer helpful and amusing content, so your own newsletter should be a must-read rather than just more clutter in someone's electronic mailbox.

Including Content in Your Store

Many business sites that include an online store take the simple path of producing the store pages based purely upon their product database. This is not a good tactic and forces them to compete purely on price. Worse, it creates an often-unfriendly shopping experience with lots of abandoned shopping carts. Some sites are so terse that customers routinely open up additional web browser windows to do research on a competitor's site as they go.

BizTips

Good online stores should be much more than just a Web-based catalog of product pictures, specifications, and "buy" buttons. Think about case studies, customer testimonials, product reviews, and similar content.

A content-centric shopping site is a much better solution, where every product listed includes extensive information, customer commentary, reviews, news about the manufacturer, and any other information you can incorporate. Not only do these then help ensure the user has a good shopping experience, but they also serve as additional content on your site, hooks through which you can gain more traffic.

Provide a User-Friendly Shopping Cart

While we're talking about online stores, let me also add that there are many very good e-commerce infrastructure firms that can supply you with a shopping cart or entire secure store for a minimal investment. Don't have your webmaster or website designer reinvent the wheel because of a perceived lack of features in the solutions they're most familiar with.

If you only have a few products available, working with a large company such as PayPal can be the fast path to processing customer credit cards and expanding your sales to the online world. Using the default PayPal merchant shopping cart system, you can have your entire merchandise line available for web sales within hours.

Content, Even During the Shopping Experience

Tying it all together, a business website can have a weblog that has teaser articles and excerpts of their e-books, with those pages including purchase links. That material appears again in the company e-mail newsletter, and the teaser articles could also be successfully syndicated to other websites, along with a link to the purchase page.

The plumber who writes the "Don't Try This At Home" weblog could use this exact technique to sell his own e-books on solving common plumbing problems, finding a good plumber, suing for damages from bad plumbing jobs, and so on. Spending four days a week on actual plumbing projects and one day a week creating various online promotions and writing e-books and new articles will invariably produce a larger and more sustainable revenue stream than spending five days of each week fixing customers' pipes.

Care should be taken to ensure that the content on your shopping and product pages doesn't lead the customer too far from the actual transaction, however. Links to product specs or reviews can pop up new windows or move to pages that include the information along with the omnipresent purchase button, but these information pages should have few links to the rest of the site.

The Least You Need to Know

- Any material you place online can be stolen by unscrupulous entrepreneurs, so it's important to protect yourself and know what to do if you do find material stolen.

- There are many legal sources of site content, from other sites to syndication networks to hiring your own writers.

- An excellent place to find hungry writers eager to be published is the local community college journalism department.

- Syndicating your own content can serve as free advertising on other websites and within newsletters.

- Publish your own newsletter with product sales and industry information. Make sure that the list is "double opt-in" to avoid anyone accusing you of sending spam.

- Even your store pages should contain sufficient content to ensure that all customer questions are answered without interrupting their shopping process.

Chapter 23

The Future of Findability

In This Chapter

- ◆ Content matters
- ◆ The benefits of organic linking
- ◆ The future of Google

The history of technology has shown time and again that no one company can retain its monopolistic hold on the industry. A cursory glance at the rise and fall of the Netscape Navigator browser, Yahoo! hierarchical website directory, VisiCalc, and Lotus 1-2-3 reveals that companies come and go with the whims and ever-changing needs of the user community.

This is true in your business segment, too. Whether you have a restaurant, a video rental store, a manufacturing facility, or a home-based weaving cooperative, competitors appear, succeed, miss changes that occur in their customer community, and fail. But not all businesses fail. Some companies ride the waves of change and continually remain on top, whether through the acquisition of smaller competitors or just a superior ability to stay plugged-in with their customers.

You're more likely to have a successful company, too, because you're exploring different ways to grow and expand your business, identify new product lines, become more involved with your customers, and rethink marketing and sales in this new web-based information age.

The last few hundred pages have been focused on how to work with Google and use its tools and software to attain your business goals and grow your business with Google. Some day another search engine will eclipse Google, however, and become the site of choice for finding out about your industry, your product line, and your company.

Your need for findability won't diminish when that happens. The techniques explored herein have been developed to improve your ranking with all search engines. By following the legitimate suggestions and eschewing the inappropriate tricks, by genuinely building a good, interesting, information-packed website, you'll always come out on top.

If the possibility of Google losing its top position in the search engine world concerns you, remember that Google has hundreds of engineers perpetually tinkering with the relevance score formula, identifying automatic methods for detecting SEO tricks, and trying to get closer and closer to the mythical perfect search engine with optimal results for every search.

BizTips

Flip back to Chapter 15 to learn more about the Google dance and how it affects search result rankings.

When you start paying attention to your ranking in the results for a specific keyword search, you may be surprised to see that your ranking fluctuates over time. That change, the result of a Google dance, is symptomatic of continual modifications to their relevance scoring.

An axiom of the restaurant business is "you're only as good as the last meal you served." Restaurant owners are always thinking about what the kitchen is serving today. Not yesterday, not a month ago, not a year ago, but right now. They know that the best way to have a successful restaurant isn't to worry about food critics and what happened last week, but to make today's meal the best it can be, to create a compelling and enticing dining experience for their customers.

Business websites are in the same situation. There are two extensions to the axiom that I suggest apply here: Your website is only as interesting as your newest content, and the best websites are full of compelling information. It's *not* about design, graphics, technology, or even advertising. The path to a successful long-term business website is all about creating and maintaining interesting and engaging content.

It's All About Content!

When I present business seminars about effective website design, I'm always amazed by how few participants have added even a single sentence of content to their site in the previous 60 days. Invariably, they don't understand the web or their customers: It's all about content.

Companies Don't Leverage Their Content Online

It's also astonishing that there are so many content-creating organizations that don't realize that they are sitting on a proverbial gold mine. Instead, they publish their newsletters, magazines, and newspapers but don't make their content available online. Or, in a misguided attempt to monetize their websites, they keep their content open to the public for a few days, then drop it into a for-pay research archive.

Organizations that could have thousands of industry- or region-specific articles instead relegate themselves to niche players by only thinking short-term and missing the opportunity to leverage their invaluable content.

How could they capitalize on their archives? For one, simply having more content online will inevitably lead to more traffic on the website, and if each article includes links to the latest news and the rest of the site, then that traffic will pour onto the rest of the site, too. To monetize the individual pages directly, Google AdSense, discussed in Chapter 19, is an excellent option.

As a middle ground, publishing companies could offer the first three to four paragraphs of their older content online for free, and then charge a small access fee to people interested in reading the remainder of the article.

There's also a synergistic partnership opportunity. A regional business paper could license its content to local companies in return for an affiliatelike relationship, where the publication is paid a commission for each customer who finds the business because of the licensed articles. This is a win-win relationship because the

BizTips

A book publisher could offer the first three to four pages of each chapter of new books online in exactly the same manner. Enough information to attract searchers and engage their interest, followed by a "read the rest of the book, buy a copy at the special discounted price of ..." link.

newspaper leverages its older articles to produce an affiliate revenue stream, and the local companies gain an excellent source of professionally written material that they can include on their sites with the express purpose of attracting more customers. (Licensing content and partnership agreements are both discussed in Chapter 22.)

It's incredibly difficult to sustain website traffic over the long term with tricks, give-aways, and other smart promotions. Websites that gain long-term adherents do so because they offer useful information that's both relevant and interesting to visitors. Even the most successful business sites don't necessarily understand this concept; people go to Amazon.com to shop, but Amazon.com does a poor job of leveraging its information to entice visitors to return.

Shopping malls, by contrast, have long ago figured out that if they can be a destination, a hang-out, and social venue, then they become an important part of the social fabric and more successful in the long term. There's something deeply significant about the parallel trends of teenagers hanging out at shopping malls and these same teenagers having more disposable income and purchasing power than ever before.

Tapping into the Zeitgeist

Translating this into the online world, it's a smart business that creates a discussion forum and helps it become a hangout for future customers. A snowboard manufacturer would be a tremendous success if it offered a discussion forum for snowboard aficionados to share their snowboarding experiences at different ski resorts throughout the world. Think about this myopically or have an old-school board, and you'd kick these people out and shut down the discussion board; they're not talking about your product, so they're wasting your resources.

Buzzwords

Look up the definition yourself, using Google! Simply search for **define:zeitgeist**. Nice secret Google feature, isn't it?

Now that you're content-savvy, however, you recognize that not only are you gaining tremendous branding and PR by association as the host of the discussion forum, but that each discussion, perhaps each individual article, is another hook in the information sea, luring another customer your way. If you add product news, links to your own snowboards, and even Google AdSense advertising to the site, people won't complain. Far from it, they'll be enticed by the product news and advertising and help you turn what could have been a cost center into a significant profit center.

What's really wonderful about creating this kind of great content is that it doesn't take long to be recognized; then you'll find that success breeds success. Newspaper and magazine articles will routinely mention your company and website. This brings more customers to your site, helps generate more content, and helps maintain your visibility in the industry.

Weblogs offer a similar opportunity for producing and maintaining a busy content-centric site that becomes a model for the rest of your industry. Add just two or three new entries each week, and in six months you'll have more content on your site than the leading publication in your segment. A year later, you'll have hundreds of web pages drawing potential customers to your site, customers that arrive because of your efforts to create a great website, not your optimization tricks or willingness to pay for advertising.

Optimizing the Organic Way

Forward-thinking members of the search engine optimization community talk about *organic linking* as an important method of gaining good PageRank. In this case, organic doesn't have anything to do with pesticides or genetically modified organisms; it's referring to sites built page-by-page rather than massive sites built from a database.

Organic linking is the opposite of link farms, in a sense. Link farms, you'll recall, are sites that consist entirely of pages that point to other websites. A typical link farm page will have many hundreds of links and offer zero value in terms of increasing your inbound link count (which is a factor in Google's PageRank calculation).

BizTips

Belay the fancy nomenclature: organic website linking just means that you link to sites that your customers and visitors would find useful and informative.

If we put aside the world of search engine optimization for a moment and think about the halcyon, ideal past of the web, before search engines, websites linked to other websites because they liked the content or company. Sites didn't "exchange" links and there weren't enough different sites to produce pages with more than a hundred links on a given industry or region. You apply organic linking to your website by only linking to sites that you would logically reference. If you're an optometrist, then links to other optical professionals and related businesses make sense and are "organic." Linking to your sister's cat hotel, however, may seem logical to you, but is a thematically irrelevant and therefore nonorganic link.

Does this mean that you should only link to sites that are in your industry or profession? I don't think so. But it is worth being reticent about pointing to completely unrelated websites.

A logical extension to organic linking is organic page design, something that SEO insiders are starting to ponder. The reason that so many of the site optimization tricks are a problem is because they're not organic: no normal web designer specifies white text on a white background, uses a dozen title tags, or engages in keyword stuffing.

> **BizTips** _____
>
> One way to think about the Google PageRank is that it's an organic linking count, and the Google relevance score is an organic content measurement.

Organic page design is also a good rule of thumb for your own web design and web optimization efforts. If you're doing something or adding something that wouldn't normally be found on a web page, then it's probably not a good idea to proceed.

Organic websites grow through the addition of—no surprise—new content. As has occurred so many times previously in this book, we're back to this fundamental method of building a good business website.

Through the Looking Glass: The Future of Google

With a tremendously successful initial public stock offering, Google seems set to stay the leader in the search engine space for quite a few years. Success generates attention, and in this case, also produces hundreds of people trying to figure out how Google works so they can circumvent the system.

After all, this isn't the *Complete Idiot's Guide to Growing Your Business with MSN Search* or with Yahoo! Search or similar search engines. But in five years? Who knows …

The Problem of Affiliate Websites

One of the greatest threats to Google has already been discussed in Chapter 20: affiliate programs. The focus was on whether you should offer an affiliate program, so the problem of affiliate websites and their impact on Google wasn't discussed. Affiliate programs allow the affiliates to use any information on the parent site, including product photographs, product descriptions, and trade and customer reviews. This has produced thousands of affiliate sites that are clones of the merchant sponsoring the affiliate program.

Product searches on Google now match dozens, if not hundreds, of affiliate websites that offer exactly the same information as the company sponsoring the affiliate program. Compounding the problem, busy affiliates are also typically well-versed in search engine optimization techniques. The combination of the two means that there are many searches where the first 5, 10, or even 50 Google search results are the same information on different affiliate websites.

Figure 23.1 shows the search for "GMAT book" on Google. Thirteen of the top 20 matches are Amazon.com affiliates, and one of the affiliate links is actually ranked higher in the results than a book that matches on the Amazon.com website.

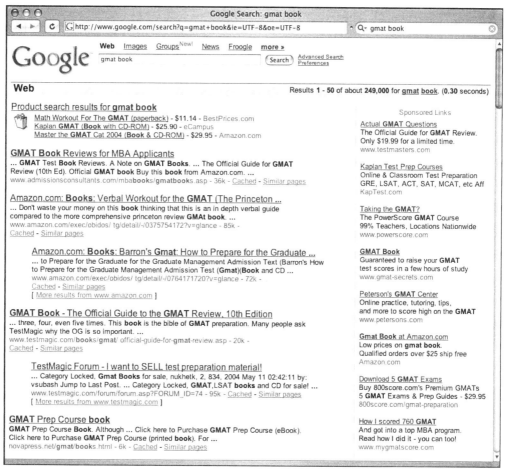

Figure 23.1: Some search spaces are polluted with affiliate and associate pages, making it exceptionally difficult to find genuine content through Google.

How Affiliates Corrupt AdWords

There's nothing prohibiting AdWords customers from buying keywords associated with products, then having an AdWords link that goes directly to Amazon.com or eBay. A search for the sixth volume of the popular Harry Potter series, *Harry Potter and the Half-Blood Prince*, also produces an extensive list of AdWords advertisements. There are nine advertisements shown on the first two results pages, of which seven are Amazon.com affiliates.

BizTips

Affiliate ads with AdWords are required to include *aff, affil,* or *assoc,* so that they're easily distinguished from nonaffiliate advertisements.

Book searches produce Amazon.com affiliate links. Product searches produce eBay affiliate links instead. The search results page for "Barbie doll" includes 45 AdWords ads, of which almost half, 18, are eBay affiliates. The preponderance of affiliate ads forces legitimate businesses to compete with these affiliates when bidding for AdWords keywords and, more importantly, producing web pages that are not just findable, but *more findable*, that is, higher ranked, than affiliate pages.

Memo

As this book went to press, Google changed its policy on affiliate AdWords accounts and now limits AdWords results to only one direct affiliate link. This is a step in the right direction, but mostly just means that affiliates will have to build rudimentary websites that contain the links, rather than just connect directly from Google to eBay, Amazon.com, or similar sites.

The challenge of separating out the proverbial wheat from the chaff, the legitimate organic content pages from those sites produced en masse by affiliates, is the core challenge for Google at this point in time. It's a key reason why their top position in the search engine world might be ephemeral.

Facing the Competition

Google doesn't have a corner on the market for smart search engine algorithms, well-integrated site features, and sophisticated search capabilities. Yahoo!, America Online, Microsoft MSN Network, and even Amazon.com have been aggressively developing their own competing search engines, complete with similar text-only advertisements and sophisticated relevance-scoring systems.

Google could also fall into the trap that Yahoo! did in the last few years, losing focus on their core property in the interest of developing more and more varied tools and capabilities. The Yahoo! website directory has become almost completely marginalized in the last few years as Yahoo! has grown from a web directory into a massive multimedia conglomerate, opening up the door for competitors such as the Open Directory Project, DMOZ, and about.com.

When Amazon.com introduced "search in the book" capabilities, it didn't take long for the Amazon.com engineers to recognize that it was the cornerstone of an interesting and valuable alternative to Google search. Amazon.com introduced a search service called A9 (www.a9.com) that offers search results that integrate both printed book content and web-based content.

Google's response to A9 has been to announce a massive plan to scan and incorporate the content of millions of volumes from academic libraries to its search corpus. Will the addition of this data improve overall search results? It doesn't seem like it matters, somehow. This is more like the battle of the Internet Titans and the probability that the customer—and customer experience—will be forgotten increases with each new announcement and capability.

There are many competitive pressures that are threatening Google and it's not only probable that other search engines will move into the public zeitgeist, but possible that they'll eclipse Google and become the search destination of choice for your potential customers.

As you continue to develop your business website and come up with a plan for increasing your online presence through sharing your expertise, it's critical that you therefore don't work in an exclusively Google-centric manner.

Here are some brief reminders of these general optimization strategies:

- Build your business website with lots of content.

- Consider creating a pair of websites, one informational, and one that serves as more of a product catalog.

- Request links from other sites in your industry and link listing pages like the Open Directory that have topical link pages of value.

- Don't link to other websites unless they actually offer value to your customers or visitors.

- Optimize your web pages using the techniques discussed herein, but avoid all tricks and anything that wouldn't ordinarily—"organically"—be found on a web page.

- Add content frequently, and keep all your old content online. Hundreds of pages are always better than tens of pages.

Don't Write Off Google Yet

Google isn't going to fade away, and its team of engineers is busy working on solving just these problems as they also expand the search service into new document types and new informational archives.

For example, early in 2005 Google changed the method by which affiliates can bid on AdWords ad spots, making it easier for legitimate businesses to have a high AdWords ranking without exceeding their cost-per-click budget.

For the purposes of your business, though, it doesn't matter who wins, or who is the most popular search engine at any given time.

Build the best website you can, add content as frequently as possible, spend the time to find the most popular discussion lists and share your expertise, and you'll grow your business with Google, with MSN Search, with Yahoo!, with AOL Search, and with the entire web community.

The Least You Need to Know

◆ Content makes the web go around. Whatever happens in the world of search engines, sites with more content will see more success than sites with too little content.

◆ Organic links are links that point to your site from other sites that are contextually similar. You should practice organic linking off your site, too. Don't link to unrelated websites.

◆ You can always evaluate your web page modifications by asking if they would occur naturally on the web. If they wouldn't, they're not "organic" and should be avoided.

◆ Google won't always be the top search engine, so it's critical you build the best site you can, eschewing all Google-specific tricks or techniques.

Websites Worth Exploring

The following is a quick reference list of all the websites mentioned in the book, organized by category.

The World of Search Engines

search.aol.com
The America Online search engine, this sees a phenomenal amount of traffic from all the AOL users.

search.msn.com
Microsoft's MSN search engine, this will be the one to watch as a possible Google-killer.

www.a9.com
A fascinating search engine from Amazon.com that lets you search the web and thousands of books simultaneously.

www.dmoz.org
The Open Directory Project. DMOZ sprung out of the ashes of the late, ignored Yahoo! directory of websites.

www.google.com
The king of the search engine hill. It's Google. What else do I need to say?

www.yahoo.com
After using the Google engine for years, Yahoo! woke up one day and realized that they needed their own. Worth exploring because Yahoo! can integrate a lot of unique information sources into their results.

Building an Online Store

smallbusiness.yahoo.com/merchant
Your first stop if you want to build an online store using the popular Yahoo! Shopping system. Worth having a rudimentary store here, even if your main e-commerce site is elsewhere online.

www.amazon.com/marketplace
The Amazon Marketplace is another good option for building a store, though it can be a bit confusing.

stores.ebay.com
You can have a store on eBay as a marketing strategy, too, even if you just have fixed-price goods.

www.froogle.com
Froogle is a catalog search system integrated into Google and you can include your product line information without charge. Well worth doing.

Discussion Boards and Mailing Lists

lists.topica.com
Thousands of different mailing lists on almost any topic imaginable, though the search engine is quite poor.

groups.google.com
An excellent interface to the world of Usenet discussion groups and Google-hosted mailing lists, with an archive of millions of discussion articles.

groups.yahoo.com
One of the premier sources for finding industry and topical mailing lists, Yahoo! hosts tens of thousands of active discussions.

The World of Blogging

www.blogger.com
A Google company, Blogger is a simple way to experiment with the world of weblogs, though it's not suitable for business weblogs.

daypop.com
feedster.com
infopop.com
syndic8.com
technorati.com
Weblog article aggregators, you can search Daypop, Feedster, InfoPop, Syndic8, or Technorati to learn about bloggers who are writing about your company, products, or industry.

www.movabletype.org
One of the premier weblog software vendors, Movable Type is powerful, sophisticated, and difficult to configure properly.

www.typepad.com
Typepad is the hosted version of Movable Type, a service more akin to Blogger, where you can create your own weblog on their system rather than hosting it yourself. Since they let you use your own domain name, this is a good entry point for a business-oriented weblog.

www.wordpress.org
A popular alternative weblog package, many journalists use Wordpress as the foundation of their weblogs.

Affiliate and Advertising Reference Sites

adwords.google.com
The Google AdWords program lets you pay for text ads that only display in relevant contexts on Google's search results pages and pages in the AdSense network. A critical ingredient to any successful web business.

www.cj.com
Commission Junction is the leader in the world of affiliate marketing, and whether you're a merchant interested in adding your company to their list of affiliates or want to just sign up to be an affiliate, CJ's the place to start.

www.google.com/adsense/
AdSense is the yang to AdWord's yin, a program where contextually relevant text ads can be included on specific pages on your own site. When someone clicks on the advertisement, you earn a small commission.

www.myap.com
My Affiliate Program is a smaller but powerful affiliate management system ideal for merchants experimenting with using affiliate programs to expand their sales force in a cost-effective manner.

www.wordtracker.com
Whether you're trying to identify how your customers perform online searches or pick the very best keywords for your own text ads, WordTracker offers superb data and takes this critical step of building an ad campaign out of the dark.

Finding Staff

www.craigslist.com
A true Internet phenomenon, Craigslist is a remarkably humble website that is an excellent tool for finding help with your web and business projects.

www.elance.com
If you'd like to identify outsourcing options from overseas, eLance is a good place to start. There are many web and business people from India, the Eastern Soviet nations, and Asia who bid on projects through this site.

Content Sources

ezinearticles.com
ideamarketers.com
isyndicate.com
mediapeak.com
All of these sites offer fresh content for your own website for free. They also offer a venue for you to publish your own materials and build additional backlinks to your business website.

The Author's Websites

www.askdavetaylor.com
A technical and business Q&A site, Ask Dave Taylor is referenced extensively in this book and demonstrates many best practices.

www.colorado-portraits.com
The author as award-winning photographer. A simple site that has nonetheless been optimized for search engine placement.

www.findability.info
This is the home of the supplemental content for this book.

www.intuitive.com
The author's main website, with extensive articles, reference materials, and even a public reading library to attract visitors.

www.intuitive.com/blog/
The Intuitive Life weblog is one of six weblogs that the author maintains and uses to manage the information on the site.

www.RealLifeDebt.com
A topic-specific website, this information source also serves as a research test bed for search engine techniques with its hundreds of pages of content, popular weblog, paid advertising, Google AdSense, and more. Another site worth studying for good techniques.

Exemplary Websites

www.ask-leo.com
Another technical Q&A website, by an expert in the world of Windows and Microsoft products.

www.askthebuilder.com
Ask The Builder is a superb example of how a general contractor rethought his business for the twenty-first century and became a wildly successful information publisher.

www.bestwebbuys.com
With its price comparison system and multiple data sources all smoothly integrated into each page, Best Web Buys is an excellent example of an affiliate site.

www.flowersfast.com
It's hard to differentiate floral websites, particularly since so many are affiliates of the FTD service, but Flowers Fast demonstrates many smart strategies in this regard and is worth visiting.

www.laborposter.com
Sometimes a very specific site for a very specific product can yield excellent results. LaborPoster.com is actually a page on a much larger business website, but it helps searchers identify and purchase posters online.

www.lockergnome.com
An excellent information resource, Lockergnome has long been on the forefront of weblog and RSS technologies, and its methods of leveraging content across multiple media are superb.

www.myweddingfavors.com
An example of an attractive and highly effective business website built around the Yahoo! Shopping system.

www.thisistrue.com
Popular stories, topical content, and a simple search engine–friendly design all contribute to making This Is True an extremely successful business website. When you visit, notice how products are promoted within the context of freely shared information.

Glossary

AdSense   An advertising network run by Google that allows you to add contextually relevant ads to pages on your own site. It is the presentation side of AdWords.

AdWords   A keyword-based advertising network that enables you to advertise directly on relevant search results pages and on other content pages throughout the web through the AdSense network.

affiliate websites   A business site built around one or more affiliate programs. These sites are characterized by having no original content, and currently they adversely impact product search results.

applet   A small, portable program that's intended to be downloaded to the visitor's computer and run. It then produces and controls some of the material on the web page. Many applets offer exciting visual effects, sounds, and animation, but it's important to balance eye candy versus findability.

backlink   A page that points to a given web page.

bandwidth   The amount of traffic your site sees. Think of it as water flowing through a pipe: To be able to have more water go through the pipe, you need to enlarge the pipe. If you receive sufficient traffic to require a bigger pipe (that is, more bandwidth to your server), you can easily end up paying hundreds or thousands more each month.

blog   *See* weblog.

click-through rate (CTR)   The percentage of people who click on a link out of the total number who see the link. In advertising terms, CTR measures how well the advertisement is targeted: A higher CTR is more desirable.

cloaking   In online marketing terms, cloaking is the trick of presenting a different version of a web page to a search engine spider than that which the visitor will actually see. This is a dangerous and prohibited technique.

conversion rate   The relationship between the people who visit a page or site and those that engage in a desired behavior. Typically this measures purchasers versus visitors, and a high conversion rate is more desirable.

cookie   A cookie is a message sent from a web server to a visitor's computer that's then saved on the computer and sent back to the website on the next visit. This is used for tracking visitors, remembering login accounts, and similar tasks.

cost per click (CPC)   In advertising terms, cost per click is the amount of money that the advertiser agrees to pay each time someone clicks on their advertisement and goes to their website.

CPM   CPM is cost per thousand. The "M" comes from the Latin *mil*, thousand, just as a *millimeter* is a thousandth of a meter, not a millionth. Here's how Google explains it: "CPM is a useful way to compare revenue across different channels and advertising programs. It is calculated by dividing total earnings by the number of impressions in thousands. For example, if a publisher earned $180 from 45,000 impressions, the CPM would equal $180/45, or $4.00."

crawler   A software application that extracts links from web pages and then visits those pages, extracting both content information and links.

deep linking   When one website points to the home page of another site, that's called a link. When one site points to a specific subpage on another site, a page other than the home page, that's considered a "deep" link. The further away from the home page the link points (determined by the number of clicks required to find it), the deeper the link is considered.

differentiators   Differentiators are those characteristics of your business that are different from those of your competitors. For example, Southwest Airline's unassigned seating strategy is an important differentiator in the airline industry, and Apple Computer's emphasis on the design of their products differentiates them from their competitors.

doorway page   A web page created specifically to rate highly for a given keyword or key phrase, it invariably leads visitors to a different web page that's part of the real website. These are also known as bridge pages and gateway pages.

double opt-in mailing lists   A mailing list where people request to be added and then are on the list is an "opt-in" list, and it's prone to sabotage by having one person sign up another. A double opt-in list is one where each person who signs up is e-mailed a confirmation message that they must respond favorably to before they're actually added to the list.

ego bidding   Refers to bidding whatever price is necessary to have your advertisement appear in the #1 position on AdWords and similar pay-per-click ad networks.

evergreen content   Just as evergreen trees never lose their leaves, evergreen content is material that will be as relevant in a year as it is today. A website with evergreen content will become a resource for industry and customers alike.

e-zine   An e-zine is an electronic magazine that's distributed purely through the Internet, typically as an electronic mailing list.

gateway page   *See* doorway page

Google dance   The Google dance is a sporadic adjustment to the Google relevance formula that results in your pages being ranked higher or lower for specific keyword searches.

heuristics   Heuristics are the set of evaluatory formulas that Google applies when it analyzes a web page to figure out the main subject or theme of the page.

HTML   *Hypertext markup language*, the language that web designers use to create web pages. It's not terribly difficult to learn and there are some very sophisticated tools that make producing simple HTML as easy as typing in Microsoft Word.

interrupt-driven advertising   Advertising that interrupts what you're doing and forces you to view the advertisement. Television commercials are interrupt-driven advertising, while sponsor billboards on the side of a soccer field are not.

keyword stuffing   A malicious practice, keyword stuffing is using tricks to increase the *keyword density* of certain keywords on a page without those keywords being visible to the user. This can be done by putting these keywords within comments, making up fake HTML tags that are ignored by browsers but seen by search engines, and so on. Keyword stuffing is a bad idea, and if a crawler like Googlebot detects it on your page, it'll toss the page out of the database entirely.

lateral search   Lateral searches produce thematically related keywords by identifying the most commonly occurring words or phrases on web pages that also match your specific search term. A lateral search for Coca-cola could produce additional keywords *Coke*, *Pepsi*, and *soda*, for example.

link farm   A website built exclusively of pages that are lists of links to other sites without any content of their own. They exist purely to increase the inbound link count for other sites and should be avoided.

meta tag   One of a class of special HTML markup tags that weren't included in the original language definition. They all start with the word "meta," hence the name.

negative keyword   A word or phrase for which, if it's included in the search query, your advertisement shouldn't be shown. You can either use these as block words in AdWords so that your ad will never show up with these searches, or bid a minimum amount on these keywords just to see what happens. A knife seller would identify "make" as a negative keyword to avoid matching searches for "how to make a knife".

organic linking   The practice of linking only to sites that you would logically reference and that are contextually relevant to your industry or profession.

PageRank   All web pages in the Google database are assigned a "PageRank," a measure of their relevance and relative importance for specific keywords and key phrases. Among the variables that are part of the PageRank formula are the number of other web pages that point to the page, the frequency of the keyword or key phrase on the page, and whether the keywords or key phrases are emphasized on the page. PageRank is such an important topic that it is explored in Chapter 5.

robot   *See* crawler

secondary pages   Any page other than the home page on a website. Secondary pages are traditionally thought of as pages that the visitor has to "click through" to get to, though with the rise of search engines, all pages are really primary pages on a site.

secure server   Web browsers communicate with remote web servers using a simple protocol called *hypertext transport protocol*. It's not secure and any information sent that way can theoretically be intercepted en route. The secure alternative is called SSL, the secure socket layer. You're using SSL every time the website addresses changes from an "http:" to an "https:".

SEO   An acronym for "search engine optimization."

SERP   An acronym that you frequently see in discussions about search engine placement, SERP stands for "Search Engine Results Page."

signature block   A sequence of three to five lines of text that is automatically appended to each and every message you send out, whether to individuals or mailing lists.

SKU   A stock-keeping unit; a unique identifier that allows both merchandise and inventory control.

spam   Unsolicited communication from a company to an individual, most typically through electronic mail. You never want to engage in this or give any potential customer reason to think you might be spamming them. To avoid that, ensure you only maintain double opt-in mailing lists.

spider   *See* crawler

sustainable differentiators   A differentiator is something that lets customers see how you are different from your competitors, and a *sustainable differentiator* is a differentiator that you continue to leverage even after your competitors realize how smart your differentiator is and seek to use it themselves. It's much harder to have a sustainable differentiator. Consider how other airlines now have low-cost shuttle services with seating similar to that of Southwest Airlines, and how Apple's design success has spawned dozens of look-alike PC manufacturers. This is where branding proves important, because brands have legal protection. Pepsi can't advertise themselves as "The Real Thing," and Chevy isn't "Built Ford Tough."

weblog   Weblogs, also known informally as "blogs," started out as informal online diaries, but weblog management tools have since evolved to where they now offer an ingenious method of managing a website where the *content* is separated out from the *underlying technology*. The tremendous upside is that weblog authors can write a few paragraphs of text as if they were composing an e-mail message and have the tools automatically turn their message into attractive and cross-linked material on the website. Weblogs embody many important concepts that help you learn how to grow your business with Google. See Chapter 15 for more details.

Index

A

A9 search service
  (Amazon.com), 299
About.com, submitting
  websites to, 188-189
Abracat, AdHound, 105
accounts, Google AdWords,
  29
ad blocks (AdSense), 237
  configuration, 237-239
  where to add ad blocks,
    244
ad campaigns, Google
  AdWords, 220
  AdGroups, 221-222
  daily budget, 225
  editing and modifying
    campaign settings,
    225-228
  language and location tar-
    geting, 221
  maximum cost-per-click
    bid, 223-225
  monitoring, 231-232
  setting per-keyword maxi-
    mum cost-per-click,
    228-231
  specification of keywords,
    223
  writing ad copy, 232-233
ad trackers, monitoring competitors, 105-106
AdGroups, 221-222
AdHound (Abracat), 105
AdSense (Google AdSense),
  30-32, 236-248
  ad blocks, 237

avoiding ads from com-
    petitors, 245-247
  business focus, 243-244
  configuring ad blocks,
    237-239
  maximizing click-through
    rates, 240-241
  revenue, 241-243
  utilization for Search, 245
  where to add ad blocks,
    244
advanced Google searches,
  40-46
  "|" notation, 41
  logical "or," 41
  minus sign, 40
  parentheses, 41
  plus sign, 40
  quoting, 43
  special search notations,
    43-45
  word order, 45-46
Advantage (Amazon), 194
advertising
  Google AdSense, 236-248
    ad blocks, 237
    avoiding ads from com-
      petitors, 245-247
    business focus, 243-244
    configuring ad blocks,
      237-239
    maximizing click-
      through rates, 240-241
    revenue, 241-243
    utilization for Search,
      245
    where to add ad blocks,
      244

Google AdWords, 213-215
    ad campaigns, 220-233
    keywords, 215-220
    interrupt-driven advertis-
      ing, 213-214
AdWords (Google AdWords),
  22, 28, 213
  ad campaigns, 220
    AdGroups, 221-222
    daily budget, 225
    editing and modifying
      campaign settings,
      225-228
    language and location
      targeting, 221
    maximum cost-per-click
      bid, 223-225
    monitoring, 231-232
    setting per-keyword
      maximum cost-per-
      click, 228-231
    specification of key-
      words, 223
    writing ad copy,
      232-233
  affiliate programs, 298
  keyword research tool, 237
  keywords, 215-216
    keyword research tool,
      219-220
    WordTracker, 216-219
  specific searches, 29
affiliate programs, 250-260,
  296-298
  adding affiliate
    products/services to sites,
    257
  AdWords, 298
  Amazon.com, 250

application requirements, 257
Commission Junction, 252
PayPal, 251
sample affiliates, 258-259
signing up, 259-260
SKUs (stock keeping units), 251
TOS agreements, 252
 acceptable promotional techniques, 255-256
 acceptable sites, 253-254
 commission structure and payment, 256
 ownership of intellectual property, 254-255
Yahoo!, 252
Age of Information, 4
ALT text, 270
Amazon
 A9 search service, 299
 affiliate program, 250
 diversification, 62
 one-click purchasing, 87
animated graphics, 126
applets, 163
application requirements, affiliate programs, 257
Artdolls website, 84
Ask Dave Taylor website, 11
Ask The Builder website, 90
assessment of your business, 61
 competitors, 67-69
 current Internet strategy, 8
  brand identity, 11
  e-mail and one-to-one communication, 8
  newsletters and publishing venues, 9-10
  online store, 10
  website, 10

customers, 12
differentiators, 6-8, 64-67
focus, 62-64
goals, 69-70
Atom, 182
authors, republishing, 281
automatic refresh, 268

B

backlink farming tools, 271-272
bandwidth, 15, 177
benefits of Google, 3
Blogger, 32-33
blogosphere, 104
blogs, 14, 32-33
 as content management systems, 178-180
  incorporation in site, 180
  RSS feeds, 181-183
  writing for weblogs, 184
 information sharing, 209-210
 learning what customers are discussing, 117
 submitting to blog indices, 191-192
 tracking new competitors, 104
brand identity, assessing business Internet strategy, 11
breadcrumb trails, 165
bridge pages, 267
Brin, Sergey, 37
broad matches, AdWords keyword phrases, 223
building business websites, 121-135
 avoiding design fads, 125-127

avoiding ethnocentric sites, 133
calls to action, 129-130
collaboration with experts, 124
five simple ideas, 134-135
keeping site on topic, 122-123
limiting complexity, 124
minimizing off-site links, 131
responsiveness to customers, 132-133
search engine–friendly sites, 127
secure servers, 129
selling company to visitors, 130-132
trustworthiness, 127-128
business assessment, 61
 competitors, 67-69
 current Internet strategy, 8
  brand identity, 11
  e-mail and one-to-one communication, 8
  newsletters and publishing venues, 9-10
  online store, 10
  website, 10
 customers, 12
 differentiators, 6-8, 64-67
 focus, 62-64
 goals, 69-70
business names/slogans, 74-75
business websites, 121-122
 appeal to clients, 82-83
 avoiding design fads, 125-127
 avoiding ethnocentric sites, 133
 calls to action, 129-130

collaboration with experts, 124

content, 86
  core content, 87-89
  development, 174-178
  findability, 89-90
  informational articles, 90-91
  management systems, 178-184

design, 161
  keyword density, 166-167
  link exchanges, 169
  meta tags, 165-166
  naming links and pages effectively, 167
  page design, 162-164
  page titles, 164-165
  thematically related inbound links, 168

five simple ideas, 134-135

information sharing, 200-201
  discussion boards, 207-208
  industry experts, 201-202
  mailing lists, 202-207
  Usenet groups, 210-211
  weblogs, 209-210

integration of online and offline content, 137-138
  customer service, 149
  information sources, 148-149
  promotion of website in physical world, 140-141
  providing frequently asked questions, 142-148
  visual consistency across media, 138-140

keeping site on topic, 122-123

limiting complexity, 124

minimizing off-site links, 131

multiple sites, 93-94

responsiveness to customers, 132-133

search engine–friendly sites, 127

secondary pages, 83-84

secure servers, 129

selling company to visitors, 130-132

submitting to search engines, 186
  About.com, 188-189
  Open Directory Project, 187-188
  topical web directories, 189-191
  Yahoo! Directory, 186-187

tools to avoid, 271-273

tricks to avoid, 265
  different pages for different visitors, 267-268
  doorway pages, 267
  duplicate content, 270
  excess links, 269
  hidden or cloaked text, 266
  keyword stuffing, 266-267
  limiting ALT text and META keywords, 270
  refresh pages, 268
  SEO content pages, 269
  TITLE tags, 271

trustworthiness, 127-128

updates, 92

C

calls to action, building business websites, 129-130

Campaign Daily Budget (Google AdWords), 226

Campaign Summary (Google AdWords), 226

capturing queries, 115-116

Cascading Style Sheet Web design technology, 127

cease-and-desist letters, 279

channels (AdSense), 241

Chevron Corporation, differentiators, 65

city/regional accounts (Google AdWords), 29

classified ads, monitoring competitors, 105-106

click-through rates (AdSense). *See* CTR

ClickThruStats website, 232

cloaked text, 266

Commission Junction, 250-252
  affiliate programs, 258-259
  signing up, 259-260

commission structure, TOS agreements (affiliate programs), 256

commoditization, differentiators, 66

communication, customer communications, 156-160

competitors, 67
  avoiding ads (AdSense), 245-247
  differentiators, 6
  discussion boards, 106-107
  evolution of markets, 68
  future of Google, 298-299
  identification
    evaluating competitors, 100-101

global businesses,
99-100
local businesses, 96-99
lessons learned, 68-69
monitoring classified ads,
105-106
tracking
Google News Alerts,
101-102
Usenet, 103-104
weblogs, 104
configurations, AdSense ad
blocks, 237-239
content, 293
business websites, 86
core content, 87-89
findability, 89-90
informational articles,
90-91
testimonials, 87
copyright law, 278-280
discussion boards, 294-295
discussion forums, 176-177
evergreen content, 277
finding content for site,
178
games, 177-178
integration of online and
offline content, 137
customer service, 149
information sources,
148-149
promotion of website in
physical world,
140-141
providing frequently
asked questions,
142-148
visual consistency across
media, 138-140
leveraging content online,
293-294

licensing
excerpts, 282
finding authors to
republish, 281
hiring writers, 283-284
republishing magazine
articles, 280-281
syndication programs,
282
management systems,
weblogs, 178-184
online stores, 288-289
publishing e-mail newsletters, 286-287
surveys, 177-178
syndication, 284-286
updates, 174-176
web pages
avoiding design excess,
163-164
influence on relevance
scoring, 57
cookie tracking (affiliate programs), 260
copyright
laws, 278-280
protection, 91
symbol, 278
core business, 61-62
competitors, 67-69
differentiators, 64-67
focus, 62-64
goals, 69-70
core content, business websites, 87-89
cost centers, 24
cost per thousand. *See* CPM
costs, traffic, 15-16
CPM (cost per thousand),
241
*Creating Cool Web Sites with
HTML, XHTML and CSS*,
121
cross-linking, 192-193

CTR (click-through rates),
240-241
current Internet strategy,
business assessment, 8
brand identity, 11
e-mail and one-to-one
communication, 8
newsletters and publishing
venues, 9-10
online store, 10
website, 10
customers
attracting to website,
17-18
being your own customer,
35-36
building buzz about prod-
ucts, services ideas, 19-21
business assessment, 12
customer service, 149
discussion boards, 116-117
driving to products in
store, 18-19
focus on customer desires,
64
learning what customers
seek, 111
queries from personal
site, 115-116
Wordtracker, 111-115
mailing lists, 118
maximizing value of mar-
keting and PR, 22
responsiveness to, 132-133
traffic costs, 15-16
understanding your cus-
tomers, 110-111
weblogs, 117
website appeal, 82-83
customized accounts (Google
AdWords), 29

D

daily budget, ad campaigns, 225
deep links, 83
design of websites, 161
  fads, 125-127
  keyword density, 166-167
  link exchanges, 169
  meta tags, 165-166
  naming links and pages effectively, 167
  page design, 162-164
  page titles, 164-165
  thematically related inbound links, 168
designers (website), 161
development
  business websites, 161
    keyword density, 166-167
    meta tags, 165-166
    naming links and pages effectively, 167
    page design, 162-164
    page titles, 164-165
    thematically related inbound links, 168
  content, 137
    customer service, 149
    information sources, 148-149
    promotion of website in physical world, 140-141
    providing frequently asked questions, 142-148
    visual consistency across media, 138-140

differentiators, 6-8, 64-67
Digital Ocean website, 131
directories
  submitting websites to
    About.com, 188-189
    Open Directory Project, 187-188
    topical web directories, 189-191
    Yahoo! Directory, 186-187
  topical website directories, 4
  weblogs, 191-192
discussion boards, 294-295
  content development, 176-177
  information sharing, 207-208
  learning what customers are discussing, 116-117
  monitoring competitors, 106-107
distribution lists, 287
diversification, 24, 62-63
DMOZ (Open Directory Project), 187-188
Dogpile (search engine), 112
domain name system, 72-73
  findability, 75-76
  Internet-friendly business names and slogans, 74-75
  obtaining a domain name, 77-80
  trademarks, 76
doorway pages, 267
dotcom crash, 72
double opt-in requirement (distribution lists), 158, 287
duplicate content, 270

E

eBay, 194-195
Edit Campaign Settings link (Google AdWords), 226
Edit Campaign Settings page (Google AdWords), 227
editing ad campaigns, 225, 228
ego bidding, 225
e-mail
  as advertisements, 203-204
  assessing business Internet strategy, 8
  newsletters, 286-287
ethnocentric sites, 133
etiquette, mailing lists, 206-207
evaluation of competitors, 100-101
evergreen content, 277
evolution of markets, competitors, 68
exact matches, AdWords keyword phrases, 223
excerpts, publishing on website, 282
excess links, 269
exchange of links
  cross-linking, 192-193
  web page design, 169
experts, information sharing, 201-202
EzineArticles.com database, 282

F

fads, 125-127
FC Now weblog, 180
Feedster, 117
Feedster News Alerts, 104

findability, 4-5
  being your own customer, 35-36
  business website content, 89-90
  domain names, 75-76
  Google searches, 36
    advanced Google searches, 40-46
    how customers find you, 39-40
    narrowing search with more words, 39
    one- or two-word searches, 38
    PageRank, 37
    web page searches, 38
  weblogs, 13-15
  websites, 9
Flash (Macromedia Flash), 126
focus, business assessment, 62-64
formula
  PageRank, 48-52
  relevance scoring, 54-57
    content and structure of web page, 57
    graphical links, 54
    inbound links, 54
    internal links, 56
    nondescriptive links, 55
    text links, 54-56
Frequently Asked Questions
  information sharing, 200
  integration of online and offline content
    question and answer formats, 142-145
    weblogs as Q&A alternatives, 146-148
  Usenet groups, 210
frictionless commerce, 87
Froogle, 33-34, 197-198
future of Google, 296-300

G

games, content development, 177-178
gateway pages, 267
Geneology.com affiliate program, 255
global businesses, identification of competitors, 99-100
global/nationwide accounts (Google AdWords), 29
Gmail, 26-27
goals (company), 69-70
Good, Robin, 192
Google AdSense, 30-32, 236-248
  avoiding ads from competitors, 245-247
  business focus, 243-244
  configuring ad blocks, 237-239
  maximizing click-through rates, 240-241
  revenue, 241-243
  utilization for Search, 245
  where to add ad blocks, 244
Google AdWords, 28-29, 213-215
  ad campaigns, 220
    AdGroups, 221-222
    daily budget, 225
    editing and modifying campaign settings, 225-228
    language and location targeting, 221
    maximum cost-per-click bid, 223-225
    monitoring, 231-232
    setting per-keyword maximum cost-per-click, 228-231

specification of keywords, 223
    writing ad copy, 232-233
  customized accounts, 29
  global/nationwide accounts, 29
  keywords, 215
    keyword research tool, 219-220
    WordTracker, 216-219
  regional/city accounts, 29
  specific searches, 29
Google dance, 173-174
Google Groups, 116
Google Labs, 25
Google News Alerts, 101-102
Google Press Center, 155
Googlebot, 53, 174
graphical links, relevance scoring formula, 54
Groups (Google Groups), 116

H

hallway pages, 267
heuristics, 28
Hewlett, Bill, 36
Hewlett-Packard. *See* HP
hidden text, 266
hiring writers, licensing content, 283-284
home page (Google), 25
HP (Hewlett-Packard), 36
HTML text links, 55
HTML-based newsletters, 157
http (hypertext transport protocol), 129
hypertext transport protocol. *See* http
hyphenated domain names, 75

I

ideas, increasing community interest, 19-21
identification of competitors
    evaluating competitors, 100-101
    global businesses, 99-100
    local businesses, 96-99
inbound links
    cross-linking, 192-193
    relevance scoring formula, 54
    web page design, 168-169
industry awards, 148
industry experts, information sharing, 201-202
InfoPop, 177
information sharing, 200-201
    discussion boards, 207-208
    industry experts, 201-202
    mailing lists, 202
        e-mail as advertisements, 203-204
        etiquette, 206-207
        searching for, 206-207
        signatures, 204-205
    Usenet groups, 210-211
    weblogs, 209-210
information sources, 90-91, 148-149
integration of online and offline content, 137
    customer service, 149
    information sources, 148-149
    promotion of website in physical world, 140-141
    providing frequently asked questions, 142
        question and answer formats, 142-145

weblogs as Q&A alternatives, 146-148
visual consistency across media, 138-140
intellectual property, ownership, 254-255
internal links, 56
Internet strategy, business assessment, 8
    brand identity, 11
    e-mail and one-to-one communication, 8
    newsletters and publishing venues, 9-10
    online store, 10
    website, 10
interrupt-driven advertising, 213-214
intitle: searches (advanced Google searches), 44
Intuitive Life Business Blog articles, 92
inurl: searches (advanced Google searches), 44
Invision Power Services, 177

J

Java-based menu bars, 163
JavaScript menu pop-ups, 163
job listings, monitoring competitors, 105-106

K

KEI Analysis (Wordtracker), 114
key phrases, advanced Google searches, 43
Keyhole, 25
keyword research tool (AdWords), 219-220, 237

keywords
    ad campaigns, 223
    density, 166-167
    domain name findability, 75-76
    Google AdWords, 215
        keyword research tool, 219-220, 237
        WordTracker, 216-219
    ranking for obscure keywords, 264-265
    stuffing, 166, 266-267

L

Labs (Google Labs), 25
Lamberg, Paul, 123
landing pages, 160
lateral searches (Wordtracker), 113
laws, copyright, 278-280
layout, web pages, 57
licensing content
    excerpts, 282
    finding authors to republish, 281
    hiring writers, 283-284
    republishing magazine articles, 280-281
    syndication programs, 282
link farms, 264, 295
LinkShare, 250
List Apart, A, 127
local businesses, 96-99
logical "or," advanced Google searches, 41

M

Macromedia Flash, 126
magazine articles, republishing, 280-281

mailing lists
information sharing, 202
e-mail as advertise-
ments, 203-204
etiquette, 206-207
searching for lists,
206-207
signatures, 204-205
learning what customers
are discussing, 118
topical mailing lists, 107
management, content,
178-184
market evolution, competitors, 68
marketing
expanding online presence
newsletters and cus-
tomer communica-
tions, 156-158
press releases, 155
product-based websites,
153-155
sponsorship of newslet-
ters and sites, 159-160
expenditures, 152-153
maximizing value, 22
role in website content
development, 139
transforming positive feedback into marketing col-
lateral, 21
Marketplace (Amazon), 194
MassageSpecialists website,
84
maximum cost-per-click bid
(ad campaigns), 223-225
Men's Warehouse, differentiators, 65
meta refresh, 268
META tags, 165-166, 270
Metacrawler (search engine),
112
Microsoft MSN Search, 4

mini-stores, 193
eBay, 194-195
Froogle Merchant
Program, 197-198
Yahoo! Shop, 195-197
minus sign, advanced Google
searches, 40
modifying ad campaigns,
225-228
monitoring AdWords cam-
paigns, 231-232
MSN Search, 4, 58
multiple websites, 93-94
MyAffiliateProgram, 250
Myst Technology, 180

N

names
business, 74-75
links and pages, 167
narrowing Google searches,
39
nationwide/global accounts
(Google AdWords), 29
navigation toolbars, 163
negative keywords, 219
Netnews Tracker, 104
networked ad distribution
system (AdSense), 30-32
NewsGator Online, 183
newsletters
assessing business Internet
strategy, 9-10
HTML-based newsletters,
157
integration of online and
offline content, 156
avoiding spam label,
158
sponsorships, 159-160
writing styles, 157-158
publishing own e-mail
newsletters, 286-287

"next bench" concept, 36
nondescriptive links, 55
Nordstrom, differentiators,
65
notations, Google search
notations, 43-45

O

obscure keywords ranking,
264-265
obtaining a domain name,
77-80
offline content, integration
with online content,
137-138
customer service, 149
information sources,
148-149
promotion of website in
physical world, 140-141
providing frequently asked
questions, 142-148
visual consistency across
media, 138-140
off-site links, 131
one-word searches, 38
one-click purchasing
(Amazon), 87
one-to-one communication, 8
online content, integration
with offline content,
137-138
customer service, 149
information sources,
148-149
promotion of website in
physical world, 140-141
providing frequently asked
questions, 142-148
visual consistency across
media, 138-140
online diaries, blogs, 14

online stores, 193
assessing business Internet strategy, 10
content, 288-289
eBay, 194-195
Froogle Merchant Program, 197-198
Yahoo! Shop, 195-197
Open Directory Project, 187-188
opt-in lists, 158
optimization strategies, 299
organic linking, 295-296
Orkut, 34
Other World Computing, 287
ownership of intellectual property, 254-255

P

Packard, David, 36
page impressions (AdSense), 241
Page Relevance Score, 37
page titles, 164-165
Page, Larry, 37
PageRank, 37, 48-52
parentheses, advanced Google searches, 41
pay for placement scams, 262-264
payment structure, TOS agreements (affiliate programs), 256
PayPal, 251
perceived scarcity, 27
Performics, 250
pipe symbol, advanced Google searches, 41
plug-ins, 126
plural keyword searches, 217
plus sign, advanced Google searches, 40

pop-up windows, 127
position analysis tools, 271
position articles, 148
positive feedback, 21
PR, maximizing value, 22
press releases, 148, 155
Proctor & Gamble, 153
product literature, 148
product-based websites, 153-155
products
advertising
Google AdSense, 236-248
Google AdWords, 213-233
Froogle database, 33-34
increasing community interest, 19-21
selling via online stores, 193
eBay, 194-195
Froogle Merchant Program, 197-198
Yahoo! Shop, 195-197
profit centers, 24
promotional mistakes
link farms, 264
pay for placement scams, 262-264
ranking for obscure keywords, 264-265
tools to avoid, 271-273
tricks to avoid on website, 265
different pages for different visitors, 267-268
doorway pages, 267
duplicate content, 270
excess links, 269
hidden or cloaked text, 266

keyword stuffing, 266-267
limiting ALT text and META keywords, 270
refresh pages, 268
SEO content pages, 269
TITLE tags, 271
publishing
e-mail newsletters, 286-287
venues, 9-10
punctuation, advanced Google searches
"|" notation, 41
logical "or," 41
minus sign, 40
parentheses, 41
plus sign, 40
quoting, 43

Q

Q&A alternatives, weblogs, 146-148
qualified traffic, 15
queries, tracking, 115-116
question and answer formats (frequently asked questions), 142-145
quoting, advanced Google searches, 43

R

radio ad test, domain names, 73
ranking for obscure keywords, 264-265
Real-Life-Debt.com website, 258
refresh pages, 268
regional/city accounts (Google AdWords), 29
registration, domain names, 77-80

relevance scoring
formula, 54-57
content and structure of
web page, 57
graphical links, 54
inbound links, 54
internal links, 56
nondescriptive links, 55
text links, 54-56
Google dance, 173-174
republishing
authors, 281
magazine articles, 280-281
responsiveness to customers,
132-133
revenue (AdSense), 241-243
RSS feeds, 181-183

S

scams
link farms, 264
pay for placement scams,
262-264
ranking for obscure key-
words, 264-265
Scholar Search, 34
Search, AdSense utilization,
245
search engine optimization
experts. *See* SEO experts
search engine results page.
See SERP
search engines
building business websites,
127
Dogpile, 112
Metacrawler, 112
MSN Search, 58
submitting websites to
About.com, 188-189
Open Directory Project,
187-188

topical web directories,
189-191
Yahoo! Directory,
186-187
Yahoo!, 37, 58
searches, 36
advanced Google searches
"|" notation, 41
logical "or," 41
minus sign, 40
parentheses, 41
plus sign, 40
quoting, 43
special search notations,
43-45
word order, 45-46
domain name findability,
75-76
how customers find you,
39-40
mailing lists, 206-207
narrowing search with
more words, 39
one- or two-word searches,
38
PageRank, 37
web page searches, 38
secondary pages, 83-84
secure servers, 129
secure socket layer. *See* SSL
selling products
Froogle database, 33-34
online stores, 193
eBay, 194-195
Froogle Merchant
Program, 197-198
Yahoo! Shop, 195-197
SEO content pages, 269
SEO (search engine optimization) experts, 48, 162
SERP (search engine results
page), 264
servers, secure, 129

sharing information, 200
discussion boards, 207-208
industry experts, 201-202
mailing lists, 202
e-mail as advertise-
ments, 203-204
etiquette, 206-207
searching for, 206-207
signatures, 204-205
Usenet groups, 210-211
weblogs, 209-210
shopping, online stores, 193
eBay, 194-195
Froogle Merchant
Program, 33-34, 197-198
Yahoo! Shop, 195-197
shopping cart systems
online stores, 288
PayPal, 251
signatures, mailing lists,
204-205
signing up, affiliate programs,
259-260
singular keyword searches,
217
SiteBuilder (Yahoo!), 195
SKUs (stock keeping units),
affiliate programs, 251
Slashdot effect, 15
slogans, 74-75
spammers, 133
spec sheets, 148
spiders, 52-53
Sponsored Links tool, 221
sponsorships, newsletters,
159-160
squatters (domain names), 73
SSL (secure socket layer), 129
Starbucks, differentiators, 65
stock keeping units. *See* SKUs
stores, online, 193
eBay, 194-195
Froogle Merchant
Program, 197-198
Yahoo! Shop, 195-197

strategies
    current Internet, 8-11
    diversification, 24
    versus tactics, 63-64
surveys, content development, 177-178
sustainable differentiators, 7, 66-67
syndication programs, 282-286

T

tactics versus strategies, 63-64
Teaching Company, The, 16
technologies, 25
    Froogle, 33-34
    Google AdSense, 30-32
    Google AdWords, 28-29
    Google Labs, 25
    weblogs, 32-33
Technorati, 117
Techron, Chevron Corporation differentiators, 66
terms of service agreements. *See* TOS agreements
testimonials, 87, 148
testing, advertising, 232
text links
    relevance scoring formula, 54-56
    web page design, 168-169
thematically related inbound links, 168
thesaurus searches (Wordtracker), 113
thieves (content), copyright laws, 279
ThinkGeek, 255
This is True website, 87
TITLE tags, 271

TiVo site, 143
TLDs (top-level domains), 72
tools, 25
    Froogle, 33-34
    Google AdSense, 30-32
    Google AdWords, 28-29
    Google Labs, 25
    weblogs, 32-33
top-level domains. *See* TLDs
Topica, searching for mailing lists, 206
topical mailing lists, 107
topical website directories, 4, 189-191
TOS (terms of service) agreements, affiliate programs, 252
    acceptable promotional techniques, 255-256
    acceptable sites, 253-254
    commission structure and payment, 256
    ownership of intellectual property, 254-255
tracking competitors
    classified ads, 105-106
    discussion boards, 106-107
    Google News Alerts, 101-102
    Usenet, 103-104
    weblogs, 104
trademarks (domain names), 76
traffic, 15-16
trees (domain name trees), 72
TTC (*The Teaching Company*), 16
Turbo Lister program (eBay), 195
two-word searches, 38

U–V

U.S. Copyright Office, 278
updates
    business websites, 92
    content development, 174-176
Usenet
    information sharing, 210-211
    tracking new competitors, 103-104
user-friendly shopping carts, 288

visibility, 4-5
visual consistency across media, 138-140

W

Wal-Mart, diversification, 62
Wall Street Journal website, 165
weblogs, 14, 32-33
    as content management systems, 178-179
      incorporation in site, 180
      RSS feeds, 181-183
      writing for weblogs, 184
    information sharing, 209-210
    learning what customers are discussing, 117
    as Q&A alternatives, 146-148
    submitting to blog indices, 191-192
    tracking new competitors, 104
WebPosition Gold, 271

websites
Artdolls, 84
Ask Dave Taylor!, 11
Ask The Builder, 90
Blogger, 33
business
appeal to clients, 82-83
assessing business
Internet strategy, 10
attracting customers,
17-18
avoiding design fads,
125-127
avoiding ethnocentric
sites, 133
calls to action, 129-130
collaboration with
experts, 124
content, 86-91, 174-184
five simple ideas,
134-135
information sharing,
200-211
integration of online
and offline content,
137-149
keeping site on topic,
122-123
keyword density,
166-167
limiting complexity, 124
link exchanges, 169
meta tags, 165-166
minimizing off-site
links, 131
multiple sites, 93-94
naming links and pages
effectively, 167
page design, 162-164
page titles, 164-165
responsiveness to cus-
tomers, 132-133
search engine–friendly
sites, 127

secondary pages, 83-84
secure servers, 129
selling company to visi-
tors, 130-132
submitting to search
engines, 186-191
thematically related
inbound links, 168
tools to avoid, 271-273
tricks to avoid, 265-271
trustworthiness,
127-128
updates, 92
ClickThruStats, 232
Commission Junction, 252
content, 57
design, 162
avoiding applets and
navigation toolbars,
163
design excess, 163-164
keyword density,
166-167
meta tags, 165-166
naming links and pages
effectively, 167
page titles, 164-165
thematically related
inbound links, 168
designers, 161
Digital Ocean, 131
EzineArticles.com, 282
Feedster News Alerts, 104
findability, 9
Google Press Center, 155
Google searches, 38
InfoPop, 177
Invision Power Services,
177
MassageSpecialists, 84
Myst Technology, 180
Netnews Tracker, 104
Paul Lamberg, 123
product-based websites,
153-155

Real-Life-Debt, 258
Robin Good, 192
Sponsored Links tool, 221
This is True, 87
TiVo, 143
Topica, 206
topical directories, 4
Wall Street Journal, 165
WordTracker, 215
Yahoo! Groups, 206
white papers, 148
whois system, 78
word order, Google searches,
45-46
Wordtracker, 111-115,
215-219
writers, licensing content,
283-284
writing
ad copy (AdWords cam-
paigns), 232-233
styles, newsletters, 157-158

X–Y–Z

Yahoo!, 4, 37, 58
affiliate program, 252
Groups, searching for
mailing lists, 206
SiteBuilder, 195
submitting websites to,
186-187
Yahoo! Shop, 195-197

Check Out These
Best-Selling
COMPLETE IDIOT'S GUIDES®

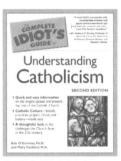

Understanding
Catholicism
SECOND EDITION

Bob O'Gorman, Ph.D.
and Mary Faulkner, M.A.

1-59257-085-2
$18.95

Learning
Spanish
THIRD EDITION

Gail Stein

0-02-864451-4
$18.95

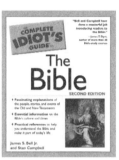

The
Bible
SECOND EDITION

James S. Bell Jr.
and Stan Campbell

0-02-864382-8
$18.95

Being a
Groom
SECOND EDITION

Jennifer Lata Rung
and Mark Rung

0-02-864456-5
$9.95

Grammar
and Style
SECOND EDITION

Laurie E. Rozakis, Ph.D.

1-59257-115-8
$16.95

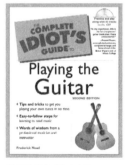

Playing the
Guitar
SECOND EDITION

Frederick Noad

0-02-864244-9
$21.95 w/CD

Personal Finance
in Your **20s & 30s**
SECOND EDITION

Sarah Young Fisher
and Susan Shelly

0-02-864374-7
$19.95

**Knitting and
Crocheting**
SECOND EDITION
Illustrated

Barbara Breiter and Gail Diven

1-59257-089-5
$16.95

The **Perfect
Resume**
THIRD EDITION

Susan Ireland

0-02-864440-9
$14.95

**Buying and
Selling a Home**
FOURTH EDITION

Shelley O'Hara
and Nancy D. Lewis

1-59257-120-4
$18.95

**Low-Carb
Meals**

Lucy Beale and
Sandy G. Couvillon, M.S., L.D.N., R.D.

1-59257-180-8
$18.95

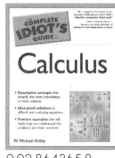

Calculus

W. Michael Kelley

0-02-864365-8
$18.95